Workshop on Computation and Written Language (CAWL 2023)

AA001763

Toronto, Canada
14 July 2023

ISBN: 978-1-7138-8223-7

Printed from e-media with permission by:

Curran Associates, Inc.
57 Morehouse Lane
Red Hook, NY 12571

Some format issues inherent in the e-media version may also appear in this print version.

Copyright© (2023) by the Association for Computational Linguistics
All rights reserved.

Printed with permission by Curran Associates, Inc. (2024)

For permission requests, please contact the Association for Computational Linguistics at the address below.

Association for Computational Linguistics
209 N. Eighth Street
Stroudsburg, Pennsylvania 18360

Phone: 1-570-476-8006
Fax: 1-570-476-0860

acl@aclweb.org

Additional copies of this publication are available from:

Curran Associates, Inc.
57 Morehouse Lane
Red Hook, NY 12571 USA
Phone: 845-758-0400
Fax: 845-758-2633
Email: curran@proceedings.com
Web: www.proceedings.com

CAWL 2023

The Workshop on Computation and Written Language (CAWL)

Proceedings of the Workshop

July 14, 2023

The CAWL organizers gratefully acknowledge the support from the following sponsors.

Google

©2023 Association for Computational Linguistics

Order copies of this and other ACL proceedings from:

Association for Computational Linguistics (ACL)
209 N. Eighth Street
Stroudsburg, PA 18360
USA
Tel: +1-570-476-8006
Fax: +1-570-476-0860
acl@aclweb.org

Introduction

We are pleased to bring you these Proceedings of the Workshop on Computation and Written Language (CAWL), held in Toronto on July 14, 2023. We received 17 paper submissions, of which 11 were chosen to appear in the workshop. Additionally, we include a position paper from organizers and the abstracts of our two invited talks.

Most work on NLP focuses on language in its canonical written form. This has often led researchers to ignore the differences between written and spoken language or, worse, to conflate the two. Instances of conflation are statements like "Chinese is a logographic language" or "Persian is a right-to-left language", variants of which can be found frequently in the ACL anthology. These statements confuse properties of the language with properties of its writing system. Ignoring differences between written and spoken language leads, among other things, to conflating different words that are spelled the same, or treating as different, words that have multiple spellings.

Furthermore, methods for dealing with written language issues (e.g., various kinds of normalization or conversion) or for recognizing text input (e.g., OCR & handwriting recognition or text entry methods) are often regarded as precursors to NLP rather than as fundamental parts of the enterprise, despite the fact that most NLP methods rely centrally on representations derived from text rather than (spoken) language. This general lack of consideration of writing has led to much of the research on such topics to largely appear outside of ACL venues, in conferences or journals of neighboring fields such as speech technology (e.g., text normalization) or human-computer interaction (e.g., text entry).

We are excited to bring together researchers working on various aspects of these topics, and hope that this might be the means for creating a persistant community within ACL focused on these topics.

We would like to thank the members of the Program Committee for completing their reviews promptly, and for providing useful feedback for deciding on the program and preparing the final versions of the papers. Special thanks to Nizar Habash for helping with organizational issues. Thanks also to our invited speakers, Mark Aronoff and Amalia Gnanadesikan, and to the authors of the interesting papers we are presenting in this volume.

Kyle Gorman, Brian Roark, and Richard Sproat
Organizers of the workshop

Program Committee

Organizers

Kyle Gorman, The Graduate Center, City University of New York
Brian Roark, Google Inc.
Richard Sproat, Google, Japan

Program Committee

Manex Agirrezabal, University of Copenhagen
Sina Ahmadi, George Mason University
Cecilia Ovesdotter Alm, Rochester Institute of Technology
Steven Bedrick, Oregon Health & Science University
Taylor Berg-kirkpatrick, University of California San Diego
Dan Garrette, Google Research
Alexander Gutkin, Google
Nizar Habash, New York University Abu Dhabi
Yannis Haralambous, IMT Atlantique & CNRS LabSTICC
Cassandra L. Jacobs, University at Buffalo
Martin Jansche, Amazon
George Kiraz, Institute for Advanced Study
Christo Kirov, Google
Grzegorz Kondrak, University of Alberta
Yang Li, Northwestern Polytechnical University
Constantine Lignos, Brandeis University
Zoey Liu, Department of Linguistics, University of Florida
Gerald Penn, University of Toronto
Yuval Pinter, Ben-Gurion University of the Negev
William Poser, freelance
Emily Prud'hommeaux, Boston College
Shruti Rijhwani, Google
Maria Ryskina, Massachusetts Institute of Technology
Lane Schwartz, University of Alaska Fairbanks
Djamé Seddah, Inria
Shuming Shi, Tencent AI Lab
David Smith, Northeastern University
Kumiko Tanaka-ishii, Waseda University
Annalu Waller, University of Dundee

Invited Talks

Paradise Lost: How the Alphabet Fell from Perfection

Mark Aronoff
Stony Brook University

Abstract: The original alphabet, devised by Semitic speakers in Egypt ca. 1800 BCE, was a perfect 1-1 mapping between individual letters and individual sounds. All alphabets and similar systems are descended from this original invention. Very few alphabets today retain a perfect 1-1 mapping. How far have alphabets diverged from perfection since? Modern alphabetic systems have letter-to-phoneme mappings of up to 4-1. These included Italian (one of the most regular) and English (perhaps the least regular). English also shows a high number of mappings to single morphs (stems and affixes). Korean, the only alphabetic system that groups letters into syllables, shows an interaction between morphemes and syllabic grouping.

How Linguistic are Writing Systems?

Amalia Gnanadesikan
University of Maryland

Abstract: Theoretical linguists have long denied that writing is language, while NLP research has tended to conflate writing and spoken language. The truth is more complex than either view. Writing imposes a linguistic analysis on spoken language, dividing a continuous speech stream into segments, syllables, morphemes and/or words. These elements are not simply representational. Writing systems impose their own linguistic structure, for example by requiring syllables to meet well-formedness conditions even when the spoken syllables violate these conditions. Writing systems also include linguistic categories that are not used in the languages for which they are designed, such as graphic classifiers used in writing non-classifier languages or graphic inflectional morphology used for languages with virtually no inflectional morphology.

Table of Contents

Program

Friday, July 14, 2023

09:00 - 09:05 *Opening Remarks,* Organizers

09:05 - 09:15 *Position Paper*

Myths about Writing Systems in Speech & Language Technology
Kyle Gorman and Richard Sproat

09:15 - 10:15 *Invited talk, Mark Aronoff: Paradise Lost: How the Alphabet Fell from Perfection*

10:15 - 10:30 *Morning Talks*

The Hidden Folk: Linguistic Properties Encoded in Multilingual Contextual Character Representations
Manex Agirrezabal, Sidsel Boldsen and Nora Hollenstein

10:30 - 11:00 *Coffee Break*

11:00 - 12:00 *Morning talks (continued)*

Preserving the Authenticity of Handwritten Learner Language: Annotation Guidelines for Creating Transcripts Retaining Orthographic Features
Christian Gold, Ronja Laarmann-quante and Torsten Zesch

Exploring the Impact of Transliteration on NLP Performance for Low-Resource Languages: The Case of Maltese and Arabic
Kurt Micallef, Fadhl Eryani, Nizar Habash, Houda Bouamor and Claudia Borg

Distinguishing Romanized Hindi from Romanized Urdu
Elizabeth Nielsen, Christo Kirov and Brian Roark

12:00 - 13:30 *Lunch Break*

13:30 - 14:30 *Invited Talk, Amalia Gnanadesikan: How Linguistic are Writing Systems?*

14:30 - 15:25 *Afternoon talks*

Friday, July 14, 2023 (continued)

	Back-Transliteration of English Loanwords in Japanese Yuying Ren
	Pronunciation Ambiguities in Japanese Kanji Wen Zhang
	Lenient Evaluation of Japanese Speech Recognition: Modeling Naturally Occurring Spelling Inconsistency Shigeki Karita, Richard Sproat and Haruko Ishikawa
15:25 - 16:00	*Coffee Break*
16:00 - 17:15	*Afternoon talks (continued)*
	Disambiguating Numeral Sequences to Decipher Ancient Accounting Corpora Logan Born, M. Willis Monroe, Kathryn Kelley and Anoop Sarkar
	Decipherment of Lost Ancient Scripts as Combinatorial Optimisation Using Coupled Simulated Annealing Fabio Tamburini
	Learning the Character Inventories of Undeciphered Scripts Using Unsupervised Deep Clustering Logan Born, M. Willis Monroe, Kathryn Kelley and Anoop Sarkar
	A Mutual Information-based Approach to Quantifying Logography in Japanese and Sumerian Noah Hermalin
17:15 - 17:30	*Closing Remarks,* Organizers

Myths about writing systems in speech & language technology

Kyle Gorman[*†] **and Richard Sproat**[†]
[*]CUNY Graduate Center
[†]Google LLC

Abstract

Natural language processing is largely focused on written text processing. However, many computational linguists tacitly endorse myths about the nature of writing. We highlight two of these myths—the conflation of language and writing, and the notion that Chinese, Japanese, and Korean writing is *ideographic*—and suggest how the community can dispel them.

1 Introduction

For a variety of historical and sociological reasons, *natural language processing* usually denotes the processing of *written* text, with work on spoken and signed language—as well as "multimodal" research—largely consigned to other venues. This largely unacknowledged focus on written language affects how computational linguists understand the nature of language itself. In this position paper, we argue that the field of natural language processing is beholden to certain misconceptions about the nature of writing and its relationship to other forms of language. We then make concrete suggestions as to how authors and editors can respond to these myths. We recognize that at least some of the issues we discuss may be obvious to the reader. If that is the case, we beg the reader's forgiveness. However, we think what we have to say here needs to be said.

2 Writing as a technology

Human language is notoriously hard to define, but we adopt a standard "cognitive" definition: the ability to learn and use systems of conventionalized externalized mental propositions. This ability is acquired, more or less effortlessly, by all typically developing humans barring gross sensory or motor impairments, and evolved sometime in the early prehistory of man. Writing, in contrast, is not a cognitive ability per se, but rather a technology which allows for the creation of durable visible records of language (Gelb, 1963, 11f.). Use of this technology can only be mastered by conscious, determined study[1] and has developed independently only a few times—in Mesopotamia and Egypt, China, and Central America—and in each case represents the dawn of human history in that region.

A writing system is, at its base, a linguistic analysis of the language it is used to write. (Indeed, the scribes of ancient Mesopotamia and Egypt are history's first linguists.) These analyses may seem quite naïve to the trained linguist, but the design of even the earliest writing systems hinge on sophisticated insights that presage the comparatively recent discoveries of the phoneme, mora, and morpheme.[2] For this reason, typologies of writing systems (e.g., Sproat, 2000; Rogers, 2005) are largely oriented around what types of linguistic units underlie the writing system's analysis.

3 Conflation and confusion

Language and writing may be ontologically incommensurate objects, but all known forms of writing are parasitic on spoken language. This is contrary to *standard language ideologies* (in the sense of Lippi-Green, 1997) which tend

[1]See, for example, Dehaene (2009) for an in-depth discussion of how parts of the brain which evolved for other purposes are co-opted in reading.

[2]Neural networks that process raw text—codepoint by codepoint or byte by byte—are sometimes said to work *from scratch* (e.g. Collobert et al., 2011). The implication seems to be that by doing away with explicit tokenization and related preprocessing steps, one has eliminated the need for linguistic analysis altogether. But since writing itself is a vernacular form of linguistic analysis, these could be said to work *from characters* or *from bytes* (e.g. Gillick et al., 2016; Li et al., 2019), but they certainly do not work from scratch.

Proceedings of the Workshop on Computation and Written Language (CAWL 2023), pages 1–5
July 14, 2023 ©2023 Association for Computational Linguistics

to value written over spoken language, but it seems an unavoidable conclusion.

NLP researchers commonly conflate a language and the writing system(s) used to write it. Consider the following quotations, all taken from papers hosted on the ACL Anthology.[3]

"Right-to-left" As is well-known, Arabic, Hebrew, and Persian are written and read right-to-left.

> ...*right to left* languages such as **Arabic** and **Hebrew**...

> Since **Persian** is a *right-to-left* language...

However, there is nothing about the **languages themselves** that is right-to-left. Furthermore, note that in Unicode, the right-to-left property of these scripts is purely an issue for text entry and rendering engines, since the codepoints are in the same logical order as text written left-to-right.

"Consonantal" Every language has consonants, so presumably the author below is referring to the consonantal alphabetic (or *abjad*) script used to write Arabic.

> One more idiosyncrasy of the **Arabic** language is that it is a *consonantal* language...

One does not ordinarily indicate short vowels in Arabic, except in certain pedagogical and religious texts. While the templatic word formation processes in Semitic languages might make them uniquely suited for this type of "defective" writing, many languages which lack this property—including Persian, Urdu, and until 1928, Turkish—are or were written using an Arabic-based consonantal script without great difficulty. This alone shows that there is nothing particularly "consonantal" about the Arabic language.

"Syllabic" Much like the presence of consonants, division of spoken language into syllables seems to be a linguistic universal, so it is not clear why the authors quoted below have chosen to highlight this property.

> ...**French** is a *syllabic* language...

> ...**Linear B**, a *syllabic* language...

> **Mandarin** is a tonal and *syllabic* language...

> **Punjabi** is a *syllabic* language...

Indeed, Punjabi is notable for having two major—and rather different—writing systems, the Gurmukhi alphasyllabary (or *abugida*) and the Shahmukhi consonantal alphabet. Neither of these systems use the phonological syllable as an orthographic unit, though alphasyllabaries have been characterized as using so-called *orthographic syllables.*

Chinese Finally, one can find a number of conflicting statements about the nature of Chinese in the ACL Anthology.

> **Chinese** is a *morphemic* language.

> **Chinese** is a *logographic* language...

> ...**Chinese** is *ideographic*

> It's well known that **Chinese** is an *ideographic* language...

> ...**Chinese**, **Japanese** and other *ideographic* languages.

We now turn to the question of what kind of writing system Chinese really is.

4 Ideography and CJK

We acknowledge that there exist many symbol systems which are purely *ideographic* (or *semasiographic*), without any direct reference to spoken language (Sproat, 2023). However, DeFrancis (1989, ch. 2) shows that these fail to satisfy any reasonable definition of writing. There have also been heroic attempts to develop purely ideographic writing systems, most notably Blissymbolics (Bliss, 1965). While carefully designed, such systems struggle with encoding categories like:

- colors; e.g., *chartreuse*, *royal blue*
- proper names; e.g., *Kyle*, *Richard*, *Park Slope*, *Shibuya*
- non-imageable predicates; e.g., *imagine*, *consternation*

[3]We deliberately omit citations for these quotations. We do not wish to draw undue negative attention to particular authors, but simply to illustrate how widespread this confusion is within our community.

- subtle connotative differences; e.g., *salt* vs. *sodium chloride* vs. *NaCl*.

Dependency on spoken language appears to be inherent to the design of writing. Despite this, it is very common to find statements in the literature that suggest that some writing systems, especially those used for Chinese, Japanese, or Korean, are *ideographic*. We demonstrate this with a survey of the literature in subsection 4.4, but first we present a brief synopsis of how Chinese, Japanese and Korean writing actually work.

4.1 Chinese writing

As argued by DeFrancis (1989, ch. 3), Chinese writing is best described as *morphosyllabic*. With only rare exceptions, each Chinese character represents a single phonological syllable, and in most cases corresponds to a single morpheme as well. Some characters, such as 人 *rén* 'person' are nondecomposable in that they represent the respective morpheme, and cannot be broken down into parts that have any meaning on their own. However *most* characters that have ever been invented—roughly 90%, by some estimates—are *semantic-phonetic* compounds that can be decomposed into a portion that represents something about the meaning and another portion that represents something about the pronunciation. For example, 鯉 *lǐ* 'carp', can be broken down into 魚, meaning 'fish' and 里, which here is being used for its pronunciation *lǐ*.[4] In most cases the pronunciation hint provided by the phonetic component is not nearly as good as in the case of 鯉, but the crucial point is that despite the common myth that Chinese writing is *ideographic*, in fact it depends heavily on phonology.

4.2 Japanese writing

The adaptation of Chinese writing to Japanese is more complex. In Japanese, *kanji* are used both to represent words or morphemes of Chinese origin, as well as native words. In the former case, the same semantic-phonetic principles carry over in that the phonetic component serves the purpose of hinting at the (Sino-Japanese) reading of the morpheme. In the latter case, the Chinese phonetic component is generally useless. For example the reading of 鯉 'carp' in Japanese is *koi*. In such cases, the kanji comes unanalyzable, like 人 'person' in Chinese, in that there is no phonetic cue to the reading (though the semantic component still has some function): 鯉 is just used as a whole to represent the morpheme *koi*. But notice that the unit represented is still a linguistic unit—a morpheme—not an idea (cf. Joyce, 2011). Apart from kanji, a large portion of Japanese writing is covered by *hiragana* and *katakana*, two (moraic) syllabaries that were historically derived from using Chinese characters purely for their pronunciation, and are now reasonably transparent, phonemic systems. That said, there are cases where the Japanese use of kanji is nearly semasiographic. One case is where different kanji are used to spell different senses of the same etymon. For example 泊まる *tomaru* 'stay, stop at a lodging' is probably the same word as 止まる *tomaru* 'stop, come to a halt', but the two spellings reflect different senses. Another case involves *jukujikun*, native Japanese words that are written with multiple kanji purely for their meaning. For example *sanma* 'Pacific saury', has a kanji spelling 秋刀魚 whose individual kanji convey the meaning 'autumn sword fish'. Since saury are long silver fish usually caught in the autumn, this spelling certainly evokes the meaning, but none of the kanji individually correspond to any linguistic unit. However, this reflects a small portion of the writing system, and the vast majority of Japanese writing can still be characterized as phonological or morphological.

4.3 Korean writing

Chinese characters were used widely in the history of Korean. Adaptations of Chinese writing to Korean were very similar to what one finds in Modern Japanese; see Handel (2019) for an in-depth discussion. In contrast, Modern Korean makes very sparing use of Chinese characters, and then only for morphemes of Chinese origin; e.g., 男 *nam* 'male' and 女 *yeo* 'female' on bathroom signs, or 小 *so* 'small', 中 *jung* 'medium', and 大 *dae* 'large' for serving sizes in restaurants. Nearly all Korean text

[4]There are also quite a few characters that are decomposable into two or more bits that represent the meaning, but unlike semantic-phonetic compounds, these have not been a major source of new characters in the last few millennia.

nowadays is written in *hangul*, the alphabetic writing system developed in the 15th century under King Sejong. Korean writing is thus essentially phonological.

4.4 Methods

Since the ideography myth is so pervasive in the speech and language processing community, it seems useful to try to understand what authors wish to convey when they incorrectly describe a language or writing system as *ideographic*. Therefore, we conducted an exhaustive survey of the ACL Anthology[5] for the words *ideograph*, *idiograph* [sic], and *ideographic*. There is little speech processing work published in the Anthology, and there is no single central repository for research on this topic. To survey speech research, the search terms *"ideographic" "speech recognition"* and *"ideographic" "speech synthesis"* were entered into Google Scholar.[6] As anticipated, this procedure retrieved examples from the proceedings of conferences like ICASSP, INTERSPEECH, and ASRU, and journals like *Computer Speech & Language*. ACL Anthology papers were excluded from this latter sample.

50 papers, all published 2003–2022, were selected randomly from each of the two samples. We then examined the surrounding context in which ideography is mentioned, and manually coded the following:

- which languages and/or writing systems this term refers to,
- whether or not language and writing is conflated, and
- the authors' apparent reason for mentioning ideography.

One author [KG] coded the Anthology sample, and another [RS] coded the Scholar sample.

4.5 Results

Three general trends emerge. First, as shown in Table 1, Chinese and Japanese are by far the most common languages to be described as ideographic. Three sources described Korean as ideographic. As we noted above (subsection 4.3), modern Korean writing makes limited use of Chinese characters, but it is not clear why this is qualitatively different than, for example, English's ideographic use of the dollar and pound signs in currency expressions like *$4.20*. Akkadian cuneiform and Egyptian hieroglyphs are both mentioned; these would probably be regarded as mixed writing systems, (cf. Hermalin this volume and Sproat and Gutkin 2021 for recent attempts to quantitatively characterize such scripts).

	Anthology	Scholar
Chinese	31	37
Japanese	20	21
(others)	8	1

Table 1: The counts of languages and/or writing systems described as "ideographic" (etc.) in a sample of 100 speech & language processing papers, published 2003–2022 in either the ACL Anthology or in speech research venues via Google Scholar.

More bafflingly, the undeciphered Proto-Elamite script, known to us from Early Bronze Age inscriptions in Iran, is similarly described, as is Dutch, and the entire Indo-Aryan language family. Secondly, 23 of the 100 papers are quite explicit in incorrectly conflating writing and language (i.e., describing Chinese as an *ideographic language*). Third, 69 of the 100 papers which mention ideography appear to do so as a means to describe—or simply introduce—the Han characters used in Chinese, Japanese, and Korean. However, we note some correctly describe symbols such as $, &, and Arabic numbers as *ideographic*.

5 Conclusions

We have shown that researchers in speech and language processing frequently conflate writing and language, a mistake that is often accompanied by misunderstandings about the nature of writing itself or misinformation about the nature of specific writing systems.

We recognize that many researchers may lack the necessary background in writing systems, and this is unsurprising given that the history and structure of writing is not widely taught, at least at North American universities. For researchers who wish to learn more about writing systems, we recommend two texts: Rogers (2005) provides an accessible introduction to the typology of writing sys-

[5] `https://aclanthology.org/`
[6] `https://scholar.google.com`

tems, and Gnanadesikan (2009) gives an easy-to-read introduction to the history of writing.

Editors and reviewers should pay more attention the use of inappropriate terminology used to describe writing systems as a simple matter of scientific communication. Describing the Arabic and Chinese languages as *right-to-left* or *ideographic* wrongly conflates of writing and language; these are the sort of mistakes that simply should not be made by specialists in our field.

We conclude with one concrete suggestion: we recommend the Unicode Consortium remove incorrect uses of the term *ideograph* in the standard (Unicode Consortium, 2021). As the they admit in their FAQ on CJK languages, this term does not accurately reflect the nature of these characters, but they claim the "term is now so pervasive in the standard that it cannot be abandoned or replaced."[7] However, we submit that the standard's description of Han characters as *CJK Unified Ideographs* is perhaps the primary channel by which the myth has been propagated amongst technologists, and a correction and *mea culpa* would do much to publicize the issue and dispel this myth. Handel (2019), for instance, proposes the term *sinographs*, and there are other sensible alternatives.

Acknowledgments

Thanks to Brian Roark, Daniel Yakubov, and audiences at Grapholinguistics in the 21st Century for comments on this work.

References

Charles K. Bliss. 1965. *Semantography (Blissymbolics)*, 2nd enlarged edition. Semantography (Blissymbolics) Publications.

Ronan Collobert, Jason Weston, Léon Bottou, Michael Karlen, Koray Kavukcuoglu, and Pavel Kuksa. 2011. Natural language processing (almost) from scratch. *Journal of Machine Learning Research*, 12:2493–2537.

John DeFrancis. 1989. *Visible Speech: The Diverse Oneness of Writing Systems.* University of Hawaii Press.

Stanislas Dehaene. 2009. *Reading in the Brain: The Science and Evolution of a Human Invention.* Viking.

[7]`https://unicode.org/faq/han_cjk.html`

I. J. Gelb. 1963. *A Study of Writing*, 2nd edition. University of Chicago Press.

Dan Gillick, Cliff Brunk, Oriol Vinyals, and Amarnag Subramanya. 2016. Multilingual language processing from bytes. In *Proceedings of the 2016 Conference of the North American Chapter of the Association for Computational Linguistics: Human Language Technologies*, pages 1296–1306.

Amalia E. Gnanadesikan. 2009. *The Writing Revolution: Cuneiform to the Internet.* Wiley-Blackwell.

Zev Handel. 2019. *Sinography: The Borrowing and Adaptation of the Chinese Script.* Brill.

Noah Hermalin. 2023. A mutual information-based approach to quantifying logography in Japanese and Sumerian. In *Proceedings of the ACL Workshop on Computation and Written Language.*

Terry Joyce. 2011. The significance of the morphographic principle for the classification of writing systems. *Written Language and Literacy*, 14(1):58–81.

Bo Li, Yu Zhang, Tara Sainath, Yonghui Wu, and William Chan. 2019. Bytes are all you need: end-to-end multilingual speech recognition and synthesis with bytes. In *ICASSP 2019-2019 IEEE International Conference on Acoustics, Speech and Signal Processing*, pages 5621–5625.

Rosina Lippi-Green. 1997. *English with an Accent: Language, Ideology, and Discrimination in the United States.* Routledge.

Henry Rogers. 2005. *Writing Systems: A Linguistic Approach.* Blackwell.

Richard Sproat. 2000. *A Computational Theory of Writing Systems.* Cambridge University Press.

Richard Sproat. 2023. *Symbols: An Evolutionary History from the Stone Age to the Future.* SpringerNature.

Richard Sproat and Alexander Gutkin. 2021. The taxonomy of writing systems: how to measure how logographic a system is. *Computational Linguistics*, 47(3):477–528.

Unicode Consortium. 2021. *The Unicode® Standard: Version 14.0: Core Specification.* Unicode Consortium.

The Hidden Folk: Linguistic Properties encoded in Multilingual Contextual Character Representations

Manex Agirrezabal and **Sidsel Boldsen** and **Nora Hollenstein**
Centre for Language Technology
Department of Nordic Studies and Linguistics
University of Copenhagen
{sbol,manex.aguirrezabal,nora.hollenstein}@hum.ku.dk

Abstract

To gain a better understanding of the linguistic information encoded in character-based language models, we probe the multilingual contextual CANINE model. We design a range of phonetic probing tasks in six Nordic languages, including Faroese as an additional zero-shot instance. We observe that some phonetic information is indeed encoded in the character representations, as consonants and vowels can be well distinguished using a linear classifier. Furthermore, results for the Danish and Norwegian language seem to be worse for the consonant/vowel distinction in comparison to other languages. The information encoded in these representations can also be learned in a zero-shot scenario, as Faroese shows a reasonably good performance in the same vowel/consonant distinction task.

1 Introduction

Subword and character sequence information is crucial in state-of-the-art neural language models (Sennrich et al., 2016; Kudo, 2018) because it improves their generalization and robustness capabilities (Xue et al., 2022; Tay et al., 2021). Additionally, character-level features are beneficial for morphologically rich and low-resource languages (Papay et al., 2018; Riabi et al., 2021). However, there is a lack of interpretability methods for character-based models. Only a few approaches have tried to understand the linguistic information encoded in character embeddings and cross-lingual approaches must be evaluated more rigorously by considering typology and linguistic distance (Artetxe et al., 2020). Therefore, in this work, we analyze how much phonetic information is encoded in contextualized multilingual character embeddings from the CANINE language model (Clark et al., 2022).

Based on six Nordic languages, we extract phonetic features for characters in context through unsupervised grapheme-to-phoneme alignment and design a set of probing tasks. We explore the character representations in two different evaluation scenarios, a traditional train/test split scenario and a leave-one-letter-out scenario. We find that phonetic information on a global level (e.g., vowel and consonant detection) is encoded accurately in the character representations and more mixed results are achieved on lower-level probing tasks such as consonant voicing and manner, or vowel height and roundness. We also see that this information is transferred to the related zero-shot language Faroese. Our code is available online[1].

2 Related Work

We discuss previous work in this area by focusing on existing multilingual character language models and the interpretability of these models.

Building Character-Level Models Subword and character-level information is exhibiting great benefits for computational language models (Bostrom and Durrett, 2020; Zhang et al., 2021). With the rise of multilingual models, pre-trained simultaneously on 100+ languages, these are also being adapted for and augmented with character-level information (Xue et al., 2022; Tay et al., 2021). We choose to work with the CANINE model by Clark et al. (2022), because it is a strongly performing neural encoder which operates directly on character sequences, i.e., without explicit tokenization or vocabulary, and incorporates a pre-training strategy operating directly on characters.

Understanding Character-Level Models Because of their popularity and lack of interpretability, many researchers have attempted to understand what is behind word and letter representations. A number of probing tasks have been employed to extract knowledge from contextualized word representations (e.g. Liu et al. 2019). For character

[1] https://github.com/manexagirrezabal/hidden_folk_repository

Proceedings of the Workshop on Computation and Written Language (CAWL 2023), pages 6–13
July 14, 2023 ©2023 Association for Computational Linguistics

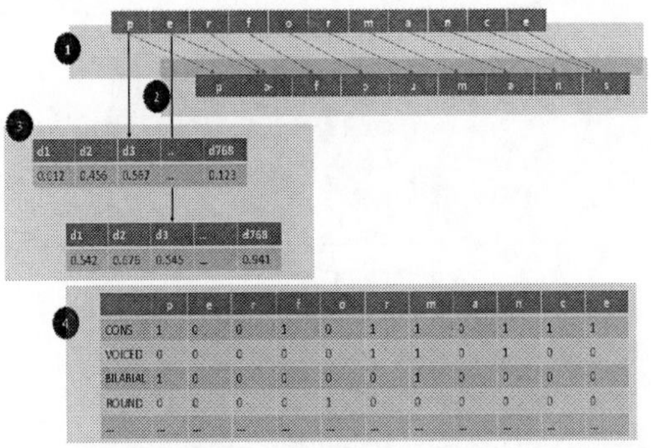

Figure 1: This figure represents how we process our textual data. The alignment between graphs and phones is done using m2m-aligner (1). We extract the phones from Wikipron (2). We obtain the Canine embeddings (768 dimension representation) (3). Finally, we get the phonemic information of letters using the `ipapy` package from Python (4).

representations, there are works in which the authors attempt to interpret the individual character-level hidden state contributions (Pinter et al., 2019; Kementchedjhieva and Lopez, 2018). In our case, though, we employ probing as the mechanism to interpret the representations. Recent work probes word-level representation with respect to their knowledge about characters. For instance, Kaushal and Mahowald (2022) predict the presence of a particular character in a token showing that large models robustly encode this information across various scripts. Additionally, Itzhak and Levy (2021) test the "spelling abilities" of language models showing that the embedding layers of RoBERTa and GPT-2 learn the internal character composition of whole words to a surprising extent, without seeing the characters coupled with the tokens during training.

Specifically on character-level models, Boldsen et al. (2022) compare perceptual representations to character embeddings. Their cross-lingual analysis shows that character representations correlate with phonological representations for languages using an alphabetic script and implies a relationship between the information encoded in the embeddings and the orthographic transparency of the languages. Furthermore, Hahn and Baroni (2019) probe character models in a cognitively realistic task on data with removed word boundaries showing that recurrent LMs learn morphological, syntactic and semantic aspects even on unsegmented text. These findings encourage the exploration of character and phoneme-level learning.

3 Contextualized Character Embeddings

We extract character embeddings (in the context of full words) from the CANINE model. In this section, we present the multilingual data and the embedding extraction.

Data Since character-level features are important for morphologically rich and low-resource languages (Lauscher et al., 2020; Garrette and Baldridge, 2013), we choose a set of six Nordic languages for our experiments: Danish (da), Swedish (sv), Norwegian (nb), Finnish (fi), Icelandic (is) and Faroese (fo). Five of the languages are included in the training data of the character language model (da sv, nb, fi and is). Additionally, we use Faroese to test performance of multilingual zero-shot embeddings. The starting point for extracting character embeddings is a frequency list for each language (see Table 1). We select the 10000 most frequent words of every language and then randomly sample 3000 of these words and retrieve embeddings for all characters in these 3000 words. This implies that more frequent characters in a given language will be better represented in the embeddings. Note that word length will affect the number of character embeddings extracted.

Model We extract contextualized embeddings from the CANINE model (Clark et al., 2022). CANINE is a neural encoder which operates directly on character-level without requiring an explicit tokenization strategy or a pre-defined vocabulary. We choose this model since it showed superior performance on multilingual downstream tasks. CANINE has been trained on data from 104 languages.[2] While it performs well on NLP tasks, it has not yet been explored which type of linguistic information is encoded in these pre-trained character representations. We use the HuggingFace checkpoint of the CANINE model with autoregressive character loss.[3] We input words to the model, and use the last hidden state of a character in the context of the word it occurs in as a contextualized character embedding ($d = 768$).

4 Phonetic Feature Extraction

In order to extract phonetic features from characters, we need to know how a specific letter should be

[2]The CANINE model is pretrained on on the multilingual Wikipedia data of mBERT.

[3]`https://huggingface.co/google/canine-c`

pronounced. We do that by aligning the characters with the string of phones as given by Wikipron. As the number of letters and phones may not match, we align them using `m2m-aligner` (Jiampojamarn et al., 2007), an unsupervised model that is based on Expectation-Maximization. Then, we use the `ipapy` toolkit to obtain phonetic features for each phone. We describe this process below.

Pipeline We use the aligner to obtain phonetic features for characters in all six languages. First, we obtain a dictionary for each language from Wikipron (Lee et al., 2020),[4] and then, we align graphemes to phones using `m2m-aligner`.[5] Wikipron includes both phonemic and phonetic representations of words, which they refer to broad and narrow, respectively. As the model for extracting features works at a phonetic level, we use the phonetic representations (narrow). In the next step, we use the `ipapy`[6] toolkit to extract phonetic features for each phone.

Finally, the IPA features are merged with the CANINE character representations. This process results in one dataset per language, consisting of 6067 characters in 899 words for Danish, 700 characters in 135 words for Faroese, 4698 characterss in 745 words for Finnish, 268 characters in 43 words for Icelandic, 302 characters in 57 words for Norwegian, and 312 character in 58 words for Swedish. The reason for the drastic decrease in samples for some of the language is the small size of the pronunciation dictionaries.

5 Probing

In this section, we describe the probing tasks and the evaluation scenarios that we devise to test the extracted character embeddings.

We design 23 tasks to investigate the phonological knowledge encoded in the multilingual character representations. The tasks are split into three categories: global features (e.g., is this character a vowel or not?), consonant features (e.g., is the manner of articulation of this consonant plosive or not?[7], and vowel features (e.g., is this vowel pronounced as a rounded vowel?[8] The probing tasks have the structure $F : X \rightarrow Y$, where given a set of character representations X, we want to find the best mapping F that relates X to a set of target features Y using a supervised Logistic Regression classification model.

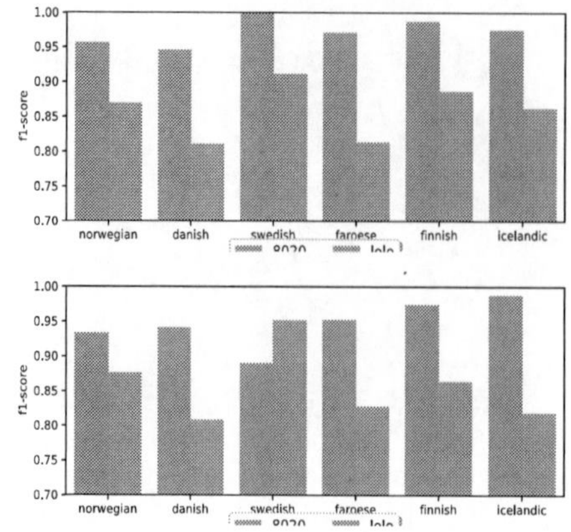

Figure 2: Weighted F1-scores for two global features: vowel prediction (top) and consonant predictions (bottom). Exact numbers in Appendix A.4.

As discussed by Hewitt and Liang (2019), it is important to take into account the expressivity of a probing task, since overly expressive probes, i.e., too many possible mappings for $F : X \rightarrow Y$, does not reveal much about the internal feature representations. Therefore, we test the all probing classifiers in two evaluation scenarios: (i) 80/20, a random 80% training and 20% test split of the data, and (ii) LoLo, a leave-one-letter-out training and test split. The 80/20 setup implies that the same characters (in different contexts) can appear in the train *and* test split, resulting in a simpler probing task, whereas the LoLo setup ensures zero-shot learning for the specific character of which all representations in all contexts are held out during training.

6 Results

To understand the implicit phonetic information encoded in contextual representations, we present weighted F1-scores for a selection of features.[9] Most of the individual probing tasks show F1-scores above 0.5, which means that the models generally perform better than a random baseline.

In Figure 2, we observe the results for two global features, where we predict whether a character is a vowel (top) and whether a letter is a consonant (bottom). In each plot, we report the results of both evaluation scenarios. Faroese performs very similar

[4]Please find the size of the dictionaries in Appendix A.2.

[5]We evaluated the alignments of `m2maligner` by using a manually aligned dictionary. This is available for the Danish language (Juul, 2010), where $\sim$ 42,000 words and their phonetic transcriptions are aligned. Results show that the word error rate is below $< 2.5\%$.

[6]`https://github.com/pettarin/ipapy`

[7]In Danish, "b" in *peber* ([ˈpʰewɐ]) vs. *åben* ([ˈɔːb̥m̩])

[8]In Danish, "o" as in ballon ([b̥aˈlʌŋ]) (unrounded) vs. blod ([ˈb̥loðˀ])(rounded)

[9]See Appendix A.4 for the full results.

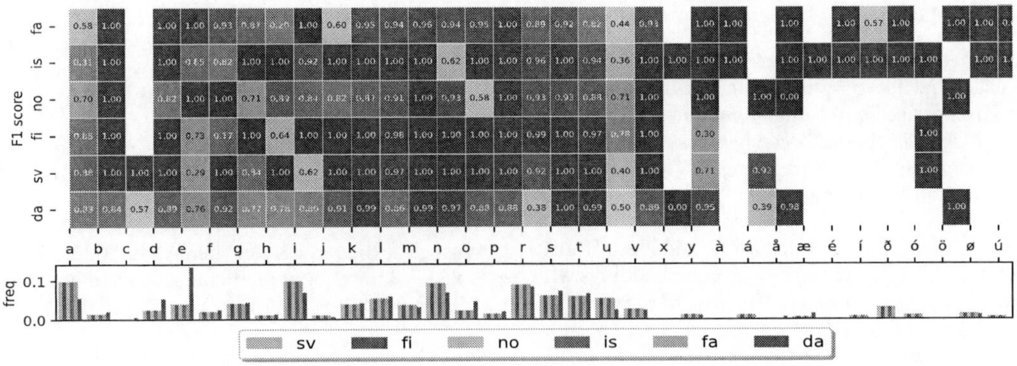

Figure 3: Heatmap for **global type vowel**. The barplot shows the frequency of the given character.

to Danish, even though the CANINE training data does not include any Faroese data. Furthermore, Norwegian and Swedish are the languages with the smallest difference between different validation methodologies (80/20 vs. LoLo).

Figure 3 shows the LoLo performance of each model for all characters and languages. The models were trained to predict whether the contextual character embedding had the label `global_type_vowel`, meaning that the character in this specific context is pronounced as a vowel. Taking a closer look at Danish and Norwegian, for instance, the F1-scores are relatively similar. This was expected given the similarities between the two languages in the written form. Although the results are similar, if we zoom in to specific character, we observe that the performance for vowels is systematically worse for Danish, which is reasonable given the complex nature of the Danish vowel system (Trecca et al., 2018).

7 Conclusions & Future Work

In this work, we design a probing mechanism to better understand information encoded in contextual character representations, for which we use two validation mechanisms. The first one, where the training data is divided into training and testing set, and the second one where we train one model for each character. The reasoning behind this is that a letter representation, even though it occurs in a different context, would have a similar representation and therefore, it would involve a kind of data leakage to the testset. We can imagine the example of the letter "a" in the words "tram" and "gas" in English. The contexts are rather different, but we would expect the representation of the letter "a" to be relatively similar, as it is pronounced similarly. Therefore, the LoLo evaluation allows us to test the representations of a character in *any* context in a zero-shot scenario.

Following this methodology, we observe that contextual character representations encode some phonetic information, supported by the probing classifier performances. This result is in line with similar works performed on less complex representations, such as *word2vec*, *PPMI+SVD* or an *RNN* encoder-decoder (Silfverberg et al., 2018), where they found that in some languages these representations showed distributional properties.

We use Wikipron data as linguistic knowledge and we align graphs and phones using an automatic aligning mechanism. We validate the aligner for Danish on manually aligned data, but other languages may have their own specific challenges. We use a wide range of phonetic probing tasks to accommodate language-specific particularities.

It is crucial that the number of positive and negative instances is checked when probing each phonetic feature. As expected, many pronunciation-related features do not occur in specific languages, and thus, this results in phonetic features with only one class, which will not shed any light on such phonetic properties. Hence, future research should address the design of these probing tasks as much as the results. Finally, since some of the datasets were relatively small, using a grapheme-to-phoneme model could increase the number of instances. Besides, these analyses could be extended to more languages to cover the full spectrum of orthographic depth.

References

Mikel Artetxe, Sebastian Ruder, Dani Yogatama, Gorka Labaka, and Eneko Agirre. 2020. A call for more rigor in unsupervised cross-lingual learning. In *Proceedings of the 58th Annual Meeting of the Association for Computational Linguistics*, pages 7375–7388, Online. Association for Computational Linguistics.

Sidsel Boldsen, Manex Agirrezabal, and Nora Hollenstein. 2022. Interpreting character embeddings with perceptual representations: The case of shape, sound, and color. In *Proceedings of the 60th Annual Meeting of the Association for Computational Linguistics (Volume 1: Long Papers)*, pages 6819–6836, Dublin, Ireland. Association for Computational Linguistics.

Kaj Bostrom and Greg Durrett. 2020. Byte pair encoding is suboptimal for language model pretraining. In *Findings of the Association for Computational Linguistics: EMNLP 2020*, pages 4617–4624, Online. Association for Computational Linguistics.

Jonathan H. Clark, Dan Garrette, Iulia Turc, and John Wieting. 2022. Canine: Pre-training an efficient tokenization-free encoder for language representation. *Transactions of the Association for Computational Linguistics*, 10:73–91.

Dan Garrette and Jason Baldridge. 2013. Learning a part-of-speech tagger from two hours of annotation. In *Proceedings of the 2013 Conference of the North American Chapter of the Association for Computational Linguistics: Human Language Technologies*, pages 138–147, Atlanta, Georgia. Association for Computational Linguistics.

Michael Hahn and Marco Baroni. 2019. Tabula nearly rasa: Probing the linguistic knowledge of character-level neural language models trained on unsegmented text. *Transactions of the Association for Computational Linguistics*, 7:467–484.

Zakaris Svabo Hansen, Heini Justinussen, and Mortan Ólason. 2004. Marking av teldutøkum tekstsavni [tagging of a digital text corpus]. *URL http://ark. axeltra. com/index. php.*

John Hewitt and Percy Liang. 2019. Designing and interpreting probes with control tasks. In *Proceedings of the 2019 Conference on Empirical Methods in Natural Language Processing and the 9th International Joint Conference on Natural Language Processing (EMNLP-IJCNLP)*, pages 2733–2743, Hong Kong, China. Association for Computational Linguistics.

Itay Itzhak and Omer Levy. 2021. Models in a spelling bee: Language models implicitly learn the character composition of tokens. *arXiv preprint arXiv:2108.11193.*

Sittichai Jiampojamarn, Grzegorz Kondrak, and Tarek Sherif. 2007. Applying many-to-many alignments and hidden markov models to letter-to-phoneme conversion. In *Human Language Technologies 2007: The Conference of the North American Chapter of the Association for Computational Linguistics; Proceedings of the Main Conference*, pages 372–379, Rochester, New York. Association for Computational Linguistics.

Holger Juul. 2010. K-a-tt-e-p-i-n-er: om komplekse bogstav-lyd-forbindelser i danske ord. *NyS*, 39:10–32.

Ayush Kaushal and Kyle Mahowald. 2022. What do tokens know about their characters and how do they know it? *arXiv preprint arXiv:2206.02608.*

Yova Kementchedjhieva and Adam Lopez. 2018. 'indicatements' that character language models learn English morpho-syntactic units and regularities. In *Proceedings of the 2018 EMNLP Workshop BlackboxNLP: Analyzing and Interpreting Neural Networks for NLP*, pages 145–153, Brussels, Belgium. Association for Computational Linguistics.

Adam Kilgarriff, Frieda Charalabopoulou, Maria Gavrilidou, Janne Bondi Johannessen, Saussan Khalil, Sofie Johansson Kokkinakis, Robert Lew, Serge Sharoff, Ravikiran Vadlapudi, and Elena Volodina. 2014. Corpus-based vocabulary lists for language learners for nine languages. *Language resources and evaluation*, 48(1):121–163.

Taku Kudo. 2018. Subword regularization: Improving neural network translation models with multiple subword candidates. In *Proceedings of the 56th Annual Meeting of the Association for Computational Linguistics (Volume 1: Long Papers)*, pages 66–75, Melbourne, Australia. Association for Computational Linguistics.

Anne Lauscher, Vinit Ravishankar, Ivan Vulić, and Goran Glavaš. 2020. From zero to hero: On the limitations of zero-shot language transfer with multilingual Transformers. In *Proceedings of the 2020 Conference on Empirical Methods in Natural Language Processing (EMNLP)*, pages 4483–4499, Online. Association for Computational Linguistics.

Jackson L. Lee, Lucas F.E. Ashby, M. Elizabeth Garza, Yeonju Lee-Sikka, Sean Miller, Alan Wong, Arya D. McCarthy, and Kyle Gorman. 2020. Massively multilingual pronunciation modeling with WikiPron. In *Proceedings of the Twelfth Language Resources and Evaluation Conference*, pages 4223–4228, Marseille, France. European Language Resources Association.

Nelson F. Liu, Matt Gardner, Yonatan Belinkov, Matthew E. Peters, and Noah A. Smith. 2019. Linguistic knowledge and transferability of contextual representations. In *Proceedings of the 2019 Conference of the North American Chapter of the Association for Computational Linguistics: Human Language Technologies, Volume 1 (Long and Short Papers)*, pages 1073–1094, Minneapolis, Minnesota. Association for Computational Linguistics.

Sigríður Ólafsdóttir, Auður Pálsdóttir, Starkaður Barkarson, and Ásdís Björg Björgvinsdóttir. 2022.

Word frequency list from the icelandic corpus for academic words (orðtíðnilisti málheildar fyrir íslenskan námsorðaforða - MÍNO). CLARIN-IS.

Sean Papay, Sebastian Padó, and Ngoc Thang Vu. 2018. Addressing low-resource scenarios with character-aware embeddings. In *Proceedings of the Second Workshop on Subword/Character LEvel Models*, pages 32–37, New Orleans. Association for Computational Linguistics.

Yuval Pinter, Marc Marone, and Jacob Eisenstein. 2019. Character eyes: Seeing language through character-level taggers. In *Proceedings of the 2019 ACL Workshop BlackboxNLP: Analyzing and Interpreting Neural Networks for NLP*, pages 95–102, Florence, Italy. Association for Computational Linguistics.

Arij Riabi, Benoît Sagot, and Djamé Seddah. 2021. Can character-based language models improve downstream task performances in low-resource and noisy language scenarios? In *Proceedings of the Seventh Workshop on Noisy User-generated Text (W-NUT 2021)*, pages 423–436, Online. Association for Computational Linguistics.

Rico Sennrich, Barry Haddow, and Alexandra Birch. 2016. Neural machine translation of rare words with subword units. In *Proceedings of the 54th Annual Meeting of the Association for Computational Linguistics (Volume 1: Long Papers)*, pages 1715–1725, Berlin, Germany. Association for Computational Linguistics.

Miikka P. Silfverberg, Lingshuang Mao, and Mans Hulden. 2018. Sound analogies with phoneme embeddings. In *Proceedings of the Society for Computation in Linguistics (SCiL) 2018*, pages 136–144.

Yi Tay, Vinh Q Tran, Sebastian Ruder, Jai Gupta, Hyung Won Chung, Dara Bahri, Zhen Qin, Simon Baumgartner, Cong Yu, and Donald Metzler. 2021. Charformer: Fast character transformers via gradient-based subword tokenization. In *International Conference on Learning Representations*.

Fabio Trecca, Dorthe Bleses, Thomas O Madsen, and Morten H Christiansen. 2018. Does sound structure affect word learning? an eye-tracking study of danish learning toddlers. *Journal of Experimental Child Psychology*, 167:180–203.

Linting Xue, Aditya Barua, Noah Constant, Rami Al-Rfou, Sharan Narang, Mihir Kale, Adam Roberts, and Colin Raffel. 2022. ByT5: Towards a token-free future with pre-trained byte-to-byte models. *Transactions of the Association for Computational Linguistics*, 10:291–306.

Xinsong Zhang, Pengshuai Li, and Hang Li. 2021. AMBERT: A pre-trained language model with multi-grained tokenization. In *Findings of the Association for Computational Linguistics: ACL-IJCNLP 2021*, pages 421–435, Online. Association for Computational Linguistics.

A Appendix

A.1 Frequency Lists

Table 1 contains the details about the frequency lists used for each language.

Language	Reference & Source
Danish	DSL frequency list by Jørg Asmussen
Faroese	Sosialurin corpus by Hansen et al. (2004)
Finnish	Parole corpus frequency list by the Institure for the Languages of Finland
Icelandic	Icelandic Corpus for Academic Words by Ólafsdóttir et al. (2022)
Norwegian	Kelly List by Kilgarriff et al. (2014)
Swedish	Kelly List by Kilgarriff et al. (2014)

Table 1: Data sources of the frequency lists for all six languages.

A.2 Pronunciation Dictionaries

Table 2 shows the size (word count) of the pronunciation dictionaries used in this work to train the `m2n-aligner` in all six languages.

Language	Words
Danish	8,219
Faroese	1,118
Finnish	80,377
Icelandic	464
Norwegian (bokmål)	604
Swedish	372

Table 2: Pronunciation dictionary size for all six languages, obtained from Lee et al. (2020).

A.3 Average word length and standard deviation

Table 3 shows the average word length and standard deviation for each language in the CANINE embeddings.

Language	mean	std.
Danish	7.5398	3.0756
Faroese	7.8557	3.6023
Finnish	7.7544	2.8365
Icelandic	8.4372	3.4093
Norwegian	7.0766	2.8401
Swedish	7.5166	3.3496

Table 3: Mean word length and standard deviation for each language in the CANINE embeddings.

A.4 Full Results

Table 4 presents the LoLo results (F1 scores) for all probing tasks and all languages.

Feature	*no*	*da*	*sv*	*fa*	*fi*	*is*
global_type_consonant	0.88	0.81	0.95	0.83	0.86	0.82
global_type_vowel	0.87	0.81	0.91	0.81	0.89	0.86
global_type_diacritic	0.87	0.56	0.80	0.96	0.78	0.86
global_type_suprasegmental	0.82	0.92	0.71	0.86	0.77	0.81
consonant_voicing_voiced	0.57	0.64	0.59	0.43	0.43	0.67
consonant_voicing_voiceless	0.57	0.65	0.66	0.39	0.43	0.50
consonant_place_alveolar	0.46	0.74	0.63	0.58	0.69	0.66
consonant_place_bilabial	0.83	0.83	0.82	0.85	0.86	0.85
consonant_place_labio-dental	0.89	0.90	0.87	0.88	0.94	0.87
consonant_place_palatal	0.92	0.96	0.96	0.95	0.95	0.89
consonant_place_velar	0.86	0.92	0.85	0.90	0.86	0.90
consonant_manner_approximant	0.86	0.86	0.96	0.91	0.87	0.95
consonant_manner_nasal	0.72	0.78	0.83	0.69	0.73	0.84
consonant_manner_non-sibilant-fricative	0.89	0.75	0.85	0.86	0.94	0.73
consonant_manner_plosive	0.64	0.57	0.62	0.52	0.67	0.54
vowel_height_close	0.63	0.77	0.89	0.82	0.48	0.84
vowel_height_close-mid	0.81	0.72	0.74	0.90	0.92	0.83
vowel_backness_front	0.51	0.54	0.41	0.37	0.33	0.53
vowel_backness_back	0.71	0.65	0.61	0.71	0.33	0.81
vowel_roundness_rounded	0.80	0.71	0.67	0.83	0.67	0.77
vowel_roundness_unrounded	0.80	0.72	0.70	0.81	0.67	0.83

Table 4: LoLo results (F1 scores, weighted) for all probing tasks and all languages.

Preserving the Authenticity of Handwritten Learner Language: Annotation Guidelines for Creating Transcripts Retaining Orthographic Features

Christian Gold[1], Ronja Laarmann-Quante[2] and Torsten Zesch[1]
[1]CATALPA, FernUniversität in Hagen, Germany,
[2]Ruhr University Bochum, Faculty of Philology, Department of Linguistics, Germany

Abstract

Handwritten texts produced by young learners often contain orthographic features like spelling errors, capitalization errors, punctuation errors, and impurities such as strikethroughs, inserts, and smudges. All of those are typically normalized or ignored in existing transcriptions. For applications like handwriting recognition with the goal of automatically analyzing a learner's language performance, however, retaining such features would be necessary. To address this, we present transcription guidelines that retain the features addressed above. Our guidelines were developed iteratively and include numerous example images to illustrate the various issues. On a subset of about 90 double-transcribed texts, we compute inter-annotator agreement and show that our guidelines can be applied with high levels of percentage agreement of about .98. Overall, we transcribed 1,350 learner texts, which is about the same size as the widely adopted handwriting recognition datasets IAM (1,500 pages) and CVL (1,600 pages). Our final corpus can be used to train a handwriting recognition system that transcribes closely to the real productions by young learners. Such a system is a prerequisite for applying automatic orthography feedback systems to handwritten texts in the future.

1 Introduction

When looking at the educational landscape, particularly with children, handwriting remains a prevalent mode of writing. As shown in Figure 2, handwritten texts contain various features such as strikethroughs, inserts, spelling errors, and smudges, which can provide additional information beyond the actual text about the writing process and the writer's skills.

When handwritten texts are transcribed, e.g. to make them accessible to digital analysis, there is always a loss of information involved, as we need to abstract from the source depending on the intended use. Different applications may require different levels of abstraction, depending on the focus of the analysis. This is similar to the transcription of spoken language, where depending on the application it may or may not be necessary to retain e.g. filler words or pauses.

In the case of handwriting, a quite common abstraction is the normalization of orthographic errors. For example, if the texts are analyzed for aspects like vocabulary, thematic coherence, or reader-orientedness (Grabowski et al., 2014), retaining spelling errors in the transcripts is not necessary and may even hamper the analyses. In contrast, preserving spelling errors in the transcripts would be crucial to assess orthographic competence and yet other analyses may require even more information from the handwriting, e.g. what pieces of information were added to a sentence after it was finished (see Figure 2 for examples of such inserts). Another task with special requirements concerning the transcripts is *handwriting recognition* (HWR). To achieve accurate HWR, it is crucial to have reliable training data that closely resembles real handwriting transcriptions which are directly linked to the corresponding image.

The requirements of the different tasks may be conflicting. For example, for analyzing text coherence, inserted pieces of text should be transcribed where the writer intended them to appear. In contrast, to serve as training data for HWR, the inserts have to be transcribed at the position where they were written in the text. Furthermore, transcribers often need to make decisions that affect later analyses. See for example Figure 1, where two letters are written on top of each other ('S' and 's', where *Schüler* 'student' with a captial 'S' would be the correct spelling).

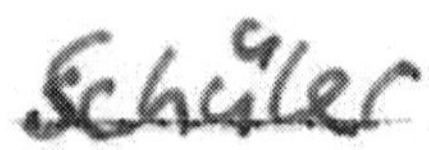

Figure 1: Handwriting sample of the word 'Schüler' with two letters written over each other.

This may be a self-correction or the writer was unsure about the correct form and provided both simultaneously. It may be viewed as an error in the context of assessing spelling competence or normalized for the purpose of analyzing a learner's vocabulary. Once the transcriber decided for a variant, information about the uncertainty is lost.

Proceedings of the Workshop on Computation and Written Language (CAWL 2023), pages 14–21
July 14, 2023 ©2023 Association for Computational Linguistics

Transcripts of handwritten texts are often produced in the context of a particular project with specific goals. However, it is a very time-consuming task requiring a lot of manual effort. It would be much more sustainable to provide a transcript that is broad enough to cover multiple use-cases.

Contribution In this paper, we present transcription guidelines for handwritten learner texts that retain various properties of the handwriting and are general enough to be used for at least two purposes: a) creating training data for HWR and b) analyzing the continuous text written by a learner with the possibility of retaining or discarding features such as strikethroughs or uncertainties which letter was written. We apply these guidelines to 1,350 pages of the FD-LEX (Becker-Mrotzek and Grabowski, 2018) dataset and show that a high agreement between two transcribers can be achieved. Furthermore, we discuss how the transcripts can be converted to two formats: a) to be suitable for HWR and b) for general text analysis. While our transcription of the FD-LEX dataset cannot be published, we publish the guidelines and the converter to foster further research.[1] A practical use-case for the HWR-converted transcripts with orthographic features present can be found in our succeeding work (Gold et al., 2023).

2 Related Work

Over the last years, numerous datasets of texts produced by language learners have been compiled. For example, some datasets aim to provide authentic records that do not normalize orthographic deviations, especially if the frequency of these deviations is negligible. Others aim at normalizing orthographic deviations to facilitate semantic analysis of the texts.

A good illustration of the approach to preserving the authenticity of handwritten manuscripts can be found in the transcription guidelines outlined in Bohnenkamp et al. (2019), which serves as a (comprehensive) exemplary model for the transcription of historical documents. The guidelines prioritize a detailed transcription of the handwriting, without any amendments to obvious errors in spelling or punctuation that might result in changes to the meaning. The detailed and time-consuming nature of these guidelines allows the preservation of a significant amount of information. Furthermore, they enable the creation of a transcript that can be analyzed with a focus on specific aspects, such as the differentiation between comments from individual authors or the use of different writing tools.

For handwritten learner content, the Grow in Grammar (GIG) Corpus, which is documented in Durrant and Brenchley (2018), comes with transcripts and a detailed transcription manual. Although not focusing on HWR, the main goal was to create an authentic record of what the learner wrote. However, annotations are often not precise enough to be usable for HWR. For example, in the case of strikethroughs, the complete sentence was flagged instead of indicating the exact position of the crossed-out words. Furthermore, the image data is not available.

Becker-Mrotzek and Grabowski (2018) released the FD-LEX dataset comprising images and their corresponding transcripts, i.e. the two key components for HWR. However, the transcripts have been orthographically normalized to focus on diagnosing and promoting sub-components of writing competence.

In a recent work (Kerz et al., 2020), the datasets GIG and FD-LEX were both comparably used to analyze the development of writing in English and German children across school grades. Although these extensive datasets were created, as orthographical errors were not present in both data, a deeper analysis of these differences could not be made.

In contrast to these datasets, several datasets targeting HWR exist. IAM (Marti and Bunke, 2002) and CVL (Kleber et al., 2013) are widely adopted in the HWR community and are frequently utilized for comparing recognition performance across various methods. They consist of image data with different segmentation levels such as text-line or word level and align with the corresponding transcripts. However, these datasets are non-learner datasets, as the texts were written by skilled writers and merely transcribed from provided texts, resulting in minimal amounts of orthographic errors.

None of the datasets had all three components - image data, a properly aligned transcript, and a transcript that retained orthographic errors - available, despite the wide range of datasets that were examined.

3 Handwritten Learner Data

For our objective of exploiting a Learner Handwritten Dataset for HWR, as described in Gold et al. (2023), we choose the dataset of FD-LEX (Becker-Mrotzek and Grabowski, 2018). The data set consists of texts from two different German school types (*Gymnasium* and *Integrierte Gesamtschule*)[2] at two different learner levels (5th and 9th grade). The FD-LEX corpus consists of 5,628 texts from 938 learners (i.e. on average 6 texts per student). Table 1 provides a detailed breakdown of attendees per system and grade. The text lengths differ from a few up to 250 words with an average of 66 words and sum up to about 373,600.

The images in FD-LEX are colored scans of white DIN-A4 paper with ruled lines and a header that includes the writer's ID. This layout is consistent throughout the entire dataset, with only a few excep-

[1] `https://github.com/catalpa-cl/learner-handwriting-recognition`

[2] The German Gymnasium is the highest of the three types of German secondary schools while the Integrierte Gesamtschule is a comprehensive school. The school type Gymnasium will be abbreviated with 'GYM' and the comprehensive school with 'IGS'.

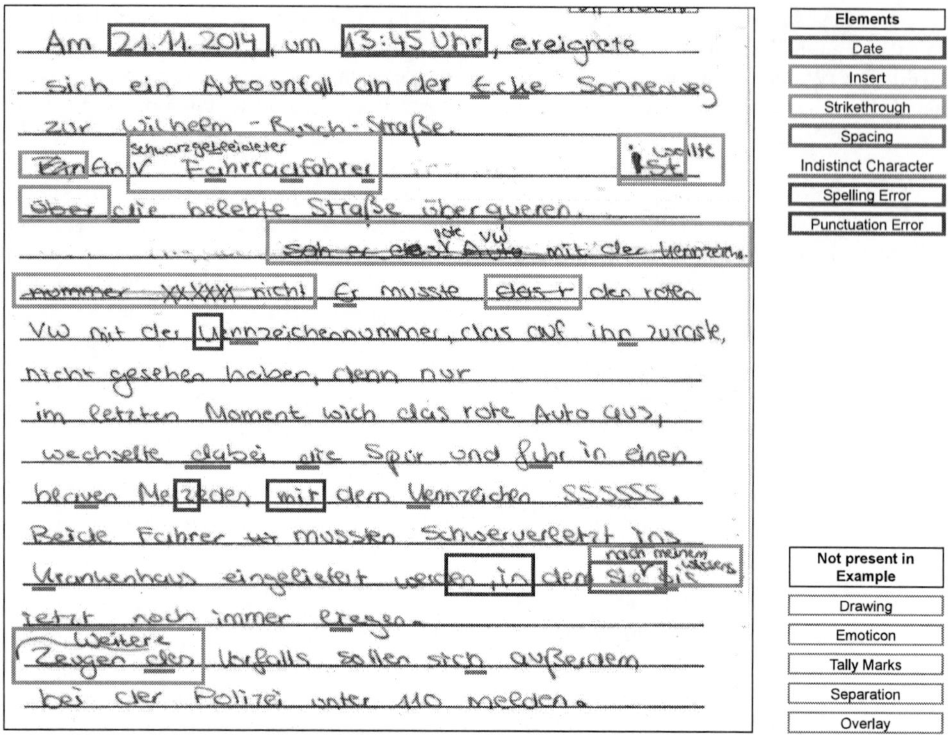

Figure 2: Handwriting sample from FD-LEX with non-normative writing practices present.

Set	GYM_5	GYM_9	IGS_5	IGS_9	Sum
1	144	90	84	72	390
2	102	96	84	108	390
3	132	138	114	60	444
4	120	138	90	90	438
5	156	132	72	84	444
6	162	120	96	114	492
7	168	144	132	120	564
8	150	132	120	120	522
9	138	144	126	114	522
10	138	144	132	132	546
11	150	120	108	90	468
12	144	84	108	72	408
Test Set	91			Total:	5628
Annotator 1	168				
Annotator 2	1092				

Table 1: The number of texts from the FD-LEX dataset used in our transcription process. Green cells indicate the subsets used for the test set which were double-transcribed, while dark orange and blue cells representing transcripts completed by Annotator 1 and Annotator 2, respectively.

tions such as rare writings on the backside or a blank white page. Figure 2 shows an example scan from this dataset.

The data from FD-LEX were collected in compliance with the relevant data protection regulations. Thus, the data were processed in such a way that the privacy and anonymity of the participating schools, classes, and students were preserved. No individual or group can be identified from the processed data, except for the fact that certain cases belong to the same school class or educational level.

The anonymized transcripts provided by Becker-Mrotzek and Grabowski (2018) normalize orthographic errors so that they cannot be directly used for our purposes. We thus had to re-transcribe the data according to our developed guidelines (preserving spelling errors, punctuation errors, and other orthographic peculiarities) as described in the next section.

4 Transcription Guidelines

The main goal of the guidelines is to ensure that the transcription reflects exactly what is written by the learner – i.e. orthography is not corrected – and where. In cases of doubt, it is necessary to reconcile what the child has written or intended to write with what a machine transcription would read. This involves careful consideration of the context and a deep understanding of the learner's level of proficiency. The transcription process should prioritize preserving the integrity of the original text and capturing the nuances of the learner's writing style, while also ensuring that the final output is legible for the handwriting recognition task.

In order to ensure consistency in the transcription process, transcribers are required to write the transcription in Excel. It is mandatory to turn off automatic error correction and automatic capitalization correction for the beginning of a text. The transcript should contain the following columns: name of the image, line num-

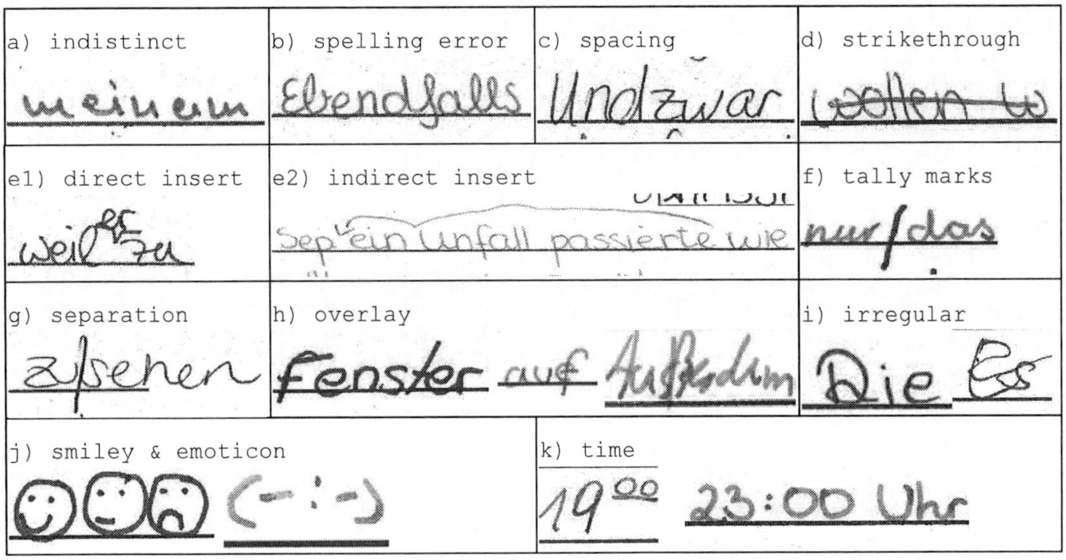

Figure 3: Examples from the FD-LEX dataset highlighting special cases of the transcription guidelines.

ber, status, content, and comment. The status column should be set to either 'ok', 'dis' (discussion), or 'err' (error). The 'dis' status indicates that the transcription requires further review, while the 'err' status indicates that the line should be disregarded.

Next, we will provide more specific guidelines on how to transcribe certain elements which are accompanied by examples in Figure 3:

Indistinct Character / Inaccuracy If a letter is written indistinctively, it is set inside of curly brackets: "{n}". (Example a: `mei{n}em`)

Spelling Error We have not corrected or tagged any types of spelling errors. Thus, they are directly transcribed as the learner wrote them. (Example b: `{Ebendfalls}` instead of `Ebenfalls`)

Spacing Inexperienced learners often struggle with producing consistent spacing in their writing. It is not uncommon to find instances where a particular letter is spaced differently from the rest of the word, necessitating the use of curly brackets for the transcription. Moreover, it is crucial to identify whether the letter is at the beginning or end of the word. This is represented by placing a space character within the curly brackets too. Compounding words can present further challenges, as learners may inadvertently leave excessive gaps between the constituent words or use insufficient spacing. (Example c: `Undzwar`)

Strikethrough If learners did not want a particular part of their content evaluated, they crossed it out. These strikethrough elements are transcribed with hashes (#). In the transcript, the number of hashes represents approximately the number of letters that were struck through. (Example d: `###### #...`)

Insert When a learner wanted to add content afterwards, the person used inserts. A small number of words or letters to be inserted are usually located at the targeted position and are transcribed in curly brackets with a "less than" symbol on the left of the content (example e1: `weil {<er} zu`). If an insert is dislocated, the targeted location is tagged using the word "insert" in curly brackets, followed by the number of the indirect insert on the page and the signaling character (often asterisks are used), if there is one (`{insert1}`). The insertion content is tagged likewise with the preceding `insert1` and if present, a signaling character. (Example e2: `Sep.{insert1} ein Unfall passierte {insert1 wie}`)

Regular Punctuation Mark In accordance with grammatical rules, regular punctuation marks such as stops (.), commas (,), and exclamation marks (!) are placed directly adjacent to the last written word. However, it should be noted that learners may sometimes place them differently, e.g. with more spacing, which is then ignored.

Tally Marks In some cases, the learner had to count the written words and marked them with tally marks '|'. These are transcribed in curly brackets according to the direction of the stroke, followed by an ampersand. (Example f: `nur {/&} das`)

Separation of a Word into two Words One type of correction made by the writer is adding a separator between two words that were originally written together because the learner intended them to be separate afterwards. Both words are transcribed separately and a separation sequence '|-' is placed into curly brackets. (Example g: `zu {|-} sehen`)

Overlay Another correction made by a learner is the overlaying of letters. In this case, both letters are placed in curly brackets and connected by a plus sign: `{F+f}`. The correct letter is written to the left of the plus and to the right is the incorrect one. (Examples h: `{F+f}enster; au{f+e}; Auß{ß+ss}erdem`)

Irregular Letter We found some special letters like letters with additional artifacts or even unusual versions of letters. These are transcribed with a plus sign to the right within curly brackets like: `{D+}`. (Examples i: `{D+}ie; {E+}s`)

Emoticon / Smiley Despite a large number of different emoticons, we decided to transcribe every emoticon in curly brackets with the same icon: ('U+1F642'). (First example j) Certain combinations of characters can be meant as smileys. These are transcribed as they appear. (Second example j: `(-:-)`)

Drawing A few learners put down larger drawings extending over several lines. If there is text before as well as after the drawing, each of the drawn lines are given an error status, and they are transcribed as three hashes (###) and a comment with a reference to the drawing. In the same style, if no text follows below the drawing, only one line is added to the transcript.

Time & Date In most cases, the information on time and date is transcribed as it appears. However, in some cases, the minutes are underlined, which is then ignored in the transcript. (Examples k: `1900; 23:00 Uhr`)

4.1 Format Conversion

We developed two converters to process the transcribed text: 1) to preprocess it for use in HWR and 2) to extract the continuous text for an assessment of e.g. the content of the text. In Figure 4 we can see the transcripts and converted variants of the example page in Figure 2.

To prepare the text for HWR, the converter removes curly brackets and all indicator signs (e.g. '&' for a tally mark, '<' for a direct insert, or '-' for separation). The converted version from (1) can be seen (1a) in Figure 4.

While indirect inserts were transcribed where they appear on the page, which is necessary for the HWR, the converter for extracting the continuous text inserts them at the position where they were intended to be (see (1b) in Figure 4). The converter also removes line breaks, which is not desirable for the HWR converter. Furthermore, strikethroughs are removed and in case of uncertainties which letter was meant, only the one that the transcriber indicated as most probable (the first named) is retained. Our current version of the converter does not include a spelling correction mechanism, although it could be a possible future extension. The highlighted words in (1b) show where the output of this converter differs from the original FD-LEX transcript,

IAA A1/A2	Accuracy w	Accuracy w/o {}	Kappa w	Kappa w/o {}	# chars (texts)
GYM-5_1	.95	.99	.94	.98	15,700 (36)
GYM-9_1	.90	.99	.90	.98	15,000 (19)
IGS-5_4	.85	.97	.84	.97	6,300 (18)
IGS-9_4	.86	.98	.85	.98	6,900 (18)
All	.89	.98	.89	.98	43,900 (91)

Table 2: Comparison of percentage agreement and Kappa scores with and without curly brackets { } between two annotators with number of texts and number of characters.

which is shown in (2) in Figure 4. We can see that besides the line breaks, the main difference is that in our transcript, spelling and grammar errors are retained.

Both converters, along with the transcription guidelines, are hosted on GitHub[3].

5 Transcription Analysis

In this transcription project, a total of 1,350 handwritten learner pages were transcribed, resulting in about 13,300 lines of text in total. A subset of about 90 pages was transcribed by two annotators and a gold transcription was created by an adjudicator for improved accuracy.

5.1 Inter-Annotator Agreement

We computed the inter-annotator agreement (IAA) to ensure that the guidelines allow for consistent transcriptions. We utilized the Python library LingPy (List and Forkel, 2019) to align the two transcripts character-wise and computed in how many cases both annotators used the same character. We report both percentage agreement and Cohen's Kappa but given the high number of different characters to choose from, chance agreement is very low, so the two values are very similar.

In order to ensure ongoing high consistency between the two annotators, we continually monitored and checked the agreement between their transcriptions over time, which resulted in 4 subsets. Table 2 shows a high level of agreement between the two annotators, with a percentage agreement of approximately 89%.

To account for the difficulty of deciphering some characters in the texts, our guidelines allow for the use of curly brackets to mark cases where the character was indistinct or difficult to read. Because the interpretation of these characters can vary depending on the annotator's individual perception and understanding, it is somewhat subjective. Therefore, we also calculated the agreement when curly brackets are ignored. This resulted in a very high agreement score of 98%, showing that most of the disagreements resulted just from marking incertainty.

[3]https://github.com/catalpa-cl/learner-handwriting-recognition

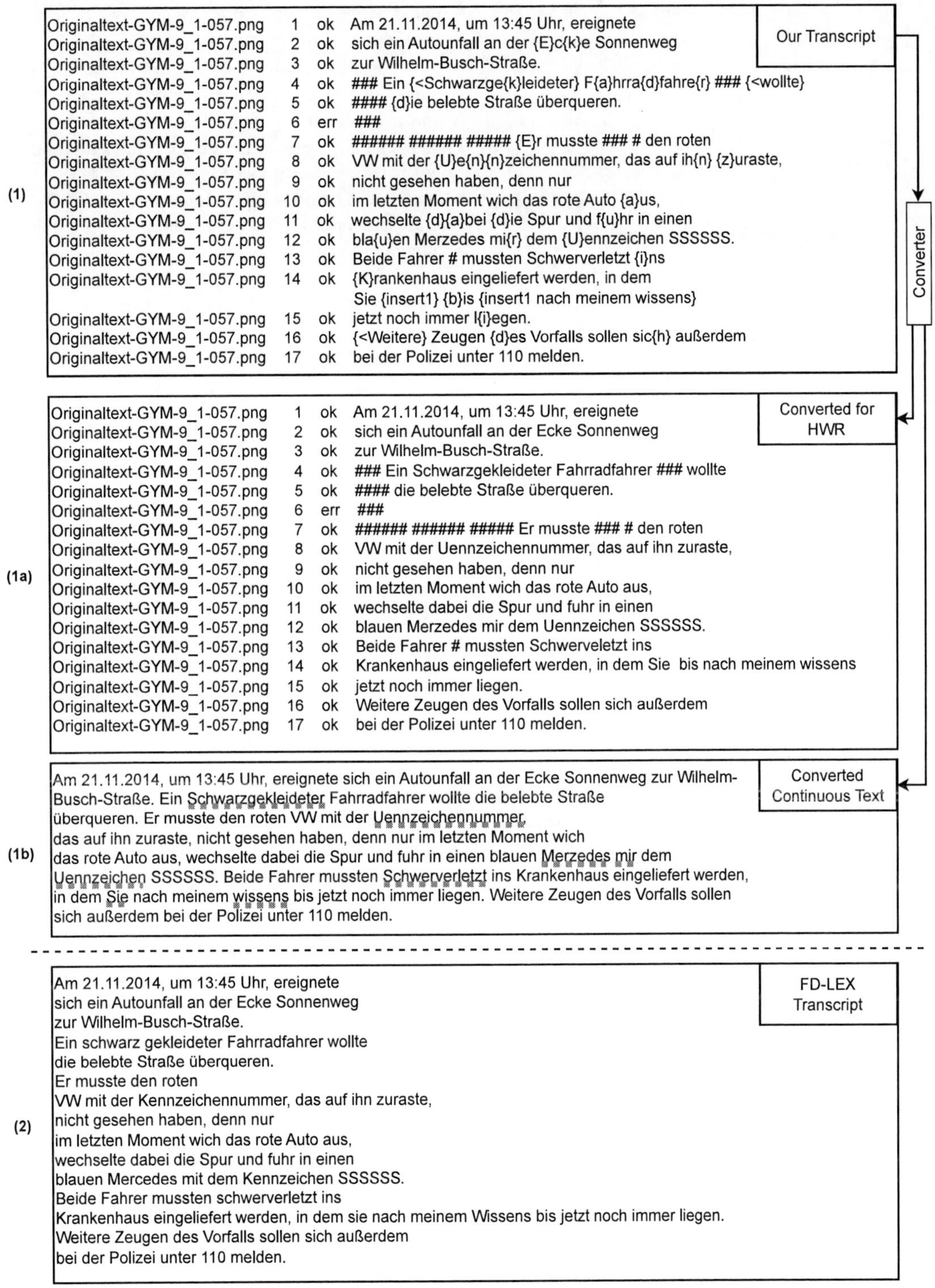

Figure 4: Our transcript (1) from the example page in Figure 2, the converted variants for HWR (1a) and continuous text (1b), and the original transcript of FD-LEX (2). Highlighted words in (1b) show the difference to (2).

IAA Anno. <>Gold	Anno.	Accuracy w	Accuracy w/o	Kappa w	Kappa w/o
GYM-5_1 Set 1 - 17 pages	A1	.93	.98	.93	.98
	A2	.96	.99	.96	.97
GYM-5_1 Set 2 - 19 pages	A1	.97	.99	.96	.99
	A2	.98	1.0	.98	1.0
GYM-9_1	A1	.91	.98	.90	.98
	A2	.98	1.0	.98	1.0
IGS-5_4	A1	.87	.98	.87	.97
	A2	.96	1.0	.95	1.0
IGS-9_4	A1	.87	.98	.87	.98
	A2	.96	.99	.96	.99
Average	A1	.91	.98	.91	.98
	A2	.97	.99	1.0	.99
	Both	.94	.98	.94	.99

Table 3: Performance evaluation of annotators A1 and A2 compared to gold label with and without curly brackets {}.

Addressed Issue	Frequency
unclear characters	25,420
strikethrough (word)	1,511
strikethrough (char in word)	1,631
overlay	809
direct inserts	458
indirect inserts	149
tally marks	31
separator	19
emoji	15

Table 4: Breakdown of the frequency of various non-normative writing practices in 1,350 pages, as identified by our transcription guidelines. These practices include unclear characters, inserts, strikethroughs, emojis, tally marks, separators, and overlays.

To create a single version that represents the most accurate transcription of the content, the two versions were merged into a gold-standard version by an adjudicator. We then evaluated the performance of both annotators, A1 and A2, by comparing their transcriptions to the gold standard using the same evaluation metrics as before. The results, presented in Table 3, show that on average, A1 had a slightly lower level of agreement with the gold standard than A2. Nevertheless, the overall level of agreement between the two annotators and the gold label was high, with a score of 94% and 99% without curly brackets.

5.2 Dataset Statistics

The transcriptions mark particular features of handwriting. The frequency of these can be seen in Table 4. One of the most notable features was the presence of a significant number of unclear characters, which amounted to over 25,400 instances within the whole transcribes dataset. Another notable feature is the presence of over 1,500 instances of strikethrough words, and about 1,600 single characters were struck out.

Furthermore, there were 800 instances of overlays, which occurred when the writer wrote over a previously written text. These overlays made it difficult to discern the intended characters or words, and required the annotators to carefully examine the image and use their best judgment to transcribe the correct characters. The most frequent overlays are upper and lower case variants like 'S+s', 'A+a', 'M+m', 'E+e', and 'F+f'. Additionally, there were over 450 direct inserts and about 150 indirect inserts, which required the annotators to transcribe the insert location and the corresponding content separately. 15 instances of emojis were found throughout the transcription.

6 Summary and Related Research Findings

In order to make handwritten texts available to automatic analyses such as an automatic feedback system for spelling errors, the texts need to be transcribed first, whereby all necessary features such as spelling errors need to be retained. A HWR system that automates such transcriptions needs images and corresponding transcripts as training data. Since no such dataset yet existed, we manually re-transcribed 1,350 pages of the learner dataset FD-LEX, while maintaining the authenticity of the handwritten texts and preserving non-normative writing practices. We developed comprehensive transcription guidelines to address issues such as spelling errors, indistinct characters, word separation, drawings, and special signs like tally marks. The transcription process resulted in a corpus that can be transformed using two converters into a version for HWR and a continuous text for content assessment. To ensure consistency, about 90 pages were double-transcribed, yielding a high IAA of about .98 at the character level.

We also investigated the frequency of certain non-normative writing practices and highlighted the benefit of having an authentic record of young learners' texts.

Based on this work, we were able to investigate handwriting recgonition of learner texts when orthographical errors are supposed to be retained (Gold et al., 2023). In this subsequent study, we used 1,350 of the transcribed pages of the FD-LEX dataset for training a handwriting recognizer and tested it on the gold transcription of the double-transcribed pages. By incorporating a language model and a dictionary that we automatically enriched with possible spelling errors, we were able to improve the recognition performance and to retain spelling errors in the transcripts.

7 Limitations

Our transcription guidelines occupy a certain position in the continuum between completely preserving the authenticity of learner handwriting and completely ignoring it. This position is motivated by our aim of capturing mainly orthographic features, which comes at the expense of other (e.g. readability, comprehension, and cohesiveness) features of the text.

In the course of this study, we only applied the guidelines to German texts. While we are quite certain that they generalize to other alphabetic languages (especially closely related ones), it cannot be ruled out that we missed some language-specific phenomena. However, these could be mitigated by augmenting the guidelines accordingly. Our guidelines are not directly applicable to other, e.g. logographic, writing systems.

8 Ethics Statement

In our work, we are using handwritten texts from the FD-LEX dataset (Becker-Mrotzek and Grabowski, 2018) which have already undergone anonymization protecting the children in the study. First, the children were instructed not to provide any personal data such as their names, schools, or addresses. Second, additional anonymization was performed by deleting image information and replacing it with the background color.

However, since our guidelines were not exclusively tailored towards FD-LEX and were designed to be applicable to a wide range of texts containing orthographic errors, we specifically address anonymization in the annotation guidelines.

To create the transcripts, we hired two annotators which were paid above the local minimum-wage standards.

Our transcripts (retaining orthographic errors) might be used to build technology assisting learners by providing automated feedback on orthographic errors. By doing so, we might also uncover learning disorders like dyslexia, which would in most cases be beneficial for better treatment, but might also have stigmatizing effects especially in cases where the system malfunctioned.

Acknowledgments

This work was conducted at "CATALPA - Center of Advanced Technology for Assisted Learning and Predictive Analytics" of the FernUniversität in Hagen, Germany.

We would like to express our sincere gratitude to the annotators: Fidan Firat and Angelika Ortner, who dedicated their time and expertise to transcribing the challenging handwritten documents used in this study. Their contributions were essential to the success of this project. We would also like to thank them for their valuable feedback, suggestions, and work to continually improve the transcription guidelines throughout the course of this study.

We would like to extend our heartfelt appreciation to Sandra Tietjens and the FD-LEX team for generously providing us with the dataset and for their invaluable support and communication throughout our research process.

References

Michael Becker-Mrotzek and Joachim Grabowski. 2018. FD-LEX (Forschungsdatenbank Lernertexte). Textkorpus Scriptoria. Köln: Mercator-Institut für Sprachförderung und Deutsch als Zweitsprache. Available at: https://fd-lex.uni-koeln.de, DOI: 10.18716/FD-LEX/861.

Anne Bohnenkamp, Silke Henke, and Fotis Jannidis. 2019. *Johann Wolfgang Goethe: Faust. Historisch-kritische Edition.* Frankfurt am Main / Weimar / Würzburg. With the assistance of Gerrit Brüning, Katrin Henzel, Christoph Leijser, Gregor Middell, Dietmar Pravida, Thorsten Vitt und Moritz Wissenbach.

P. Durrant and M. Brenchley. 2018. Growth in Grammar Corpus.

Christian Gold, Ronja Laarmann-Quante, and Torsten Zesch. 2023. Recognizing Learner Handwriting Retaining Orthographic Errors for Enabling Fine-Grained Error Feedback. In *Innovative Use of NLP for Building Educational Applications (BEA) Workshop at ACL.*

Joachim Grabowski, Michael Becker-Mrotzek, Matthias Knopp, Jörg Jost, and Christian Weinzierl. 2014. Comparing and combining different approaches to the assessment of text quality. *Methods in Writing Process Research*, pages 147–165.

Elma Kerz, Yu Qiao, Daniel Wiechmann, and Marcus Ströbel. 2020. Becoming linguistically mature: Modeling english and german children's writing development across school grades. In *Proceedings of the Fifteenth Workshop on Innovative Use of NLP for Building Educational Applications (BEA)*, pages 65–74.

Florian Kleber, Stefan Fiel, Markus Diem, and Robert Sablatnig. 2013. CVL-Database: An Off-line Database for Writer Retrieval, Writer Identification and Word Spotting. In *International Conference on Document Analysis and Recognition (ICDAR)*, pages 560–564. IEEE.

Johann-Mattis List and Robert Forkel. 2019. LingPy: A Python library for historical linguistics. v2.6.9. Leipzig: Max Planck Institute for Evolutionary Anthropology.

U-V Marti and Horst Bunke. 2002. The IAM-database: an English sentence database for offline handwriting recognition. *International Journal on Document Analysis and Recognition (IJDAR)*, 5(1):39–46.

Exploring the Impact of Transliteration on NLP Performance: Treating Maltese as an Arabic Dialect

Kurt Micallef[1] kurt.micallef@um.edu.mt
Fadhl Eryani[2,3] fadhl.eryani@nyu.edu
Nizar Habash[3] nizar.habash@nyu.edu
Houda Bouamor[4] hbouamor@cmu.edu
Claudia Borg[1] claudia.borg@um.edu.mt

[1]Department of Artificial Intelligence, University of Malta
[2]University of Tübingen
[3]Computational Approaches to Modeling Language Lab, New York University Abu Dhabi
[4]Carnegie Mellon University Qatar

Abstract

Multilingual models such as mBERT have been demonstrated to exhibit impressive cross-lingual transfer for a number of languages. Despite this, the performance drops for lower-resourced languages, especially when they are not part of the pre-training setup and when there are script differences. In this work we consider Maltese, a low-resource language of Arabic and Romance origins written in Latin script. Specifically, we investigate the impact of transliterating Maltese into Arabic scipt on a number of downstream tasks: Part-of-Speech Tagging, Dependency Parsing, and Sentiment Analysis. We compare multiple transliteration pipelines ranging from deterministic character maps to more sophisticated alternatives, including manually annotated word mappings and non-deterministic character mappings. For the latter, we show that selection techniques using n-gram language models of Tunisian Arabic, the dialect with the highest degree of mutual intelligibility to Maltese, yield better results on downstream tasks. Moreover, our experiments highlight that the use of an Arabic pre-trained model paired with transliteration outperforms mBERT. Overall, our results show that transliterating Maltese can be considered an option to improve the cross-lingual transfer capabilities.

1 Introduction

The availability of multilingual models has facilitated the development of NLP tools for many low-resource languages. Their appeal not only comes from this universal language representation but also through leveraging data from related languages (Kondratyuk and Straka, 2019; Wu and Dredze, 2019; Conneau et al., 2020). Despite this, multilingual models may fall short especially for lower-resourced languages (Wu and Dredze, 2020; Muller et al., 2021). In particular, Muller et al. (2021) show that the cross-lingual transfer capabilities are hampered due to script differences between the target language and the related language which is part of the multilingual model pre-training. However, they show that performance is dramatically improved by transliterating the target language to the same script as the related language. Unlike translation, transliteration is a relatively cheap process which maps characters in a given script to another.

In this work, we focus on Maltese, a low-resource hybrid/mixed language of Semitic origin but written in Latin script. Although it retains a strong Semitic, specifically Arabic, component in its grammar, it borrows heavily from Romance (Italian) and English. This motivates us to explore the impact that transliterating Maltese into Arabic script could have on a number of downstream tasks. Besides using large language models based on Arabic text, this experimental setup opens up interesting research questions about the impact of high ambiguity from Arabic orthographic choices, such as dropping diacritics which may lower out-of-vocabulary, but also increase ambiguity.

Despite its Arabic roots, transliterating Maltese to Arabic script is not trivial because of the strong non-Arabic influences on Maltese and its evolution independent of the Arab world for a significant number of years (Sutcliffe, 1936; Borg and Azzopardi-Alexander, 1997). That said, Arabic-transliterated Maltese can be deemed as an Arabic dialect with a higher degree of Italian code-switching. As such, unlike Muller et al. (2021), we do not just rely on multilingual language models for cross-lingual transfer, but also make use of Arabic language models, specifically CAMeLBERT (Inoue et al., 2021). We compare its performance

Proceedings of the Workshop on Computation and Written Language (CAWL 2023), pages 22–32
July 14, 2023 ©2023 Association for Computational Linguistics

to multilingual BERT (Devlin et al., 2019) and monolingual Maltese BERT (Micallef et al., 2022). Empirically, we show that there are differences in the cross-lingual transfer capabilities of Arabic models and multilingual models for Maltese.

The main contributions of this work are as follows. We present various transliteration pipelines from Maltese to Arabic script ranging from simple one-to-one character maps to more sophisticated alternatives that explore multiple possibilities or make use of manually annotated linguistic constructions. We show that the sophisticated systems are consistently better than simpler systems, quantitatively and qualitatively. We also show that despite its hybrid nature, transliterating Maltese can be considered as an option to improve the cross-lingual transfer capabilities.

The rest of the paper is organized as follows. We present a discussion of motivating linguistic background (Section 2) followed by our approach for transliterating Maltese to Arabic script (Section 3). We present our evaluation in Sections 4 and 5.

2 Linguistic Background

2.1 Arabic and Maltese

Arabic and Maltese are closely related Semitic languages. Arabic is the national language of ~360 million people across 22 countries (Eberhard et al., 2022), while Maltese is the national language of Malta and is spoken by ~500,000 people (Rosner and Borg, 2022).

The Arabic language is a collection of coexisting varieties. While Classical Arabic (CA) still survives in Muslim religious ceremonies, Modern Standard Arabic (MSA) is the official national language of the media and formal education, but neither CA nor MSA is the *mother tongue* of Arabs today. A number of dialectal Arabic (DA) varieties are primary spoken (and increasingly informally written varieties). The coexistence of MSA and DA is described as diglossia (Ferguson, 1959). Foreign languages, particularly French (in the Maghreb) and English (in the Middle East) have a strong presence in DA and result in common code-switching (Hamed et al., 2020).

The Maltese language traces its origins to medieval Sicilian Arabic. In its current form, Maltese contains elements from Arabic, Italian, and most recently English. This reflects its geography and history: the Mediterranean island of Malta is halfway between Tunisia and Italy, and historically it was under Arab rule from 870 to 1090 CE. Being the language of a Christian nation, Maltese has no CA influences, unlike other Arabic dialects with diglossia (Sutcliffe, 1936; Borg and Azzopardi-Alexander, 1997). In some simplifying respects, Maltese can be seen linguistically as a dialect of Arabic with a higher degree of code-switching to Italian. Čéplö et al. (2016) reports that mutual intelligibility between Maltese, Tunisian Arabic (TA), and Libyan Arabic (LA) ranges between 30% and 40%, with TA having the highest level of mutual intelligibility with either of the other two varieties.

2.2 Script and Orthography

The most important difference between Arabic and Maltese is the use of Arabic and Latin scripts, respectively. Furthermore, the two languages use different orthographic philosophies in how to map linguistic features (phonology and morphology) to script letters. Given the topic of this paper and to facilitate the presentation of the remaining sections, we will start with a discussion of the two scripts and the orthographic philosophies they use.

The Arabic script is used to write a number of languages from different language families, e.g. Arabic (Semitic), Persian (Indo-European), and Uyghur (Turkic). The Arabic script is mostly used as an Abjad where diacritical marks represent short vowels and consonantal doubling, although there are exceptions such as Uyghur's Arabic alphabet. Since most diacritics are optionally written in the context of the Arabic *language* (Abjad) (Habash, 2010), this leads to a high degree of ambiguity. It should be noted, however, that initial vowels are always marked by having a word initial Alif ا *A* as a diacritic carrier; and final vowels typically reflect some deeper morphological feature of the word such as a weak verbal root radical or a nominal feminine ending. Arabic effectively relies on its strong templatic morphology that allows readers to limit the ambiguity space. Arabic orthography also tends toward morphophonemic spelling which abstracts away from allomorphy, e.g. the Arabic definite determiner proclitic ال *Al* has a number of allomorphs that assimilate with word-initial coronal consonants (so-called Sun Letters) but is always written in the morphemic form: الشمس *Al+šms* /*aš+šams*/ 'the+sun'. Finally, while MSA has standard rules for orthography, DAs do not. Arabic NLP researchers have developed conventions for writing DA to allow studying spelling

(i)

	(a)	(b)	(c)	(d)	(e)	(f)	(g)
Maltese	Min	ma	jġarrabx	il-ħażin	ma	jafx	it-tajjeb
Arabic	مين *myn*	ما *mA*	يجربش *yjrb$*	الحزين *AlHzyn*	ما *mA*	يفش *yf$*	الطيب *AlTyb*
Gloss	who	not	he-experiences-not	the-bad	not	he-knows-not	the-good
Origin	AR	AR	AR	AR*	AR	AR*	AR
English	He who has not experienced what is bad cannot know the worth of what is good						

(ii)

Maltese	Il-bnedmin	kollha	jitwieldu	ħielsa	u ugwali	fid-dinjità	u d-drittijiet
Arabic	البنادمين *AlbnAdmyn*	كلها *klhA*	يتوالدوا *ytwAldwA*	خالصة *xAlSp*	واجوالي *wAjwAly*	فالدنيتا *fAldnytA*	والدريتيات *wAldrytyAt*
Gloss	the-humans	all	they-are-born	free	and equal	in-the-dignity	and the-rights
Origin	AR	AR	AR*	AR*	AR IT	AR IT	AR IT*
English	All human beings are born free and equal in dignity and rights						

Table 1: Two Maltese examples paired with their idealized Arabic script orthography. Example (i) is a traditional proverb, and example (ii) is the first sentence in the Universal Declaration of Human Rights. The tags in Origin are AR=Arabic, IT=Italian, and *=*modified.* Arabic is presented from left to right to align with Maltese. Arabic Romanization is in the Buckwalter scheme (Habash et al., 2007).

varieties (Zribi et al., 2014; Habash et al., 2018).

The Maltese script is based on the Latin script with some extension ns (*ċ*, *ġ*, *ħ*, and *ż*). The Maltese orthographic philosophy is in some way diametrically opposed to Arabic's more abstracting orthographic philosophy: Maltese tries as much as possible to reflect the phonological form of the words. There are a few exceptions to this principle, which are felicitous for our task. First, Maltese marks the form of the definite determiner with a hyphen. The number of determiner variants is quite large (∼150) due to allomorphy from phonetic assimilation and proclitics, e.g., *il-*, *l-*, *ix-*, *x-*, *is-*, *s-*, *it-*, *t-*, *id-*, *d-*, are just a few forms of the definite determiner, all of which map to Arabic ال *Al*; this is in addition to many cliticized forms such as *lill-*, *lix-*, *lis-*, *lit-*, *lid-* (all with the preposition *lil* 'for') or *tal-*, *tax-*, *tas-*, *tat-*, *tad-* (all with the preposition *ta'* 'of') (Sutcliffe, 1936). Second, Maltese writes some consonants to reflect their etymological link to Arabic, e.g. *għ* which is mostly silent and corresponds to Arabic ع/غ *E/g* (Fabri et al., 2014). Third, Maltese spells the commonly used conjunction *u* 'and' separately from the word, whereas Arabic attaches it to the following word. Finally, Maltese has access to capital letters, a concept that has no parallel in Arabic script. Capital letters are used in Maltese in similar ways to English, marking proper nouns. We leave the use of capitalization as an additional modeling feature to future work.

2.3 Phonological Differences

Maltese lost many Arabic phonological features. These include all emphatic consonants (Walter, 2006), e.g. the *s* letters in Maltese *sejf* 'dagger' and *sajf* 'summer', correspond to two letters in their Arabic cognates, سيف *sayf* and صيف *Sayf*. Other examples include the Arabic voiced pharyngeal (ع *E*) and voiced uvular (غ *g*) merging into Maltese *għ*; and the voiceless versions of both (ح *H* and خ *x*) merging into Maltese *ħ*, among others. Many of the Arabic cognates in Maltese with the Qaf consonantal variable ق *q* are spelled in Maltese with *q* although pronounced as a glottal stop (as in Urban Levantine and Egyptian Arabic), e.g. Maltese *triq* 'street' طريق *Tryq*. Due to Italian influences, the Maltese phonetic inventory has acquired a number of non-Arabic sounds such as *p*, and *v*.

Maltese has six vowels (*a*, *e*, *i*, *o*, *u*, *ie*), the first five of which may be shortened in some contexts. Standard Arabic has three short and three long vowels; while most dialects expand the set to five short and long. Arabic short vowels are generally written with diacritical marks with exceptions due to underlying derivation, or word position (initial/final) (Habash et al., 2018).

2.4 Morphological Differences

Maltese morphology shares a lot of features with Maghreb Arabic morphology, and Arabic/Semitic morphology in general. This include a rich inflectional space (person, gender, number, aspect) and many clitics that both Arabic and Maltese write as part of the word form. For example, Maltese *dar* 'house', a cognate of Arabic دار *dAr*, can be inflected into *id-dar* 'the house', *tad-dar* 'of the house', *f'dar* 'in a house', and *darha* 'her house' which correspond to Arabic الدار *AldAr*, تاع الدار *tAE AldAr*, فدار *fdAr*, and دارها *dArhA*, respectively. While Maltese marks the determiner with a hyphen, which provides a strong morphological signal (Section 2.2), it does not mark pronominal clitics or negation particles similarly. In this paper, we do not use any morphological analysis and disambiguation tools to help in transliteration. We leave this direction to future work.

2.5 Lexical Differences

While there are many shared words between Maltese and Arabic (especially Maghreb and Tunisian Arabic), there are important differences. Table 1 highlights some examples of both kinds, but these can be further broken down. First are words that undergo a major phonological shift, e.g. *jafx* 'does not know' comes from Arabic يعرفش *yErf$*. Second are words that went through a semantic shift, e.g. *ħażin* 'bad' is related to Arabic حزين *Hzyn* 'sad'. Thirdly, Maltese has many univerbation constructions which Arabic generally avoids, e.g. Maltese *waranofsinhar* 'afternoon' corresponds to three Arabic cognate words ورا نفص النهار *wrA nfS AlnhAr* 'after middle [of] the day'. Finally, Italian-origin words are all distinct from Arabic, although in some cases they may have cognates in the dialects, e.g. *kċina* 'kitchen' corresponds to TA كوجينه *kwjynh* (Aquilina, 1987, 1990).

2.6 NLP Conventions in Arabic and Maltese

NLP research conventions have developed independently in Arabic and Maltese, posing challenges to working on them jointly. For example, basic tokenization in the Universal Dependency Treebanks for Arabic follows a relatively deep morphological tokenization that separates all clitics (except the determiner), and normalizes the form of the baseword (Nivre et al., 2017; Taji et al., 2017). In contrast, Maltese tokenizes the determiner but not much more, leaving all other enclitics attached to the word and proclitics attached to the determiner (Čéplö, 2018). We follow the Maltese decisions here to simplify our training and evaluation.

3 Our Transliteration System

We present a Maltese-to-Arabic transliteration system with a number of variants that we evaluate in Sections 4 and 5. The transliteration system contains two operations: **mapping** and **ranking**. Maltese text tokens and characters are mapped from Latin script to one or more alternatives in Arabic script (Section 3.2). Then, a separate component ranks the choices or uses a deterministic hardcoded baseline (Section 3.3).

3.1 Preprocessing

As discussed in Section 2.6, we operate on tokenized Maltese to allow us to maintain label alignments from the training data of the downstream tasks. As such, Maltese texts are first tokenized using the MLRS tokenizer.[1] Next, all Maltese texts are lower-cased, since there is no casing information in Arabic; and all Latin script diacritics are removed, excluding those relevant to Maltese, namely: *ċ*, *ġ*, *ħ*, and *ż*. For example, *soċjetà* 'society', which is a remnant of Italian, is mapped to *soċjeta*, reflecting a common form of spelling such words in standard Maltese.

3.2 Character and Token Mappings

Character Mappings We list all of the Maltese-to-Arabic character mappings we consider in Table 2. Most are letter-to-letter mappings such as *k* to ك *k*, but also include the Maltese multi-character letters *ie* and *għ*. The **Basic** column indicates the most expected letter mapping based on our observations considering etymology, phonology, and Arabic letter frequencies. The additional columns in the table indicate conditional mappings as well as non-deterministic additional mappings. For vowels, we include word-initial and word-final conditional mappings; and for consonants, the second of doubled letters may be mapped to a Shadda (Arabic gemination diacritic). All Arabic diacritics are deleted after the mapping step since they are often absent in the language model training data (Habash, 2010). We use the character mappings in two ways: (a) **deterministic** mappings using only the Basic column and its associated Doubling column in Table 2, and (b) **non-deterministic** mappings using all the columns in Table 2. Our deterministic mapping does not apply context specific word-initial and word-final rules.

[1] `https://mlrs.research.um.edu.mt/`

Vowels									
Maltese	Basic		Additional		Word Initial		Word Final		
ie	ا	*A*							
a	◌َ	*a*	ا	*A*	ا، آ	*A*, |	ا، ى، ة، ه	*A*, *Y*, *p*, *h*	
e	◌َ	*a*	ا	*A*	ا	*A*	ي	*y*	
i	◌ِ	*i*	ي	*y*	ا	*A*	ي	*y*	
o	◌ُ	*u*	و	*w*	ا	*A*	و	*w*	
u	◌ُ	*u*	و	*w*	ا	*A*	و، وا، ه	*w*, *wA*, *h*	

Consonants						
Maltese	Basic		Additional		Doubling	
għ	ع	*E*	غ	*g*		
'	ع	*E*				
b	ب	*b*			◌ّ	~
ċ	تش	*t$*			◌ّ	~
c	ك	*k*			◌ّ	~
d	د	*d*	ذ، ض، ظ	***, *D*, *Z*	◌ّ	~
f	ف	*f*			◌ّ	~
ġ	ج	*j*			◌ّ	~
g	ج	*j*			◌ّ	~
h	ه	*h*			◌ّ	~
ħ	ح	*H*	خ	*x*	◌ّ	~
j	ي	*y*			◌ّ	~
k	ك	*k*			◌ّ	~
l	ل	*l*			◌ّ	~
m	م	*m*			◌ّ	~
n	ن	*n*			◌ّ	~
p	ب	*b*			◌ّ	~
q	ق	*q*			◌ّ	~
r	ر	*r*			◌ّ	~
s	س	*s*	ص	*S*	◌ّ	~
t	ت	*t*	ط	*T*	◌ّ	~
v	ف	*f*			◌ّ	~
w	و	*w*			◌ّ	~
x	ش	*$*			◌ّ	~
y	ي	*y*			◌ّ	~
ż	ز	*z*			◌ّ	~
z	دز	*dz*			◌ّ	~

Table 2: Maltese to Arabic Character Mappings (shaded regions are romanizations in the Buckwalter scheme (Habash et al., 2007)). Additional, Word Initial, and Word Final are the conditional alternatives considered for the non-deterministic mappings.

Token Mappings We augment the character-level mappings with **closed class** token-level mappings that exploit known features of Maltese orthography such as the spelling of the definite determiner, as well as the Zipfian head distribution of closed class words which we expect to help transfer learning in downstream tasks. In the settings where they are used, the token mappings take precedence over the character mappings since they match a token exactly.

We extracted all the closed class tokens from the training set portion of the MLRS POS data (Gatt and Čéplö, 2013), by filtering over the part-of-speech tag. For each of these tokens, a manual transliteration is performed by native Arabic speakers following a consistent interpretation of the Conventional Orthography for Dialectal Arabic (CODA) guidelines (Habash et al., 2018). To facilitate the interpretation of the token, annotators were provided with the POS tag, the IPA transcription (extracted using a grapheme-to-phoneme system by Borg et al. (2014)), and a sample sentence where the token is used. Native Maltese speakers were consulted for ambiguous cases.

In total, we have 691 mappings (henceforth, **Full** closed-class).[2] Examples include *fuq* `PREP` 'over', *ftit* `QUAN` 'some', *kellu* `VERB_PSEU` 'he had', and *mhux* `PRON_PERS_NEG` 'he is not', which map to فوق *fwq*, فتيت *ftyt*, كان له *kAn lh*, and ماهوش *mAhw$*, respectively. Additionally, we consider a subset of 135 mappings (henceforth, **Small** closed-class) which we restrict to the tokens containing - and/or ', such as *il-* 'the', *fis-* 'in the', and *t'* 'of', which map to ال *Al*, فال *fAl*, and تاع *tAE*, respectively. We designate not using the token mappings as **None**.

3.3 Ranking Techniques

While token mappings are essentially deterministic, character mappings produce a large lattice of combinations, e.g. Maltese *ħielsa* 'free' results in 20 forms, including خالصة *xAlSp*, حالصى *HAlSY*, خالسا *xAlsA*, حالصه *HAlSh*, and حلس *Hls*. In this section we present various ranking techniques used to select one of the alternatives for a given input.

Deterministic The use of deterministic character mappings yields a single alternative for each word, thereby not requiring any ranking.

Random A random choice is made by selecting the first alphabetically sorted token from the list of combinations. We sort to keep this technique stable across different runs.

Sub-Token Count The BERT-based language models used in the downstream task may split a given word into multiple sub-tokens (Devlin et al., 2019). We choose the mapping combination with fewer resulting sub-tokens. This idea is based on the evidence that a tokenizer that splits tokens into fewer sub-tokens correlates with better downstream performance (Rust et al., 2021).

[2]We do not use the part-of-speech information in the actual mapping process. Although there are a number of tokens that appear with different part-of-speech tags, only one of these tokens (*m'*) resulted in different transliterations: `NEG` ما *mA*, `COMP` من *mn*, and `PREP` مع *mE*. Since the `NEG` reading is the most common in our data by far, we ignore the other two.

N-gram Language Model Scores We use the word and character n-gram language models from Baimukan et al. (2022) to get **word-level** and **character-level** scores on each generated token, respectively. As highlighted in Section 2.1, due to the similarity with Maltese, we consider both the country-level Tunisian (TUN) and region-level Maghrebi (MAG) models, ending up with two sets of scores.

Some of these scores are bound to produce ties, occasionally ranking more than one token in first place. In our analysis, the word n-gram model tends to produce ties whenever the word is out of vocabulary while the sub-token count model is much more sporadic with ties. We observed that the character n-gram score almost never produced ties on the data, and so we used it as a fallback to resolve ties. Ties can further be resolved randomly if need be.

3.4 Implementation

The various mapping settings we consider in the rest of the paper select for a token-mapping setup and a ranking setup. Conceptually, putting together all of these components results in a pipeline where a token is mapped using the closed-class token mappings, backing off to the character mappings whenever the token is not found in the token mappings. This is followed by a ranking step which selects among the various options produced by the mapping component.

We implement all mappings from Section 3.2 using finite-state machinery in Pynini (Gorman, 2016). The seven basic FSTs we implement are the following: full token mappings, small token mappings, non-deterministic and deterministic multi-character mappings,[3] non-deterministic and deterministic single character mappings, and dediacritization mappings. These are then composed in succession on the fly, based on the experimental setup being used.

The generated alternatives are ranked as described in Section 3.3. The sub-token count metric is implemented using the Transformers library (Wolf et al., 2020) while the n-gram language model scores are obtained using KenLM (Heafield, 2011).

We make the code publicly available.[4]

[3]This includes multi-character letters (*ie* and *għ*) along with geminates (**Doubling**), and **Word Initial** and **Word Final** vowels from Table 2.

[4]`https://github.com/MLRS/malti_arabi_fst`

4 Downstream Task Evaluation

The transliteration system is evaluated on three downstream tasks: Part-of-Speech Tagging (**XPOS**),[5] Dependency Parsing (**DP**), and Sentiment Analysis (**SA**). Input tokens in the datasets are transliterated as discussed in Section 3, with their corresponding labels/tags remaining unchanged. Further details on the dastaset sources and processing is given in Section 4.1.

We consider three setups of token mappings, all of which use the character mappings as described in Section 3.2: the entire set of the full closed-class mappings (**Full**), the small closed-class mappings (**Small**), and no token mappings (**None**). For each of these setups, we use the ranking techniques from Section 3.3. This creates 24 distinct transliteration pipelines (3 mapping options by 8 ranking techniques), which we explore in this Section. Every dataset is transliterated through each of these pipelines, which are then used to fine-tune the language model following the setup used by Micallef et al. (2022). Each fine-tuned model is evaluated on the corresponding transliterated test set.

We systematically compare the pipelines on CAMeLBERT-Mix (Inoue et al., 2021) due to its training on dialectal data. We also fine-tune BERTu, a monolingual Maltese model (Micallef et al., 2022), and multilingual BERT (mBERT) (Devlin et al., 2019) on the datasets in the original script (untransliterated). Additionally, we consider another setup for mBERT where it is fine-tuned on transliterated Maltese. We report accuracy for XPOS Tagging, Labelled Attachment Score (LAS) for DP, and macro-averaged F1 for SA.

4.1 Datasets

We use the MUDT (Čéplö, 2018) dataset as is for the DP task. For the XPOS task, we use the MLRS POS dataset (Gatt and Čéplö, 2013), but with different splits from Micallef et al. (2022) to ensure that the instances overlapping with the MUDT data are in the same splits.

The SA dataset used (Martínez-García et al., 2021) is preprocessed and tokenized using the MLRS tokenizer. Although this task involves classifying a whole sentence, this preprocessing is done because the transliteration system operates on tokens rather than sentences. Once each token is transliterated these are joined back as a single text,

[5]XPOS refers to the language-specific tagset as opposed to UPOS, the universal tagset (Nivre et al., 2017).

Task	Dataset	Training	Validation	Testing
XPOS	MLRS POS	4,935	616	616
DP	MUDT	1,123	518	433
SA	Sentiment	595	85	171

Table 3: Dataset sizes in terms of sentences

separated by spaces. Admittedly, this results in different spacing compared to the source sentence, particularly for tokens with determiners and punctuation symbols in general. However, we fine-tune the baselines which use the original Latin script with this same pre-processing strategy.

The tokens in the MUDT and MLRS POS datasets are kept as is since these are consistent with the MLRS tokenizer. A summary of the dataset sizes is given in Table 3. To address the discrepancy in the data sizes, we also consider a lower-resourced setup where the training and validation (but not test) sets of each tasks are reduced to the smallest dataset size used in this evaluation (SA). This allows us to control for size when analysing the cross-lingual transfer capabilities.

4.2 Results

The results shown in Table 4 highlight that a combination of the full closed-class mappings and any of the non-deterministic systems achieve the best performance across all tasks. As expected, the deterministic system without any token mappings performs the worse, generally. Analysing the token and character mappings as different dimensions, reveals some interesting trends.

Token Mappings The inclusion of closed-class mappings consistently yields improvements over using no token mappings in all scenarios. In the deterministic case, the full token mappings are beneficial to surpass the non-deterministic counterpart with random ranking, in the DP and SA tasks, and are competitive against the other non-deterministic non-random scores in all tasks. The small closed-class mappings also generally improve over using no token mappings, although this is slightly detrimental in a few cases. Inspecting further the relationship between the full, small, and no token mappings, it is evident that the jumps in performance are more pronounced in the lower-resourced setup compared to the whole data setup. These findings indicate that while linguistic annotations are generally helpful, they are most useful in setups when data is scarcer.

Ranking Techniques The random ranking performs the worst of all the techniques considered for the non-deterministic character mappings but does better than the deterministic counterpart in cases where no additional tokens are present. All techniques, apart from random, perform comparably, with the word language model ranker achieving the best scores on the syntactic tasks while the character model and sub-token rankers give the best results in the semantic task.

Ranking with the Tunisian word model scores yielded the best result in 3 out of 5 task-data setups. This is likely due to the high degree of mutual intelligibility between Maltese and Tunisian Arabic as detailed in Section 2.1. Moreover, this ranking tends to give significant boosts in performance just by using the small token mappings as evidenced by the similar results obtained by the system with the full token mappings. Conversely, the Maghrebi models tend to give worse scores without any token mappings and gave a worse result than the deterministic system in one particular case in SA.

Pre-trained LMs and Transliteration Comparing the best result from each task and data size setup from Table 4 against the baselines shown in Table 5, it is evident that mBERT fine-tuned without transliteration is only better than the best transliteration pipeline in XPOS when the entire data is used. For SA and lower-resourced DP, the difference between mBERT and the best transliteration pipeline on CAMeLBERT is found to be statistically significant, using a 1-tailed t-test with a p-value of < 0.05.

In Table 5, we compare transliteration with the Tunisian word model ranking with full token mappings. It is clear that fine-tuning BERTu with the original (untransliterated) data yields the best performance overall, owing to the Maltese corpora that this model is pre-trained on. Inspecting the results obtained for mBERT, transliteration does not always improve performance compared to untransliterated fine-tuning, and can result in significant degradations as evidenced in the SA task. Since, this is counter to what Muller et al. (2021) reported, it could be attributed to the hybrid nature of Maltese. However, we posit that this is also due to the fact the mBERT was solely pre-trained on MSA. Conversely, CAMeLBERT-Mix was trained on 5.8 billion DA data, making up around a third of the entire pre-training corpus (Inoue et al., 2021). In fact, when fine-tuning with transliterated Mal-

		XPOS						DP						SA		
		Large Training			Small Training			Large Training			Small Training			Small Training		
LM	**Mapping**	**None**	**Small**	**Full**	**None**	**Small**	**Full**	**None**	**Small**	**Full**	**None**	**Small**	**Full**	**None**	**Small**	**Full**
N/A	**Deterministic**	94.4	94.2	95.2	89.8	89.7	91.5	68.8	69.7	76.4	63.4	64.3	70.9	62.7	61.2	67.0
	Random	95.6	95.6	95.9	90.7	91.0	91.8	74.0	75.1	76.0	67.2	69.0	70.3	64.3	64.2	64.7
TUN	**Char Model**	95.5	95.7	95.9	91.1	91.7	92.4	75.1	76.1	77.3	69.5	70.5	**72.4**	64.5	63.9	65.5
	Word Model	95.6	96.0	**96.1**	91.3	92.5	**92.6**	75.1	76.5	77.3	68.8	71.5	**72.4**	64.0	65.9	66.7
	Sub-Tokens	95.6	95.6	95.9	91.0	91.5	92.3	75.2	76.4	**77.5**	69.0	70.7	72.0	66.3	67.6	67.3
MAG	**Char Model**	95.5	95.5	95.9	90.7	91.3	92.4	74.9	75.6	76.7	68.6	69.5	71.7	65.1	65.3	**69.7**
	Word Model	95.3	95.7	95.7	91.2	92.2	92.4	75.2	76.7	77.0	68.8	70.8	71.8	62.5	62.4	68.7
	Sub-Tokens	95.5	95.5	95.9	90.8	91.4	92.2	74.9	76.4	77.4	68.8	70.2	71.9	66.1	65.4	69.4

Table 4: Test set results for CAMeLBERT-Mix fine-tuned on transliterated Maltese, grouped by token and character mappings. The ranking techniques are further grouped by the language model used by the primary and/or fall-back technique: no language model (N/A), Tunisian (TUN), Maghrebi (MAG). Each value is an average of 5 runs with different random seeds. The best score in a task is **bolded**, while the best results per token mappings are underlined. Color shading is done with respect to the best and worst values of each task and training size setup.

		XPOS		DP		SA
Script	**Model**	**Large**	**Small**	**Large**	**Small**	**Small**
Arabic	**CAMeLBERT**	96.1	92.6	77.3	72.4	66.7
Arabic	**mBERT**	95.9	92.1	77.7	72.0	61.6
Latin	**mBERT**	96.7	92.4	77.3	71.1	67.3
Latin	**BERTu**	98.3	97.4	88.1	86.3	83.1

Table 5: Comparison of fine-tuning on raw and transliterated Maltese using different language models. The transliteration pipeline used is the Tunisian Word Model Ranking with Full token mappings. Large and Small refers to Large Training and Small Training set ups as in Table 4.

tese, CAMeLBERT performs better than mBERT in most task-data setups. CAMeLBERT is also able to surpass or be very competitive with mBERT fine-tuned on raw Maltese. This finding gives further evidence that there is some level of mutual intelligibility between transliterated Maltese and dialectal Arabic. Moreover, making use of monolingual models should be considered for cross-lingual transfer, whenever this is available.

5 Human Readability Evaluation

In this section, we investigate how readable transliterated Maltese is to native Arabic speakers. We compare four settings: the deterministic system against the non-deterministic system (Tunisian Arabic Word Model) with both None and Full token mappings. We sample 50 instances from the MUDT training set (Čéplö, 2018). For each example, we provide the original sentence, a translation extracted from Google Translate as a reference, and each of the alternative transliterations (see example in Table 6). We hide the transliteration system information and shuffle the order in which each alternative is displayed to prevent biases. For this study we ask the evaluator, a native speaker of Tunisian Arabic, who is fluent in French and familiar with Italian, to rank the transliterations in the order of how readable the text is, where 1 is best.

Table 7 shows the average readability rank for different combinations. The results show that using the Word Model is better than the Deterministic model, and that using the token mappings is helpful. These results correlate with our empirical evaluation from Section 4.

The evaluator reported that reading Maltese written in the Arabic script allowed them to easily recognize shared words between Maltese and Tunisian Arabic. For instance, the evaluator did not recognize the Maltese word *kien*, but when transliterated into the Arabic script as كان 'he was', it was evident. However, Italian-origin words presented a reading challenge, e.g. Maltese *akkuża* (Italian *accusa*) was garbled. The evaluator also pointed out that none of the transliteration models were capable of handling

	Text	Rank
Maltese	Illum waranofsinhar il-Maġistrat Miriam Hayman iddikjarat li hemm biżżejjed provi biex il-ħames aħwa tan-negozjant George Farrugia jitqiegħdu taħt att ta' akkuża.	
English	This afternoon Magistrate Miriam Hayman has stated that there is enough evidence to put the five brothers of businessman George Farrugia under indictment.	
Word Model + Full CC	الم ورنفسنهر ال ماجسترات مريم هيمان اذكارات اللي هم بالزايد بروفي باش ال خمس اخوه تاع ال نجودزينت جورجي فرجة يتقاعده تحت ات تاع اكزة .	1
Word Model + None	الم ورنفسنهر ال ماجسترات مريم هيمان اذكارات لي هم بزايد بروفي باش ال حماس اخوه تن نجودزينت جورجي فرجة يتقاعده تحت ات تاع اكزة .	2
Deterministic + Full CC	لم ورنفسنهر ال مجسترت مرم هيمن دكيرت اللي هم بالزايد برف باش ال خمس حو تاع ال نجدزينت جرج فرج يتقاعد تحت ت تاع كز .	3
Deterministic + None	لم ورنفسنهر ل- مجسترت مرم هيمن دكيرت ل هم بزيد برف باش ل- حمس حو تن- نجدزينت جرج فرج يتقاعد تحت ت تع كز .	4

Table 6: An example of a Maltese sentence along with its English translation and the output of the four transliteration models ranked by their readability level.

Mapping	Average Rank
Word Model + Full	1.1
Deterministic + Full	2.3
Word Model + None	2.5
Deterministic + None	4.0

Table 7: Average Readability Rank

Maltese univerbations, such as *waranofsinhar* 'afternoon' (see Table 6), which made it challenging to recognize and read them accurately.

This experiment highlighted some of the many challenges in reading Maltese written in Arabic script and provided insights into the limitations of different transliteration models, and issues to consider addressing in the future.

6 Conclusion and Future Work

We presented a Maltese-to-Arabic transliteration system as a tool to leverage cross-lingual transfer from Arabic. As evidenced by our empirical results, a non-deterministic system with signals from the target language helps in choosing a better transliteration alternative, especially in ambiguous cases. Moreover, incorporating human-annotated transliterations of a set of closed-class of words is beneficial in downstream performance, especially in lower-resource settings.

Our experimental setup exploited an Arabic language model for cross-lingual transfer, instead of a multilingual model such as mBERT. Results show promising results, giving better performance than multilingual models. This echoes the findings by Wu and Dredze (2020), and we encourage further research to investigate ways to effectively leverage resources from linguistically related languages.

Future work should investigate the use of large sentence-level contexts in mapping selections. Exploring cross-lingual transfer from Italian and English is also an interesting direction, including the use of few-shot and zero-shot learning. It would be interesting to also investigate these cross-lingual transfer techniques through transliterated Arabic.

Limitations

In this work, we transliterate all Maltese words in the same manner. Given the hybrid nature of Maltese, it might be optimal to handle words which do not have an Arabic origin in a different way. Similarly, we do not treat named-entities any differently.

Moreover, we assume that the Maltese text is written using the standard orthographic rules. In turn, the system might produce spurious transliterations for cases with spelling errors. This issue also exists when the text is in raw form, but may be further exacerbated with transliteration. The character mappings could be expanded to handle dropped Maltese diacritics, such as writing *c* instead of *ċ*, but there are other cases where silent letters such as *għ* are dropped altogether, making the problem non-trivial.

Acknowledgements

We acknowledge LT-Bridge Project (GA 952194) and DFKI for access to the Virtual Laboratory. We further acknowledge funding by Malta Enterprise.

References

Joseph Aquilina. 1987. *Maltese-English Dictionary Vol. I, A-L*. Midsea Books, Valletta, Malta.

Joseph Aquilina. 1990. *Maltese-English Dictionary Vol. II, M-Z*. Midsea Books, Valletta, Malta.

Nurpeiis Baimukan, Houda Bouamor, and Nizar Habash. 2022. Hierarchical aggregation of dialectal data for Arabic dialect identification. In *Proceedings of the Thirteenth Language Resources and Evaluation Conference*, pages 4586–4596, Marseille, France. European Language Resources Association.

Albert Borg and Marie Azzopardi-Alexander. 1997. *Maltese: Descriptive Grammars*. Routledge, London and New York.

Mark Borg, Keith Bugeja, Colin Vella, Gordon Mangion, and Carmel Gafà. 2014. Preparation of a free-running text corpus for Maltese concatenative speech synthesis. *Perspectives on Maltese Linguistics, Studia Typologica*, 14:297–318. Berlin:Akademie Verlag.

Slavomír Čéplö. 2018. *Constituent order in Maltese: A quantitative analysis*. Ph.D. thesis, Charles University, Prague.

Slavomír Čéplö, Ján Bátora, Adam Benkato, Jiří Milička, Christophe Pereira, and Petr Zemánek. 2016. Mutual Intelligibility of Spoken Maltese, Libyan Arabic, and Tunisian Arabic Functionally Tested: A Pilot Study. *Folia Linguistica*, 50(2):583–628.

Alexis Conneau, Kartikay Khandelwal, Naman Goyal, Vishrav Chaudhary, Guillaume Wenzek, Francisco Guzmán, Edouard Grave, Myle Ott, Luke Zettlemoyer, and Veselin Stoyanov. 2020. Unsupervised cross-lingual representation learning at scale. In *Proceedings of the 58th Annual Meeting of the Association for Computational Linguistics*, pages 8440–8451, Online. Association for Computational Linguistics.

Jacob Devlin, Ming-Wei Chang, Kenton Lee, and Kristina Toutanova. 2019. BERT: Pre-training of deep bidirectional transformers for language understanding. In *Proceedings of the 2019 Conference of the North American Chapter of the Association for Computational Linguistics: Human Language Technologies, Volume 1 (Long and Short Papers)*, pages 4171–4186, Minneapolis, Minnesota. Association for Computational Linguistics.

David M. Eberhard, Gary F. Simons, and Charles D. Fennig. 2022. 25 edition. SIL International. [link].

Ray Fabri, Michael Gasser, Nizar Habash, George Kiraz, and Shuly Wintner. 2014. *Linguistic Introduction: The Orthography, Morphology and Syntax of Semitic Languages*, pages 3–41. Springer Berlin Heidelberg, Berlin, Heidelberg.

Charles A. Ferguson. 1959. Diglossia. *Word*, 15(2):325–340.

Albert Gatt and Slavomír Čéplö. 2013. Digital Corpora and Other Electronic Resources for Maltese. In *Proceedings of the International Conference on Corpus Linguistics*, pages 96–97. UCREL, Lancaster, UK.

Kyle Gorman. 2016. Pynini: A Python library for weighted finite-state grammar compilation. In *Proceedings of the SIGFSM Workshop on Statistical NLP and Weighted Automata*, pages 75–80, Berlin, Germany. Association for Computational Linguistics.

Nizar Habash, Fadhl Eryani, Salam Khalifa, Owen Rambow, Dana Abdulrahim, Alexander Erdmann, Reem Faraj, Wajdi Zaghouani, Houda Bouamor, Nasser Zalmout, Sara Hassan, Faisal Al-Shargi, Sakhar Alkhereyf, Basma Abdulkareem, Ramy Eskander, Mohammad Salameh, and Hind Saddiki. 2018. Unified guidelines and resources for Arabic dialect orthography. In *Proceedings of the Eleventh International Conference on Language Resources and Evaluation (LREC 2018)*, Miyazaki, Japan. European Language Resources Association (ELRA).

Nizar Habash, Abdelhadi Soudi, and Tim Buckwalter. 2007. On Arabic Transliteration. In A. van den Bosch and A. Soudi, editors, *Arabic Computational Morphology: Knowledge-based and Empirical Methods*, pages 15–22. Springer, Netherlands.

Nizar Y Habash. 2010. *Introduction to Arabic natural language processing*, volume 3. Morgan & Claypool Publishers.

Injy Hamed, Ngoc Thang Vu, and Slim Abdennadher. 2020. ArzEn: A speech corpus for code-switched Egyptian Arabic-English. In *Proceedings of the Twelfth Language Resources and Evaluation Conference*, pages 4237–4246, Marseille, France. European Language Resources Association.

Kenneth Heafield. 2011. KenLM: Faster and smaller language model queries. In *Proceedings of the Sixth Workshop on Statistical Machine Translation*, pages 187–197, Edinburgh, Scotland. Association for Computational Linguistics.

Go Inoue, Bashar Alhafni, Nurpeiis Baimukan, Houda Bouamor, and Nizar Habash. 2021. The interplay of variant, size, and task type in Arabic pre-trained language models. In *Proceedings of the Sixth Arabic Natural Language Processing Workshop*, pages 92–104, Kyiv, Ukraine (Virtual). Association for Computational Linguistics.

Dan Kondratyuk and Milan Straka. 2019. 75 languages, 1 model: Parsing Universal Dependencies universally. In *Proceedings of the 2019 Conference on Empirical Methods in Natural Language Processing and the 9th International Joint Conference on Natural Language Processing (EMNLP-IJCNLP)*, pages 2779–2795, Hong Kong, China. Association for Computational Linguistics.

Antonio Martínez-García, Toni Badia, and Jeremy Barnes. 2021. Evaluating morphological typology in zero-shot cross-lingual transfer. In *Proceedings of the 59th Annual Meeting of the Association for Computational Linguistics and the 11th International Joint Conference on Natural Language Processing (Volume 1: Long Papers)*, pages 3136–3153, Online. Association for Computational Linguistics.

Kurt Micallef, Albert Gatt, Marc Tanti, Lonneke van der Plas, and Claudia Borg. 2022. Pre-training data quality and quantity for a low-resource language: New corpus and BERT models for Maltese. In *Proceedings of the Third Workshop on Deep Learning for Low-Resource Natural Language Processing*, pages 90–101, Hybrid. Association for Computational Linguistics.

Benjamin Muller, Antonios Anastasopoulos, Benoît Sagot, and Djamé Seddah. 2021. When being unseen from mBERT is just the beginning: Handling new languages with multilingual language models. In *Proceedings of the 2021 Conference of the North American Chapter of the Association for Computational Linguistics: Human Language Technologies*, pages 448–462, Online. Association for Computational Linguistics.

Joakim Nivre, Daniel Zeman, Filip Ginter, and Francis Tyers. 2017. Universal Dependencies. In *Proceedings of the 15th Conference of the European Chapter of the Association for Computational Linguistics: Tutorial Abstracts*, Valencia, Spain. Association for Computational Linguistics.

Mike Rosner and Claudia Borg. 2022. *Report on the Maltese Language*. Language Technology Support of Europe's Languages in 2020/2021. Maria Giagkou, Stelios Piperidis, Georg Rehm, Jane Dunne (Series Editors). Available online at `https://european-language-equality.eu/deliverables/`.

Phillip Rust, Jonas Pfeiffer, Ivan Vulić, Sebastian Ruder, and Iryna Gurevych. 2021. How good is your tokenizer? on the monolingual performance of multilingual language models. In *Proceedings of the 59th Annual Meeting of the Association for Computational Linguistics and the 11th International Joint Conference on Natural Language Processing (Volume 1: Long Papers)*, pages 3118–3135, Online. Association for Computational Linguistics.

Edmund F. Sutcliffe. 1936. *A grammar of the Maltese language, with chrestomathy and vocabulary*. Oxford University Press: Humphrey Milford, London.

Dima Taji, Nizar Habash, and Daniel Zeman. 2017. Universal dependencies for Arabic. In *Proceedings of the Workshop for Arabic Natural Language Processing (WANLP)*, Valencia, Spain.

Mary Ann Walter. 2006. Pharyngealization effects in Maltese Arabic. In *Perspectives on Arabic Linguistics: Papers from the annual symposium on Arabic linguistics. Volume XVI:, Cambridge, March 2002*, volume 266, pages 161–178. John Benjamins Publishing.

Thomas Wolf, Lysandre Debut, Victor Sanh, Julien Chaumond, Clement Delangue, Anthony Moi, Pierric Cistac, Tim Rault, Remi Louf, Morgan Funtowicz, Joe Davison, Sam Shleifer, Patrick von Platen, Clara Ma, Yacine Jernite, Julien Plu, Canwen Xu, Teven Le Scao, Sylvain Gugger, Mariama Drame, Quentin Lhoest, and Alexander Rush. 2020. Transformers: State-of-the-art natural language processing. In *Proceedings of the 2020 Conference on Empirical Methods in Natural Language Processing: System Demonstrations*, pages 38–45, Online. Association for Computational Linguistics.

Shijie Wu and Mark Dredze. 2019. Beto, bentz, becas: The surprising cross-lingual effectiveness of BERT. In *Proceedings of the 2019 Conference on Empirical Methods in Natural Language Processing and the 9th International Joint Conference on Natural Language Processing (EMNLP-IJCNLP)*, pages 833–844, Hong Kong, China. Association for Computational Linguistics.

Shijie Wu and Mark Dredze. 2020. Are all languages created equal in multilingual BERT? In *Proceedings of the 5th Workshop on Representation Learning for NLP*, pages 120–130, Online. Association for Computational Linguistics.

Inès Zribi, Rahma Boujelbane, Abir Masmoudi, Mariem Ellouze, Lamia Belguith, and Nizar Habash. 2014. A conventional orthography for Tunisian Arabic. In *Proceedings of the Ninth International Conference on Language Resources and Evaluation (LREC'14)*, pages 2355–2361, Reykjavik, Iceland. European Language Resources Association (ELRA).

Distinguishing Romanized Hindi from Romanized Urdu

Elizabeth Nielsen[†] **Christo Kirov**[°] **Brian Roark**[°]
[†]School of Informatics, University of Edinburgh, UK [°]Google
e.nielsen@ed.ac.uk {ckirov,roark}@google.com

Abstract

We examine the task of distinguishing between Hindi and Urdu when those languages are romanized, i.e., written in the Latin script. Both languages are widely informally romanized, and to the extent that they are identified in the Latin script by language identification systems, they are typically conflated. In the absence of large labeled collections of such text, we consider methods for generating training data. Beginning with a small set of seed words, each of which are strongly indicative of one of the languages versus the other, we prompt a pretrained large language model (LLM) to generate romanized text. Treating text generated from an Urdu prompt as one class and text generated from a Hindi prompt as the other class, we build a binary language identification (LangID) classifier. We demonstrate that the resulting classifier distinguishes manually romanized Urdu Wikipedia text from manually romanized Hindi Wikipedia text far better than chance. We use this classifier to estimate the prevalence of Urdu in a large collection of text labeled as romanized Hindi that has been used to train large language models. These techniques can be applied to bootstrap classifiers in other cases where a dataset is known to contain multiple distinct but related classes, such as different dialects of the same language, but for which labels cannot easily be obtained.

1 Introduction

Hindi and Urdu are considered the two standardized registers of the pluricentric Hindustani language. In informal speech, they are highly mutually intelligible, to the point where it can be difficult to immediately assess which one is being spoken (Masica, 1993). Written (and more formal) Hindi and Urdu, however, have more noticeable differences. First, outside of the colloquial vocabulary commonly used in speech, they do differ in broad historical influence on the lexicon – Hindi making use of more Sanskrit-derived words and Urdu using more Arabic- or Persian-derived words. Most notably, however, the languages differ in their native scripts: Hindi is written in Devanagari, a Brahmic script, while Urdu is written in a Perso-Arabic script. Despite these stark differences, efforts have been made to unify linguistic resources for the languages (e.g., Bhatt et al., 2009; Visweswariah et al., 2010; Bhat et al., 2016, 2017).

Additionally, however, both languages are frequently written informally in the Latin script, which is known as romanization (Wellisch, 1978). Informal romanization makes text in these languages far more difficult to distinguish than when they are written in their distinct native scripts. Despite their overall linguistic similarity, Hindi and Urdu do represent different cultural contexts, and may have different patterns of expression that are useful to capture correctly. Predictive models in service of, for example, romanized text entry – perhaps providing next word prediction and other utilities that should match the user's desired language – will be expected to provide culturally appropriate predictions, which may be difficult if all Urdu and Hindi data is conflated in the training data. In general, given the larger number of speakers, romanized Hindi text may be more prevalent and thus yield degraded performance for Urdu speakers in a range of applications that process romanized text if the two languages are conflated.

In this preliminary study, we look at leveraging multilingual large language models (LLMs) that have been pretrained on data that includes (conflated) romanized Hindi and Urdu text, along with a small seed word list, to gen-

Proceedings of the Workshop on Computation and Written Language (CAWL 2023), pages 33–42
July 14, 2023 ©2023 Association for Computational Linguistics

erate training data that can capture characteristic differences between romanized Urdu and Hindi. LLMs have recently become the backbone of many state-of-the-art NLP systems performing a wide range of tasks, often after some amount of fine-tuning (see, e.g., Ruder et al. (2021) for multilingual task benchmarks). In a recent paper, Nielsen et al. (2023) demonstrated that large language models learn some degree of long-distance sensitivity to spelling convention differences in English — i.e., the T5 LLM (Raffel et al., 2020) is more likely to produce the British spelling of a word following an earlier instance of British spelling than otherwise, even though the English language pretraining data is not labeled with the particular spelling convention. Unlike the well-understood and conventional set of spelling differences distinguishing US and UK English, romanized Hindi and Urdu represent a case where (a) there is no fixed orthography, i.e., spelling varies heavily; and (b) as far as we know, there are no documented widely attested differing romanization conventions between the two languages to rely upon. We thus try to exploit any implicit knowledge about such differences that a pretrained LLM may contain, as the means to build systems that can distinguish between the two languages.

We demonstrate that a simple decision tree classifier using character n-gram features can be profitably trained on LLM generated text to distinguish romanized Hindi from romanized Urdu, even in the face of domain-mismatch, at nearly the same accuracy as that classifier's topline (i.e., when trained on domain- and annotator-matched data). Interestingly, a more powerful neural classifier, which yields a substantially higher topline accuracy, overfits on the LLM generated training data to the point of performing essentially at chance on the validation set, suggesting that the neural classifier relies too heavily on reliable yet spurious differences between the classes in the generated text. We use the resulting decision tree classifiers to estimate the prevalence of Urdu in the mC4 corpus, and also examine their most important features, yielding some potentially useful generalizations about the romanization tendencies in the two languages.

2 Background

2.1 Romanized Hindi and Urdu

As stated earlier, distinguishing between Hindi and Urdu when written in their native scripts, Devanagari and Perso-Arabic respectively, is straightforward. Informal romanization removes this key distinction between the languages, and methods for automatic identification of romanized Hindi/Urdu text often conflate the two, sometimes deliberately (Ansari et al., 2021). This is particularly true since the romanization in Hindi and Urdu is typically less transliteration (i.e., driven by writing system correspondences) than rough phonetic transcription, hence the written differences between the two languages are lessened. For example, Urdu romanizations tend to include vowels even when the vowel is omitted in the Perso-Arabic orthography.

To see examples of this, we can examine the Dakshina dataset[1] (Roark et al., 2020), which includes both single word and full sentence romanizations of Wikipedia data in 12 South Asian languages, including Hindi and Urdu. The word "گزر" (pass) is romanized in the Urdu portion of the collection as either "guzar" or (less frequently) "gujar", despite having no vowels specified in the native script. The same word in Hindi (गुज़र) is romanized in the Hindi portion of the collection once as "guzar" and once as "gujar".

Such conventions obviously make it far more difficult to distinguish romanized Hindi from Urdu than when they are written in different native scripts. Despite the lack of a widely used standardized orthography in the Latin script in the languages, there may be some romanization conventions associated with each community that would help tease them apart. As we are not aware of any previous studies describing such distinguishing features in the linguistics literature, we turn to automated, data-driven methods to find them.

Romanized Hindi is frequent enough that it is commonly included in multilingual text collections scraped from the internet, such as mC4 (Xue et al., 2021), the multilingual corpus derived from Common Crawl[2] that is used

[1] https://github.com/google-research-datasets/dakshina

[2] http://commoncrawl.org/

to train mT5 (Xue et al., 2021), the multilingual version of the T5 language model (Raffel et al., 2020). Six languages are included in that corpus in both their native script and the Latin script – Chinese, Japanese, Hindi, Greek, Russian and Bulgarian – presumably because the language identification system used to identify the languages for the collection, CLD3,[3] only includes Latin script class labels for those six languages. Given the similarity of romanized Hindi and Urdu, and the lack of romanized Urdu as an option within the system, one might expect that some fraction of the Latin script Hindi data in mC4 is in fact romanized Urdu instead.

2.2 Related work

Transliteration of informally romanized text into the native script of the language has been explored for languages making use of Perso-Arabic scripts, including Arabic (Al-Badrashiny et al., 2014), and South Asian languages Urdu and Sindhi (Roark et al., 2020), as well as languages using Brahmic scripts such as Hindi, Bengali and Tamil (Roark et al., 2020). Work has also examined directly applying NLP models to informally romanized text in Arabic (Chalabi and Gerges, 2012), Persian (Maleki and Ahrenberg, 2008) and Urdu (Bögel, 2012; Irvine et al., 2012; Rafae et al., 2015). Language identification has been shown to be a particularly tricky problem for a variety of informally romanized languages (Bögel, 2012; Banerjee et al., 2014; Das and Gambäck, 2014; Eskander et al., 2014; Adouane et al., 2016; Zhang et al., 2018; Kreutzer et al., 2022). We direct the interested reader to Roark et al. (2020) for a more extensive background on these and related topics.

The problem of distinguishing romanized Hindi and Urdu, given a small set of seed words believed to be indicative of each language – the approach we pursue in this paper – can be thought of as an instance of weak supervision, or semi-supervised learning. We have a large, unlabeled dataset assumed to contain both Hindi and Urdu, and can use the seed set to "label" a small subset of the data depending on which seed words it contains.

From here, a typical semi-supervised approach would be to try to use the distribution of unlabeled sentences around the "labeled" points to build a decision surface that separates the two classes. Various general methods exist, including transductive support vector machines (TSVM) (Vapnik, 1998), or graph-based methods within the framework of manifold regularization (Belkin et al., 2004). These classic approaches, however, may require making additional assumptions, such as defining a distance metric between data points.

In this paper, we attempt a different approach. We exploit the implicit knowledge contained in a pre-trained LLM, as well its ability to maintain context over longer spans of generated text. In particular, we prompt the model with a frame containing one of our seed words, and allow it to generate an arbitrary amount of text based on that template. Then, we simply use this generated text as labeled data and train a standard supervised classifier to decide whether new text is either Hindi or Urdu. Before presenting these methods in detail, we first present data resources (two existing and one new) used for validation.

3 Datasets

Our work makes use of three independent data sources, including a training/validation set derived from Wikipedia, a general web-scraped text collection labeled in part as being romanized Hindi, and a set of Hindi and Urdu language-indicating seed words.

Dakshina While most relevant datasets do not distinguish between romanized Hindi and romanized Urdu, the Dakshina corpus[4] (Roark et al., 2020) does distinguish between the two. It contains hand-romanized sentences (10k per language) taken from Hindi and Urdu Wikipedia articles. This makes it ideal for evaluating our language ID system. We split the Hindi and Urdu portions of the corpus into training, development, and test sets,[5] and we use the development set (965 sentences from each language) to evaluate all versions of our language ID system. We also use the training

[3]https://github.com/google/cld3

[4]https://github.com/google-research-datasets/dakshina

[5]This data split and the seed words are available at https://github.com/google-research/google-research/tree/master/distinguishing_romanized_hindi_urdu.

Hindi		Urdu		English
urja	ऊर्जा	tawanai	توانائی	energy
chhati	छाती	seena	سینا	chest
shunya	शून्य	sifar	صفر	zero
ang	अंग	aazoo	عاضو	organ
prakar	प्रकार	qisam	قسم	type

Table 1: Examples from the seed list, including romanization and native script for both Hindi and Urdu alternatives along with an English gloss.

set in one of our baselines (see Section 4.1). All of the training and validation sets are balanced between the two languages.

mC4 The mC4 corpus, described above, consists of web-scraped data divided into 101 language partitions, of which "hi-Latn," nominally corresponding to romanized Hindi, is one. However, as previously mentioned, we believe this parition is likely to contain romanized Urdu as well, which has been conflated with Hindi due to the coverage of the CLD3 LangId system used to build the corpus.

Seed words Consulting with professional linguists who are familiar with both Hindi and Urdu, we collected 147 Hindi/Urdu pairs of words that differ between the two languages, but otherwise share the same meaning and are used in mostly the same semantic contexts. These were elicited by asking for words that, if seen in romanized text, would be strongly indicative of either Urdu or Hindi. The seed words were provided in the native scripts of Hindi and Urdu along with common romanizations for those words. Table 1 presents five example pairs from the set in both Latin and native script, along with an English gloss.

4 Methods

In this paper, we focus on comparing different sources of training data for distinguishing romanized Hindi and Urdu, rather than developing new classification architectures.

As such, initial comparisons are done using a straightforward off-the-shelf decision tree classifier (Breiman et al., 1984) from Scikit-Learn[6]. This model has the advantage of being highly interpretable, which makes it simple to determine which features are most important for distinguishing Hindi from Urdu. We train the decision tree with a maximum depth of 5 nodes, and use character 1- through 4-gram features.

To see how a more complex neural model behaves, we also finetune[7] the same mT5 checkpoint we use for data generation (see Section 4.2) to act as a classifier, where the input is a romanized sequence with the added task prefix 'Classify_HIUR:', and the output is either the string 'hi' or 'ur'.

For each of the three sources of classifier training data – Dakshina, mC4 and mT5 generated text – we provide the size of the resource and example strings in Table 2.

4.1 Baselines

Dakshina Topline. We train the classifiers on the training portion of the romanized Dakshina fullstring data. The specific articles in the Hindi and Urdu portions of the data differ, but otherwise span the entire range of Wikipedia topics, so there is unlikely to a be confound due to mismatched domains. The romanizations were produced by specific sets of annotators – disjoint between the two languages – hence the text may contain individual romanization styles that can make detection easier if present in the training data. Since this kind of labeled training data — along with a strong domain-match between the training and development data — is unlikely to occur in a realistic scenario, we consider this a topline condition. Our Dakshina training corpus has a total of 15.8k sentences, with a total of 1.6M characters.

mC4 Sentences. We train our classifiers on a balanced sample of sentences taken directly from the hi-Latn portion of mC4 (which we believe contains both Hindi and Urdu). In order to distinguish Hindi-aligned and Urdu-aligned sentences from the corpus, we use a simple heuristic: We give a sentence the Hindi label if it contains at least one of our Hindi seed words, and none of our Urdu seed words. The same applies in reverse to select potential Urdu sentences. From these candidates, we select 45.9k sentences for each language. This

[6]https://scikit-learn.org/stable/modules/tree.html

[7]The number of finetuning steps varied according to training data size — 5k for the Dakshina topline, 50k for the mc4 sentences baseline, and 100k for the data generated by mT5.

Dataset	Lines	Lang	Example
Dakshina train set	15.8k	HI	kul milakar yah 800 kilometer ki unchai tak pahunchegi.
		UR	jo bulandi mein duniya mein doosre number par hai.
mC4 sentences	91.9k	HI	mainyual prakriyaon ko svachaalit kyon karen vyaapaar prakriya prabandhan sophtaveyar
		UR	aik din mujhay asad bata raha tha blue flim banay mein bht paisa hai aik flim banao tu 1lac ruppe
mT5 generated data	4.5m	HI	dva ka title oot bhi vechain wala tadap dono.
		UR	mulaqat ka abjad majamiyat duniya dono se se ghazal.

Table 2: Size of each dataset in number of lines, along with one line labeled with each language from each set. All datasets are balanced, so half the data is labeled Hindi, and half Urdu.

results in a training corpus of 91.9k sentences, with a total of 97.7M characters.

4.2 Improving language ID with generated text

In this section, we present a method for using an LLM to generate training data for identifying romanized Hindi and Urdu. As we describe in Section 2, romanized Hindi and Urdu are not easily distinguishable, and so a corpus like the romanized Hindi section of mC4 likely contains both romanized Hindi and romanized Urdu.

We perform our experiments using mT5 (Xue et al., 2021), a multilingual offshoot of the original T5 model (Raffel et al., 2020), trained on the entire mC4 dataset. mT5 is an encoder-decoder transformer architecture pre-trained on a span corruption task, a form of masked language modeling. Spans of text in the input string are replaced with a sentinel token, whose contents are recovered during decoding (e.g., "The cat in the <extra_id_0>." maps to "<extra_id_0> hat <extra_id_1>"). The model uses a 250k sentencepiece (Kudo and Richardson, 2018) vocabulary, combined with 100 additional vocabulary items to represent the text spans.

We start with a publicly available mT5 checkpoint, using the "large" configuration on the t5x (Roberts et al., 2022) codebase[8]. We fine-tune specifically on the romanized "Hindi" (hi-Latn) portion of the mC4 dataset, using the original span corruption task, for an additional 100k steps. This imparts a bias to output Hindi and Urdu content specifically, while the original checkpoint tends to generate output from a wider language distribution which is not relevant to our task.

It seems reasonable that most sentences in the hi-Latn portion of mC4 come entirely from either a Hindi or Urdu source. We hypothesize that this will allow mT5 to learn that Urdu-aligned features are more likely to co-occur with other Urdu-aligned features, rather than Hindi-aligned features, and vice versa – much as such models have been shown to learn that words written using British spelling conventions tend to co-occur with words that also follow British spelling conventions (Nielsen et al., 2023).

In order to extract the information that mT5 has learned about the features that distinguish Hindi and Urdu, we first use mT5 to generate strings. We construct prompts for generation that contain words from the list of Hindi- and Urdu-specific seed words described in Section 3. We do this by inserting these seed words into short frame sentences, with a blank span elsewhere for the model to fill in. See Table 3 for the set of frame templates — outside the seed words, the sentences are designed to be language-neutral, and to be semantically generic so as not to strongly constrain possible generated continuations. For each combination of seed word and template, we generate 1000 different continuations via random sampling — given a prompt, each subsequent symbol in a generated string is sampled from the multinomial vocabulary distribution produced by the decoder at every timestep, with decoding stopping when an end-of-string token is produced. This resulted in a total of 4.5M strings, with 54.4M total characters,

[8]https://github.com/google-research/t5x/blob/main/docs/models.md#mt5-checkpoints

Frames with Glosses
mainne[I] **SEED** aur[and] BLANK likha[wrote].
maine[I] likha[wrote] **SEED** BLANK
ye[this] kaho[say]: **SEED** BLANK
usane[he] yah[this] likha[wrote]: **SEED** BLANK
ye[these] hamaaree[our] pasandeeda[favorite] cheejen[things] hain[are]: **SEED** BLANK
maine[I] likha[wrote] **SEED** aur[and] BLANK
ye[this] kaho[say]: **SEED** aur[and] BLANK
usane[he] yah[this] likha[wrote]: **SEED** aur[and] BLANK
ye[these] hamaaree[our] pasandeeda[favorite] cheejen[things] hain[are]: **SEED** aur[and] BLANK
maine[I] likha[wrote] **SEED**, BLANK
ye[this] kaho[say]: **SEED** BLANK
usane[he] yah[this] likha[wrote]: **SEED**, BLANK
ye[these] hamaaree[our] pasandeeda[favorite] cheejen[things] hain[are]: **SEED**, BLANK

Table 3: Frames for text generation, with approximate glosses.

half of which are generated from Hindi-aligned prompts, and half from Urdu-aligned prompts. We label each generated string with the language of the seed word in the prompt, strip away any <extra_id> sentinel symbols, and then train classifiers on these labeled strings.

For example, we can make use of the second template in Table 3 and the first Hindi seed word in Table 1, to construct the specific prompt: "maine likha urja <extra_id_0>". The model would then map this input to an output that effectively fills in the blank (<extra_id_0>) at the end of the string with some amount of output text that is prompt-appropriate according to the training data.

5 Results and discussion

In this section, we first determine the language identification classification accuracy of our two classifiers when trained on three different sourcs, before attempting to estimate the amount of Urdu in the romanized Hindi section of mC4. We additionally examine the most important features of the decision tree model.

5.1 Language ID performance

Table 4 shows the accuracy of each model on the Dakshina development set, under three training conditions: training on (a) the Dakshina training set, which is the classifier's topline performance for the validation set, since the training data is matched to the validation set for annotators and domain; (b) the mC4 extracted sentences, which is a baseline method for making use of the provided seed words; and (c) the mT4 generated data.

	Accuracy	
Training data	**DT**	**mT5**
Dakshina training set (topline)	85.6	96.7
mC4 sentences (baseline)	49.0	50.8
mT5 generated data	83.4	49.2

Table 4: Accuracy on the Dakshina development set, for both Decisition Tree (DT) and finetuned mT5 (mT5) classifiers.

Examining the topline result for each classifier, i.e., training on the well-matched Dakshina training set, we can see clearly that the mT5 classifier achieves much higher accuracy (96.7%) than the decision tree classifier (85.6%). The neural classifier is simply more powerful, having access to more than just the local character n-gram features used by the decision tree model, and is able to leverage pretraining effectively. This is exactly why the Dakshina training is labeled as a topline evaluation, because strong classifiers can make use of well-matched annotator and/or domain characteristics that permit more effective discrimination between examples in the collection. The decision tree classifier fails to exploit such dependencies, hence its topline performance suffers relative to the neural model.

The mC4 trained baseline classifiers, however, perform essentially at chance (near 50% accuracy) for both classificiation methods. Interestingly, the decision tree model trained on the mT5-generated data performs quite close to the topline model for that classifier at 83.4% accuracy. The classifier manages this in spite of being trained on mT5-generated data, which, unlike the Dakshina topline, is neither domain- nor annotator-matched to the development set.

Surprisingly, the decision tree model trained on the generated data approaches the classifier's topline even though the generated data itself is not very separable — the *training* accuracy of the model is only 55%. Even though the generated data must be very noisy, there is a very large amount of it, which allows for the detection of a few signal-rich features while the remaining noise averages out.

Note that the useful features used by the decision tree model cannot just be character n-grams found in our seed words. Otherwise, the balanced mC4 baseline would have performed better than chance. The large amount of generated data must thus contain additional information, effectively extracting knowledge from the LLM.

In contrast, the neural classifier fails to rise above chance performance on the validation set in this condition. It has the capacity to memorize the training data with nearly 100% accuracy, but hovers around chance when tested on the development set. This is likely due to a domain mismatch. The dev set (as well as the mC4 data that mT5 was pre-trained on) largely consists of proper sentences, while the generated data often appears to be random word sequences, since it was produced by having mT5 fill in blanks in a generic template. Such a global mismatch is not a problem for the decision tree, since it sees all text as a bag of unordered ngram features. In this instance, performance actually seems to benefit from that simplification.

The ability of the decision tree classifier trained on mT5 generated training data to perform with relatively high accuracy on the dev set also suggests that, indeed, a substantial amount of the text labeled as romanized Hindi in mC4 is romanized Urdu. Otherwise the independently created set of prompts would not have yielded data sufficient to perform better than chance on the task. While we now have validation that this text exists, we can go further and try to estimate how much of the data is actually romanized Urdu rather than Hindi.

	Est. Urdu %
Generated data	61.1
Topline	35.0

Table 5: The percentage of mC4's romanized Hindi data that our models estimate to be Urdu.

5.2 Reconsidering mC4's Hindi section

Given our decision tree model's relatively high performance on out-of-domain language ID, we can use it to offer a tentative estimate of how prevalent Urdu text is in the "Hindi" section of mC4. This isn't easily verified, since mC4 doesn't distinguish between the two languages, but we offer these estimates in Table 5 as a suggestion of what percentage of mC4's Hindi data is actually Urdu. The higher number seems likely to be an overestimate, given differences in speaker population between the two languages, hence this is an indication that our model is somewhat biased towards Urdu (when in fact a prior bias towards Hindi is likely warranted). Further validation of this is needed.

5.3 Interpreting top features

In addition to scoring the overall performance of the language ID model, we investigate which features are most important to the decision tree model's performance. We use Gini importance to rank the features of each version of the decision tree. We then use Pearson's correlation coefficient to determine which of the two languages each feature is correlated with.

When we examine the top features for the topline model and the model trained on generated data (see Table 6), we can see some patterns emerge. Most obviously, the character v is more associated with Hindi, while q and z are more associated with Urdu. One reason for this is that the phonemes /z/ and /q/ are more frequent in words with Arabic or Persian origins. Hindi speakers are much more likely to pronounce these phonemes as [d͡ʒ] and [k] respectively (Kachru, 2006). In addition, although the phoneme /d͡ʒ/ exists in both Hindi and Urdu, as noted in Section 2, when we look at Dakshina data, we find that Urdu speak-

Generated data		Topline	
ngram	Pearson's r	ngram	Pearson's r
v	-0.46	v	-0.46
z	0.42	**q**	0.37
q	0.37	**z**	0.42
pr	-0.37	men_	-0.28
f	0.24	pra	-0.36
rez	0.01	va	-0.39
ve	-0.14	_men	-0.27
ove	-0.01	**kee**	0.24
pra	-0.36	**ovel**	0.03
a	0.01	_me_	-0.23
ohol	0.00	dh	-0.34
qu	0.09	_pra	-0.35
e	0.05	equ	-0.03
tra_	-0.17	**ee**	0.34
que	-0.04	d	-0.04

Table 6: Top 20 features for the model trained on generated data and the topline model. Note that the space character is represented here with an underscore. The features shown in **bold magenta** are correlated with the Urdu label (shown by the positive Pearson's r), and the features shown in cyan are Hindi-correlated (negative Pearson's r).

ers are more likely to transliterate it with the character *z* than *j*.

These patterns in the top features suggest that we may be able to use these features to uncover previously undocumented language variation between two related language varieties. Of course, insofar as these features have not been documented, it is difficult to evaluate how successfully they reflect meaningful variations. One direction for future work would be to verify this method on language varieties with well documented variations, such as US and UK English.

6 Conclusion

We demonstrate that it is possible to make use of pretrained large language models to generate useful training data for language identification, even if the distinction between the languages was only implicit in the pretraining data. Our method only requires a corpus of unlabelled, mixed data from the two language varieties in question and a short list of seed words from each language. It can therefore be applied in cases where only unlabeled textual data exists, including lower-resource language scenarios.

Interestingly, the combination of a powerful neural LLM for generating training data and a relatively simple decision tree classifier making use of local word-level features, yielded the best results. By focusing on local word-form features, the decision tree classifier avoided exploiting more global (but less relevant) cues in the generated strings, and thus was able to learn interesting word-level dependencies that the more powerful model simply ignored.

Future work will include manual validation and error analysis of classifier performance on a range of texts. Further, we intend to examine this method, as suggested earlier, on more clearly documented written language varieties, such as those found with US and UK English spelling differences. We also plan to investigate similar language variety confounds, such as that found between Bosnian, Croatian and Montenegrin in the Latin script.

Acknowledgements

The authors wish to thank Raymond Doctor, Cibu Johny, Anna Katanova and Alexander Gutkin for help with this project.

Ethics Statement

This work does not propose a new model or dataset, but rather probes the behavior of existing models. Thus novel ethical considerations about model behavior and dataset contents are not directly raised by this work. While not explicitly focused on ethical considerations, this paper's methods hopefully contribute to better understanding model behavior, and could be used to understand the ways in which large language models treat underrepresented and marginalized language varieties.

Limitations

Our work is focused on just a single case study of language identification of romanized text. As detailed in Section 2, distinguishing romanized Hindi and Urdu is a good candidate for a case study for several reasons, but it would be beneficial to extend this work to other language situations.

Another limitation was our choice to focus on already existing pre-trained models, rather than directly controlling the training data that is input to each model. This means some of the conclusions about the connection between training data and outcome are tentative, pending experimental confirmation.

References

Wafia Adouane, Nasredine Semmar, and Richard Johansson. 2016. Romanized Berber and romanized Arabic automatic language identification using machine learning. In *Proceedings of the Third Workshop on NLP for Similar Languages, Varieties and Dialects (VarDial3)*, pages 53–61.

Mohamed Al-Badrashiny, Ramy Eskander, Nizar Habash, and Owen Rambow. 2014. Automatic transliteration of Romanized dialectal Arabic. In *Proceedings of the Eighteenth Conference on Computational Natural Language Learning*, pages 30–38, Ann Arbor, Michigan. Association for Computational Linguistics.

Mohd Zeeshan Ansari, MM Sufyan Beg, Tanvir Ahmad, Mohd Jazib Khan, and Ghazali Wasim. 2021. Language identification of Hindi-English tweets using code-mixed BERT. In *2021 IEEE 20th International Conference on Cognitive Informatics & Cognitive Computing (ICCI* CC)*, pages 248–252. IEEE.

Somnath Banerjee, Alapan Kuila, Aniruddha Roy, Sudip Kumar Naskar, Paolo Rosso, and Sivaji Bandyopadhyay. 2014. A hybrid approach for transliterated word-level language identification: CRF with post-processing heuristics. In *Proceedings of the Forum for Information Retrieval Evaluation*, pages 54–59.

M Belkin, P Niyogi, and V Sindhwani. 2004. Manifold regularization: A geometric framework for learning from examples. Technical report, Department of Computer Science, University of Chicago TR-2004-06.

Riyaz A. Bhat, Irshad A. Bhat, Naman Jain, and Dipti Misra Sharma. 2016. A house united: Bridging the script and lexical barrier between Hindi and Urdu. In *Proceedings of COLING 2016, the 26th International Conference on Computational Linguistics: Technical Papers*, pages 397–408, Osaka, Japan. The COLING 2016 Organizing Committee.

Riyaz Ahmad Bhat, Rajesh Bhatt, Annahita Farudi, Prescott Klassen, Bhuvana Narasimhan, Martha Palmer, Owen Rambow, Dipti Misra Sharma, Ashwini Vaidya, Sri Ramagurumurthy Vishnu, and Fei Xia. 2017. The Hindi/Urdu treebank project. In Nancy Ide and James Pustejovsky, editors, *Handbook of Linguistic Annotation*, pages 659–697. Springer Netherlands, Dordrecht.

Rajesh Bhatt, Bhuvana Narasimhan, Martha Palmer, Owen Rambow, Dipti Sharma, and Fei Xia. 2009. A multi-representational and multi-layered treebank for Hindi/Urdu. In *Proceedings of the Third Linguistic Annotation Workshop (LAW III)*, pages 186–189, Suntec, Singapore. Association for Computational Linguistics.

Tina Bögel. 2012. Urdu-Roman transliteration via finite state transducers. In *FSMNLP 2012, 10th International Workshop on Finite State Methods and Natural Language Processing*, pages 25–29.

L. Breiman, Jerome H. Friedman, Richard A. Olshen, and C. J. Stone. 1984. *Classification and Regression Trees*. The Wadsworth Statistics/Probability Series. Chapman and Hall, New York.

Achraf Chalabi and Hany Gerges. 2012. Romanized Arabic transliteration. In *Proceedings of the Second Workshop on Advances in Text Input Methods*, pages 89–96, Mumbai, India. The COLING 2012 Organizing Committee.

Amitava Das and Björn Gambäck. 2014. Identifying languages at the word level in code-mixed Indian social media text. In *Proceedings of the 11th International Conference on Natural Language Processing*, pages 378–387.

Ramy Eskander, Mohamed Al-Badrashiny, Nizar Habash, and Owen Rambow. 2014. Foreign words and the automatic processing of Arabic social media text written in Roman script. In *Proceedings of the First Workshop on Computational Approaches to Code Switching*, pages 1–12, Doha, Qatar. Association for Computational Linguistics.

Ann Irvine, Jonathan Weese, and Chris Callison-Burch. 2012. Processing informal, Romanized pakistani text messages. In *Proceedings of the Second Workshop on Language in Social Media*, pages 75–78, Montréal, Canada. Association for Computational Linguistics.

Yamuna Kachru. 2006. *Hindi*. John Benjamins, Philadelphia.

Julia Kreutzer, Isaac Caswell, Lisa Wang, Ahsan Wahab, Daan van Esch, Nasanbayar Ulzii-Orshikh, Allahsera Tapo, Nishant Subramani, Artem Sokolov, Claytone Sikasote, Monang Setyawan, Supheakmungkol Sarin, Sokhar Samb, Benoît Sagot, Clara Rivera, Annette Rios, Isabel Papadimitriou, Salomey Osei, Pedro Ortiz Suarez, Iroro Orife, Kelechi Ogueji, Andre Niyongabo Rubungo, Toan Q. Nguyen, Mathias Müller, André Müller, Shamsuddeen Hassan Muhammad, Nanda Muhammad, Ayanda Mnyakeni, Jamshidbek Mirzakhalov, Tapiwanashe Matangira, Colin Leong, Nze Lawson, Sneha Kudugunta, Yacine Jernite, Mathias Jenny, Orhan Firat, Bonaventure F. P. Dossou, Sakhile Dlamini, Nisansa de Silva, Sakine

Çabuk Ballı, Stella Biderman, Alessia Battisti, Ahmed Baruwa, Ankur Bapna, Pallavi Baljekar, Israel Abebe Azime, Ayodele Awokoya, Duygu Ataman, Orevaoghene Ahia, Oghenefego Ahia, Sweta Agrawal, and Mofetoluwa Adeyemi. 2022. Quality at a glance: An audit of web-crawled multilingual datasets. *Transactions of the Association for Computational Linguistics*, 10:50–72.

Taku Kudo and John Richardson. 2018. SentencePiece: A simple and language independent subword tokenizer and detokenizer for neural text processing. In *Proceedings of the 2018 Conference on Empirical Methods in Natural Language Processing: System Demonstrations*, pages 66–71, Brussels, Belgium. Association for Computational Linguistics.

Jalal Maleki and Lars Ahrenberg. 2008. Converting Romanized Persian to the Arabic writing systems. In *Proceedings of the Sixth International Conference on Language Resources and Evaluation (LREC'08)*, Marrakech, Morocco. European Language Resources Association (ELRA).

Colin P Masica. 1993. *The Indo-Aryan languages*. Cambridge University Press.

Elizabeth Nielsen, Christo Kirov, and Brian Roark. 2023. Spelling convention sensitivity in neural language models. In *Findings of the Association for Computational Linguistics: EACL 2023*, pages 1334–1346.

Abdul Rafae, Abdul Qayyum, Muhammad Moeenuddin, Asim Karim, Hassan Sajjad, and Faisal Kamiran. 2015. An unsupervised method for discovering lexical variations in Roman Urdu informal text. In *Proceedings of the 2015 Conference on Empirical Methods in Natural Language Processing*, pages 823–828, Lisbon, Portugal. Association for Computational Linguistics.

Colin Raffel, Noam Shazeer, Adam Roberts, Katherine Lee, Sharan Narang, Michael Matena, Yanqi Zhou, Wei Li, and Peter J Liu. 2020. Exploring the limits of transfer learning with a unified text-to-text transformer. *The Journal of Machine Learning Research*, 21(1):5485–5551.

Brian Roark, Lawrence Wolf-Sonkin, Christo Kirov, Sabrina J. Mielke, Cibu Johny, Isin Demirsahin, and Keith Hall. 2020. Processing South Asian languages written in the Latin script: the Dakshina dataset. In *Proceedings of the 12th Language Resources and Evaluation Conference*, pages 2413–2423, Marseille, France. European Language Resources Association.

Adam Roberts, Hyung Won Chung, Anselm Levskaya, Gaurav Mishra, James Bradbury, Daniel Andor, Sharan Narang, Brian Lester, Colin Gaffney, Afroz Mohiuddin, Curtis Hawthorne, Aitor Lewkowycz, Alex Salcianu, Marc van Zee, Jacob Austin, Sebastian Goodman, Livio Baldini Soares, Haitang Hu, Sasha Tsvyashchenko, Aakanksha Chowdhery, Jasmijn Bastings, Jannis Bulian, Xavier Garcia, Jianmo Ni, Andrew Chen, Kathleen Kenealy, Jonathan H. Clark, Stephan Lee, Dan Garrette, James Lee-Thorp, Colin Raffel, Noam Shazeer, Marvin Ritter, Maarten Bosma, Alexandre Passos, Jeremy Maitin-Shepard, Noah Fiedel, Mark Omernick, Brennan Saeta, Ryan Sepassi, Alexander Spiridonov, Joshua Newlan, and Andrea Gesmundo. 2022. Scaling up models and data with `t5x` and `seqio`. *arXiv preprint arXiv:2203.17189*.

Sebastian Ruder, Noah Constant, Jan Botha, Aditya Siddhant, Orhan Firat, Jinlan Fu, Pengfei Liu, Junjie Hu, Dan Garrette, Graham Neubig, and Melvin Johnson. 2021. XTREME-R: Towards more challenging and nuanced multilingual evaluation. In *Proceedings of the 2021 Conference on Empirical Methods in Natural Language Processing*, pages 10215–10245, Online and Punta Cana, Dominican Republic. Association for Computational Linguistics.

Vladimir N. Vapnik. 1998. *Statistical learning theory*. Wiley, New York.

Karthik Visweswariah, Vijil Chenthamarakshan, and Nandakishore Kambhatla. 2010. Urdu and Hindi: Translation and sharing of linguistic resources. In *Coling 2010: Posters*, pages 1283–1291, Beijing, China. Coling 2010 Organizing Committee.

Hans H. Wellisch. 1978. *The Conversion of Scripts: Its Nature, History, and Utilization*. Information sciences series. John Wiley & Sons, New York.

Linting Xue, Noah Constant, Adam Roberts, Mihir Kale, Rami Al-Rfou, Aditya Siddhant, Aditya Barua, and Colin Raffel. 2021. mT5: A massively multilingual pre-trained text-to-text transformer. In *Proceedings of the 2021 Conference of the North American Chapter of the Association for Computational Linguistics: Human Language Technologies*, pages 483–498, Online. Association for Computational Linguistics.

Yuan Zhang, Jason Riesa, Daniel Gillick, Anton Bakalov, Jason Baldridge, and David Weiss. 2018. A fast, compact, accurate model for language identification of codemixed text. In *Proceedings of the 2018 Conference on Empirical Methods in Natural Language Processing*, pages 328–337, Brussels, Belgium. Association for Computational Linguistics.

Back-Transliteration of English loanwords in Japanese

Yuying Ren
The Graduate Center, City University of New York

Abstract

We propose methods for transliterating English loanwords in Japanese from their Japanese written form (katakana/romaji) to their original English written form. Our data is a Japanese-English loanwords dictionary that we have created ourselves. We employ two approaches: direct transliteration, which directly converts words from katakana to English, and indirect transliteration, which utilizes the English pronunciation as a means to convert katakana words into their corresponding English sound representations, which are subsequently converted into English words. Additionally, we compare the effectiveness of using katakana versus romaji as input characters. We develop 6 models of 2 types for our experiments: one with an English lexicon-filter, and the other without. For each type, we built 3 models, including a pair n-gram based on WFSTs and two sequence-to-sequence models leveraging LSTM and transformer. Our best performing model was the pair n-gram model with a lexicon-filter, directly transliterating from katakana to English.

1 Introduction

Loanwords have grown at a rapid pace in Japanese language since 1990s. English loanwords make up 8 percent of the Japanese vocabulary and 94 percent of all loanwords used in Japanese (Stanlaw, 2004). The excessive use of loanwords in mass media not only poses difficulties for Japanese to understand their own language (Irwin, 2011), but also creates callenges for English speakers to accurately back-transliterate the loanwords due to the significant differences in sound and written representation from their original forms.

Knight and Graehl (1998) utilized estimation-maximization to establish a mapping of the similarity between English and Japanese sounds. Among 38 phonemes they have examined, only 5 had a corresponding Japanese sound with a probability greater than .9, and 10 of them reached a probability of .8.

In terms of writing systems, Japanese has a relatively complex system. Japanese uses three sets of characters: hiragana, kanji, and katakana. Katakana is mainly used for writing foreign words and over 100 of these characters are in use. Moreover, unlike English, Japanese characters represent sounds syllabically instead of phonetically (DeFrancis, 1989). Romaji, another set of characters is informally used in Japanese, represents the Romanization of katakana. It was originally used to annotate the sounds of Japanese characters but has gained popularity as a means of typing Japanese using keyboards.

As described by Knight and Graehl (1998), the transliteration of English words to katakana is an information-losing operation from both the sound and writing system perspectives. For instance, because there is no distinction between sounds of / æ, ʌ / and / θ, s / in Japanese, the English words *bath* and *bus* are mapped to the same form in katakana: バス<ba-su>. In contrast, the word *camera* has two corresponding katakana forms: カメラ <ka-me-ra> or キャメラ <kya-me-ra>.

Due to the loss of information, back-transliteration becomes even more challenging. Nonetheless, in recent years, an increasing number of researchers have been employing NLP methods to address this issue. Many studies tackle the back-transliteration challenge as a Grapheme-to-Phoneme (G2P) problem (e.g., Jiampojamarn et al. 2010; Rosca and Breuel, 2016; Merhav and Ash, 2018), utilizing models such as WFST-based n-gram models or neural sequence-to-sequence models, which are commonly employed for the

Proceedings of the Workshop on Computation and Written Language (CAWL 2023), pages 43–49
July 14, 2023 ©2023 Association for Computational Linguistics

G2P tasks (e.g., Novak et al. 2016; Gorman et al., 2020), to address the issue.

In this paper, we approach the back-transliteration problem by building models that investigate the impact of the sound information and the use of either katakana or romaji as the input for Japanese. In addition to utilizing the n-gram and sequence-to-sequence models typically employed in G2P tasks, we introduce a novel approach by incorporating an English lexicon-filter mechanism. We expect this technique to help us generate more relevant outputs.

2 Related Work

Knight and Graehl (1998) is one of earliest works on transliteration and back-transliteration of Japanese loanwords. They utilize WFSTs to build a modular system that transliterate the katakana words to their original English forms using the sound of English words. They test their system on two relatively small datasets: a content words dictionary with 1,449 katakana-English pairs and a name list with 100 pairs. The accuracy of their method outperforms that of human translators.

Yamashita et al. (2018) not only uses phonemes to map katakana to English but also directly uses characters. They employ a bidirectional recurrent neural network (RNN), trained on a katakana-English content words dictionary, and experiment with three test datasets: a content word list, a city name list, and a restaurant name list. They use 5 similarity algorithms evaluate their model and report the top-five precision of each measurement. Interestingly, they find that the direct mapping using characters performs better than using phonemes as medium for all their measurements.

Merhav and Ash (2018)'s research primarily focusses on the transliteration of named entities from English to katakana. They employ a n-gram model with the `Phonetisaurus` library (Novak et al. 2016), an RNN model with the `seq2seq` library (Luong et al. 2017) and a transformer model with `tensor2tensor` library (Vaswani et al. 2018). They apply their transformer model to the back-transliteration task, which outperforms the other two models. They report the 1-best, 2-best, and 3-best word error rate (WER) for evaluation and the WER of the back-transliteration are averagely .2 points higher than the transliteration.

For our experiments with the no-lexicon-filter models, we adapt the implementation of the baselines in 2020 SIGMORPHON shared task [1] (Gorman et al., 2020), which consist of 3 models: a pair n-gram model built using OpenGrm toolkit (Roark et al. 2012, Gorman, 2016), and two sequence-to-sequence models with LSTM (Luong et al. 2015) and transformer (Vaswani et al. 2017) architectures that are built with the `fairseq` (Ott, et al. 2019) library.

3 Data

Our dataset is compiled from three dictionaries. First, we use the JMdict[2] (Breen, 1995), a product of the Japanese-Multilingual electronic dictionary project to extract the katakana-English word pairs. Second, we incorporate the CMUdict[3] (Weide, 2014), which provides the pronunciation of the English words. Finally, we utilize the Webster's Dictionary (Neilson and Knott, 1934) and the CMUdict to build the English lexicon-filter.

To construct our dataset, we first filter out non-loanwords such as onomatopoeias and then manually expand the abbreviated katakana words. For example, the word アメフト<a-me-fu-to> 'Ame foot', is extended to アメリカンフットボール<a-me-ri-ka-fu-to-bo-o-ru> 'American football'. Next, we utilize the CMUdict to map the sounds of English words and pair them with the corresponding katakana words. Finally, for the purpose of our experiment, we add a column of Romanized katakana words to our data by using a python library `romkan`[4]. A sample of our final dataset is shown in Table 1.

Our dataset consists 26,208 items, which we randomly divided into train, dev, and test sets. The proportions of the three sets are 80%, 10%, and 10%, respectively. It is noteworthy that 47.2% of our data consist of katakana words are mapped to multiple-word expressions in English, such as the example of American football mentioned above.

Finally, we merge the CMUdict (Weide, 2014) and Webster's dictionary (Neilson and Knott, 1934) to form an English wordlist with over 320k distinct words for building the lexicon-filter models.

[1] https://github.com/sigmorphon/2020.

[2] https://www.edrdg.org/jmdict/jmdict_whatsnew.html.

[3] http://www.speech.cs.cmu.edu/cgi-bin/cmudict.

[4] https://pypi.org/project/romkan.

katakana	romaji	English	CMU
スイーパー	suiipaa	sweeper	S W IY P ER
テニスエルボー	tenisueruboo	tennis elbow	T EH N AH S EH L B OW
...	...	...	...

Table 1. Samples of final dataset. The CMU column contains the English pronunciations.

4 Methods

4.1 Approaches

Both the direct and indirect transliteration approaches will explore the impact of using different Japanese characters: katakana and romaji as the inputs. In the direct approach, words are directly converted from their Japanese writing forms to their English forms. On the other hand, the indirect approach can be implemented in various ways. We trained models on katakana-phonemes and romaji-phonemes data, which are utilized to predict the possible pronunciations for English words in the first step. Subsequently, we train models using the phoneme-English data from the CMUdict (Weide, 2014) and employ them and the phoneme results from the first step to predict the final words in English. Figure 1 illustrates the difference between using katakana and romaji for indirect and direct approaches.

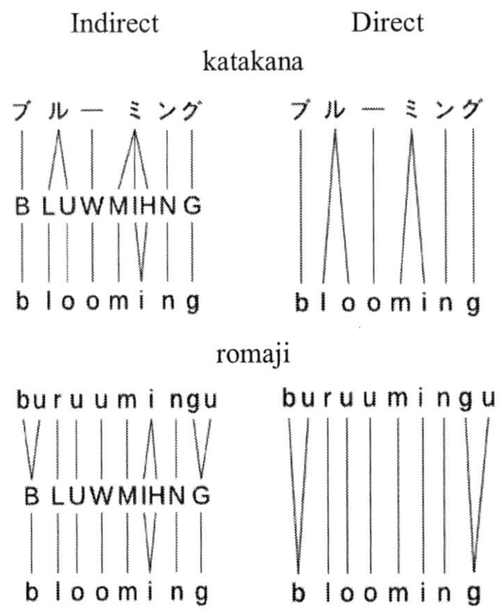

Figure 1. Demonstrations of difference between using katakana and romaji as the input for indirect (left) and direct (right) approaches.

4.2 Models

We create 2 types of models: models with an English lexicon-filter, and models without an English lexicon-filter. Within each type, we have three models, namely a pair n-gram model, and two neural sequence-to-sequence models with LSTM and transformer (Gorman et al., 2020).

The architecture of the pair n-gram model is similar to the architecture of Phonetisaurus toolkit (Novak, 2016), but it is implemented with the libraries of Pynini (Gorman, 2016), Baum-Welch, and NGram (Roark et al. 2012). We use this model to train an aligner based on WFSTs that maps katakana or romaji characters to English characters. Next, the alignments are then used to compute a higher-order n-gram model (we set the order to 8), which is converted to a final WFST. The resulting WFST can take the input words written either in katakana or romaji, and produce a weighted lattice of possible English words, the prediction is made by selecting the shortest path/s through the lattice.

The neural network models are implemented using the `fairseq` (Ott, et al. 2019) library. The LSTM-based model contains a bidirectional LSTM encoder with a single layer and a unidirectional LSTM decoder with a single layer (Luong et al., 2015). The transformer-based model (Vaswani et al. 2017) contains 4 encoder and 4 decoder layers, and both tuned using Wu et al. (2020)'s pre-layer normalization method. The two models share most of the training hyperparameters, such as the Adam optimizer (Kingma and Ba, 2015), and label-smoothed cross-entropy for regularization. We tune the models on the development dataset, with different learning rates of .001 and .005, batch sizes of 128, 256, 512, and embedding layer dimensions of 128, 256, and hidden layer units of 512, 1024. We perform early stopping in a similar way to Gorman et al. (2020), that we save every 5 checkpoints, and use the checkpoint that reached

Models		Indirect		Direct	
		katakana	romaji	katakana	romaji
LSTM	No lexicon-filter	38.38	37.96	33.12	33.42
	Lexicon-filter	34.41	33.93	26.33	25.91
Transformer	No lexicon-filter	46.70	48.95	34.30	35.41
	Lexicon-filter	41.17	43.99	24.95	25.60
Pair n-gram	No lexicon-filter	34.38	35.83	34.26	35.02
	Lexicon-filter	**30.64**	31.59	**23.01**	25.41

Table 2. WER results for all experiments.

the lowest word error rate (WER) on the development set to predict on the test set.

The implementation of the lexicon filter differs between the pair n-gram model and the sequence-to-sequence models. In the case of the pair n-gram model, we construct a FST utilizing the English wordlist data and then compose it with the output lattices. This process enables us to eliminate any predictions that are not present in the English wordlist. On the other hand, for the neural network models, we extract the top-5 predictions and use the English wordlist to filter out the predictions that include non-existent words. In all models, we retain the original outputs if all the hypotheses contain non-existent word.

5 Evaluation

We evaluate our models by reporting the word error rate (WER), which represents the percentage of predicted words that differ from the target words. A lower WER value indicates a better performance. We consider the multi-word expressions as a single entity during our evaluation, meaning that any incorrect prediction of a word in the expression results in the entire prediction being considered incorrect. Additionally, as the selection of random seed values can non-trivially affect the model's performance (Reimers and Gurevych, 2017), we opted to train each of our models with five different random seeds and present the median value of the resulting five WERs.

6 Results

Table 2 displays the results of all experiments, which demonstrate that the indirect approach performs worse than the direct approach. This finding is consistent with the results reported by Yamashita et al. (2018). However, the difference in WERs between using katakana and romaji as the input are insignificant for either approach.

In addition, it is worth noting that while the transformer models with lexicon-filter have shown better performance compared to the LSTM-based models in the direct transliteration experiments, the pair n-gram model surpassed them by a reduction of 2 to 3 points in terms of WER. This is noteworthy as transformer has generally outperformed other two models in previous G2P tasks, as well as the named entity recognition task by Merhav and Ash (2018).

Finally, the results demonstrate a significant reduction in WER for models with lexicon-filters compared to those without. Particularly for experiments with the direct approach, show a reduction of average 10 points for all models. The pair n-gram model with lexicon-filter that directly transliterate katakana to English proved to be the most robust, which achieves a WER of 23.01.

7 Discussion

Different designs in the indirect approach can yield different outcomes. Our chosen design for the experiment inherently introduces noise to the models during the conversion of phonemes to English words. Table 3 displays the WER results of experiments where words in katakana or romaji are converted into their corresponding English phonemes. The relatively high scores implies that the phonemes utilized for predicting English words, generated from the Japanese data, can significantly differ from the data used to train the phoneme-English conversion models. Yamashita et al. (2018) compared this design with an alternative approach where both Japanese and English words were converted to phonemes, and the similarity between the results was measured, which yielded better results in their study.

	katakana	romaji
LSTM	34.41	**33.65**
Transformer	42.92	46.62
Pair n-gram	**32.32**	34.26

Table 3. WER results of experiments converting Japanese loanwords to their corresponding English phonemes.

In order to assess the impact of different input characters and model architectures on solving the back-transliteration problem, we perform McNemar's tests[5] (Gillick and Cox, 1989) on the results obtained from the corresponding experiments. The null hypothesis in McNemar's test states that the two hypotheses exhibit equal accuracy and performance. In our case, we failed to reject the null hypothesis when comparing the use katakana and romaji as input characters, as well as when comparing models with lexicon-filter in the direct transliteration approach. However, it is interesting to find that pair n-gram model has surpassed the sequence-to-sequence models. Merhav and Ash (2018) has surprisingly found that their transformer model, which is typically known for its ability to handle long term dependencies, outperformed their WFST-based n-gram model in their named entity transliteration task with relatively small input sizes. Based on this finding, we divide our results into two categories: small and large input size, using the median as the threshold. We then compare the WER of the transformer and pair n-gram models within each category. We observe that while the two models exhibited similar WER on the small input size data, there was a significant difference on the large input size data, where the pair n-gram model outperformed the transformer model with a WER that was approximately 10 percent lower.

Upon analyzing the errors in our predictions, we examine the results generated by the pair n-gram model with the lexicon filter that used katakana as input. We identify two major types of the errors: the spelling errors and the word delimiter errors. Some of the spelling errors are attributed to the phonetic distinctions between Japanese and English, as discussed previously in this paper. For instance, the word *lighter* is predicted as *writer* due to the lack of distinguish between the sounds of / l, ɹ / in Japanese. Other spelling errors can arise from the English homophones such as the target-hypothesis pair of *site* and *sight*.

Word delimiter errors occur when the predicted words are correct, but the position of the whitespace is incorrect, such as the pairs of *fireman* and *fire man* or *homegrown terror* and *home grown terror*. These errors account for 10% of the total errors and accepting them could reduce the WER by 2 to 3 points.

8 Conclusion

Our study investigated the factors affecting the back-transliteration of English loanwords in Japanese. Specifically, we constructed models to compare the use of characters for direct transliteration versus the use of sounds as a medium, as well as the use of katakana versus romaji as input sources. We built 6 models with 2 types: models with lexicon-filter and those without lexicon-filter. For each type, we built two neural sequence-to-sequence models as well as a pair n-gram model. Our results revealed that models with lexicon-filter exhibited significant improvement in performance, with an average reduction of 10 points in WER. The most robust model we achieved was the pair n-gram model with lexicon-filter for the katakana-to-English transliteration, which produced a WER of 23.01. There are some areas for potential improvement in the future, such as integrating spelling correction models and incorporating word frequency computation. Moreover, we envision the integration of our model to address other challenges, including machine translation and entity matching.

Limitations

There remains a problem we have yet to address: the abbreviation of loanwords in Japanese. Japanese often abbreviates multi-word expressions after transliterating them into katakana. For example, スマートホン <su-ma-a-to-ho-n> 'smart phone' becomes スマホ <su-ma-ho>. For our method, we manually extended these abbreviated words to their full forms, but automating this process would be preferable due to the prevalence of these words in Japanese. However, back-

[5] We adapt Gorman and Bedrick's implementation of the test: https://github.com/kylebgorman/SOTA-taggers.

transliterating them presents challenges as they deviate further from their original English forms.

We designed our method to specifically focus on back-transliterating of content words, unlike many other studies that focused on the name entities data. This is because the loanwords of content words are prevalent in Japanese. However, names are also challenging as they are in other languages. Previous studies have suggested that a more sophisticated method may be necessary for back-transliterating names.

Acknowledgment

I would like to express my sincere gratitude to Dr. Kyle Gorman, who has generously shared his invaluable knowledge with me throughout this project. His expertise and insights have been instrumental in shaping the direction and improving the outcomes of this research.

Ethics Statement

The data used in this study are collected from sources that are publicly available and has been used in accordance with the terms of the respective licenses.

References

Jim Breen. 1995. Building an Electronic Japanese-English dictionary. In Japanese Studies Association of Australia Conference. Citeseer.

Brian Roark, Richard Sproat, Cyril Allauzen, Michael Riley, Jeffrey Sorensen, and Terry Tai. 2012. The OpenGrm open-source finite-state grammar software libraries. In Proceedings of the ACL 2012 System Demonstrations, pages 61–66, Jeju Island, Korea. Association for Computational Linguistics.

DeFrancis, J. (1989). *Visible speech: The diverse oneness of writing systems.* University of Hawaii Press.

Gillick, L., & Cox, S.J. (1989). Some statistical issues in the comparison of speech recognition algorithms. International Conference on Acoustics, Speech, and Signal Processing, 532-535 vol.1.

Irwin, Mark. (2011). Loanwords in Japanese. Amsterdam; Philadelphia: John Benjamins Pub. Co.

Jackson L. Lee, Lucas F.E. Ashby, M. Elizabeth Garza, Yeonju Lee-Sikka, Sean Miller, Alan Wong, Arya D. McCarthy, and Kyle Gorman. 2020. Massively Multilingual Pronunciation Modeling with WikiPron. In *Proceedings of the Twelfth Language Resources and Evaluation Conference*, pages 4223–4228, Marseille, France. European Language Resources Association.

Kevin Knight and Jonathan Graehl. 1997. Machine Transliteration. In 35th Annual Meeting of the Association for Computational Linguistics and 8th Conference of the European Chapter of the Association for Computational Linguistics, pages 128–135, Madrid, Spain. Association for Computational Linguistics.

Kingma, D. P., & Ba, J. (2014). Adam: A method for stochastic optimization. arXiv preprint arXiv:1412.6980.

Kyle Gorman. 2016. Pynini: A Python library for weighted finite-state grammar compilation. In *Proceedings of the SIGFSM Workshop on Statistical NLP and Weighted Automata*, pages 75–80, Berlin, Germany. Association for Computational Linguistics.

Kyle Gorman, Lucas F.E. Ashby, Aaron Goyzueta, Arya McCarthy, Shijie Wu, and Daniel You. 2020. The SIGMORPHON 2020 Shared Task on Multilingual Grapheme-to-Phoneme Conversion. In Proceedings of the 17th SIGMORPHON Workshop on Computational Research in Phonetics, Phonology, and Morphology, pages 40–50, Online. Association for Computational Linguistics.

Michiharu Yamashita, Hideki Awashima, and Hidekazu Oiwa. 2018. A Comparison of Entity Matching Methods between English and Japanese Katakana. In Proceedings of the Fifteenth Workshop on Computational Research in Phonetics, Phonology, and Morphology, pages 84–92, Brussels, Belgium. Association for Computational Linguistics.

Myle Ott, Sergey Edunov, Alexei Baevski, Angela Fan, Sam Gross, Nathan Ng, David Grangier, and Michael Auli. 2019. fairseq: A Fast, Extensible Toolkit for Sequence Modeling. In Proceedings of the 2019 Conference of the North American Chapter of the Association for Computational Linguistics (Demonstrations), pages 48–53, Minneapolis, Minnesota. Association for Computational Linguistics.

Novak, J. R., Minematsu, N., & Hirose, K. (2016). Phonetisaurus: Exploring grapheme-to-phoneme conversion with joint n-gram models in the WFST framework. Natural Language Engineering, 22(6), 907-938.

Nils Reimers and Iryna Gurevych. 2017. Reporting Score Distributions Makes a Difference: Performance Study of LSTM-networks for Sequence Tagging. In Proceedings of the 2017 Conference on Empirical Methods in Natural Language Processing, pages 338–348, Copenhagen, Denmark. Association for Computational Linguistics.

Rosca, M., & Breuel, T. (2016). Sequence-to-sequence neural network models for transliteration. arXiv preprint arXiv:1610.09565.

Shijie Wu, Ryan Cotterell, and Mans Hulden. 2020. Applying the transformer to character-level transduction. arXiv:2005.10213.

Sittichai Jiampojamarn, Kenneth Dwyer, Shane Bergsma, Aditya Bhargava, Qing Dou, Mi-Young Kim, and Grzegorz Kondrak. 2010. Transliteration Generation and Mining with Limited Training Resources. In *Proceedings of the 2010 Named Entities Workshop*, pages 39–47, Uppsala, Sweden. Association for Computational Linguistics.

Stanlaw, J. (2004). Japanese English: Language and Culture Contact. Hong Kong University Press.

Thang Luong, Hieu Pham, and Christopher D. Manning. 2015. Effective Approaches to Attention-based Neural Machine Translation. In *Proceedings of the 2015 Conference on Empirical Methods in Natural Language Processing*, pages 1412–1421, Lisbon, Portugal. Association for Computational Linguistics.

Vaswani, A., Bengio, S., Brevdo, E., Chollet, F., Gomez, A. N., Gouws, S., ... & Uszkoreit, J. (2018). Tensor2tensor for neural machine translation. *arXiv preprint arXiv:1803.07416.*

Vaswani, A., Shazeer, N., Parmar, N., Uszkoreit, J., Jones, L., Gomez, A. N., ... & Polosukhin, I. (2017). Attention is all you need. Advances in neural information processing systems, 30.

Weide, R. (2014). The CMU pronunciation dictionary, release 0.7b.

Neilson, W.A. and Knott, T.A (editors). 1934. *Webster's New International Dictionary*. 2nd edition. G. & C. Merriam.

Yuval Merhav and Stephen Ash. 2018. Design Challenges in Named Entity Transliteration. In Proceedings of the 27th International Conference on Computational Linguistics, pages 630–640, Santa Fe, New Mexico, USA. Association for Computational Linguistics.

Pronunciation Ambiguities in Japanese *Kanji*

Wen Zhang
The Graduate Center, City University of New York
wenzhang0222@gmail.com

Abstract

Japanese writing is a complex system, and a large part of the complexity resides in the use of *kanji*. A single *kanji* character in modern Japanese may have multiple pronunciations, either as native vocabulary or as words borrowed from Chinese. This causes a problem for text-to-speech synthesis (TTS) because the system has to predict which pronunciation of each *kanji* character is appropriate in the context. The problem is called homograph disambiguation. To solve the problem, this research provides a new annotated Japanese single *kanji* character pronunciation data set and describes an experiment using the logistic regression (LR) classifier. A baseline is computed to compare with the LR classifier accuracy. This experiment provides the first experimental research in Japanese single *kanji* homograph disambiguation. The annotated Japanese data is freely released to the public to support further work.

1 Introduction

Japanese uses a mixed writing system with three distinct scripts and one romanization. *Kanji* 漢字 is the writing script that borrows directly from Chinese characters which were introduced in Japan from China through Korea from the third century CE. There are 2,136 commonly used *kanji* characters termed *Joyo kanji* in present-day Japanese.[1] A single *kanji* character in modern Japanese may have multiple pronunciations derived from the linguistic history of the *kanji* characters as either native vocabulary words or as terms borrowed from Chinese. For instance, the *kanji* character 山 'mountain' can be read as either the native Japanese word *yama* or the Chinese-derived term *san*. The native Japanese pronunciations of the *kanji* character 文 'letter, sentence, writings' are *humi*, *aya*, and *kaza*, while Chinese borrowed pronunciations are *bun* and *mon*. Because a *kanji* character has multiple pronunciations, to predict the appropriate pronunciation for each *kanji* character, a text-to-speech synthesis engine must select the appropriate reading. This is a form of homograph disambiguation.

This research is a computational study of Japanese *kanji* homograph disambiguation. Recent research in homograph disambiguation in Japanese is limited because of the lack of extensive data sets that include comprehensive pronunciations for the most commonly used *kanji* characters. The goal of this research is to fill this void, make new data sets to conduct the analysis of *kanji* characters with multiple pronunciations, and use the computational methodology to test the data set to lay a foundation for computational research on Japanese *kanji* homographs in the future.

1.1 Japanese writing scripts

The Japanese writing system uses three different scripts, Chinese characters (*kanji*), and two *kana* systems: *hiragana* and *katakana*, which are derivatives of Chinese characters. *Hiragana* resulted from the cursive style of writing Chinese characters, while *katakana* developed from the abbreviation of Chinese characters. Roughly speaking, *kanji* are used for content words such as nouns, stems of adjectives，and verbs, whereas *hiragana* is used for writing grammatical words

[1] https://kanji.jitenon.jp/cat/joyo.html

Proceedings of the Workshop on Computation and Written Language (CAWL 2023), pages 50–60
July 14, 2023 ©2023 Association for Computational Linguistics

(case markers and other 'small' words). *Katakana* is almost exclusively used today to write foreign words and names such as Tennessee テネシー *teneshii* (Sproat, 2009: 47).

In addition to the three writing scripts that originate in Chinese characters, *romaji* is another phonetic writing script using the Roman alphabets. Thus, Japanese essentially has four ways to write the language. For instance, the word for 'mountain' can be written as 山 in *kanji*, as やま in *hiragana*, as ヤマ in *katakana*, and *yama* in *romaji*. For more details, see Zhang (2023: 4f.).

1.2 *Kanji*

The following sections introduce the *kanji* pronunciation ambiguities.

1.2.1 *On* readings and *kun* readings

Over time as Chinese characters were adapted to Japanese, the characters came to be associated with native Japanese words as well. For instance, the Chinese character for *shān* 山 was borrowed and used to write the newly created Japanese morpheme /*san*/. However, the Japanese already had the word *yama* 'mountain'. The character 山 was also used to write the native word *yama*. Present-day Japanese has kept both terms for 'mountain' but uses them in different contexts. For instance, by itself, the signifier 'mountain' is usually referred to as *yama*, but Mt. Fuji is *Fujisan*. The *kanji* character 人 'people, person' has two borrowed pronunciations: *nin* and *jin*, and one native Japanese pronunciation *hito*; the *kanji* character 者 'person' has one borrowed pronunciation *sha*, and one native pronunciation *mono*. A majority of *kanji* characters have one or more Chinese-derived readings, and one or more native readings (Sproat et al., 2021). [2] The borrowed readings and native ones are known as *on* readings and *kun* readings, respectively. The readings in speech are not a problem, however, when given the written form first, for instance, both *san* and *yama* are written as 山, one must decide, depending on the context of each occasion, whether the character should be pronounced as *san* or *yama*. The multiple context-based pronunciations of a single *kanji* make Japanese text a challenge.

1.2.2 Multiple *on* readings

In general, a given *kanji* character may have several different Sino-Japanese readings reflecting the different stages at which the *kanji* character was borrowed from Chinese (Sproat, 2009: 47; Olinsky, 2000). Many Chinese words were assimilated into Japanese along with their characters and sounds during three unique historical periods. Each of these three periods of linguistic exchange are marked by a specific system of pronunciation. The three systems are *Go'on* 'Go pronunciations', *Kan'on* 'Kan pronunciations', and *To'on* 'To pronunciations'. For instance, the *kanji* character 行 has several *on* readings: *gyo*, *ko*, and *an*. For more details, see Zhang (2023: 7f.).

1.2.3 Multiple *kun* readings

The Chinese character borrowing has experienced at least three booms, and the cycles of *kanji* borrowing led to multiple usages for each single *kanji* character. In other words, one *kanji* character can hold multiple Japanese native readings with disparate associated meanings. For instance, the *kanji* character 生 has several *kun* readings each with a different meaning: *iki* 'live, exist', *hae* 'grass grows', *nama* 'raw', and *u* 'to produce, give birth to'; 生 can also be read as *ha*, *o*, *ki*, *inochi*, *ubu*, and *na*.

1.2.4 Personal name readings

Personal name readings are a reading category different from *on* readings and *kun* readings. A *kanji* character has diverse readings in personal names which are different from its *on* readings and *kun* readings. For instance, the *kanji* character 一 has several personal name readings: *i*, *osamu*, *ka*, *kazu*, and *katsu*. For more details, see Zhang (2023: 9f.).

1.2.5 Reading ambiguities

Each single *kanji* character, generally, has at least one *on* and at least one *kun* reading. Because a *kanji* character has multiple readings, and each reading is used in different senses, when encountering a *kanji* character, one needs to figure out an appropriate contextual reading for the *kanji* character. For instance, the *kanji* character 行 is

[2] There is a *kanji* category called 和製漢語 *wasei kango* 'Japanese-made Chinese-character-based words'. *Wasei kango* are words that are composed of Chinese morphemes but were made by the Japanese rather than borrowed from Chinese. The items have *kanji* forms and most of them are read based on the *kun* reading rules, e.g., 蛯 *ebi* 'shrimp', 躾 *shitsuke* 'upbringing', and 凧 *tako* 'kite'. A few of them have both *on* reading and *kun* reading, e.g., 雫 *da* (*on* reading), *shizuku* (*kun* reading) 'driblet', and 鱈 *setsu* (*on* reading), *tara* (*kun* reading) 'cod'.

pronounced *gyo* in 修行 *shugyo* 'ascetic practices, training', *ko* in 行動 *kodo* 'action', and *an* in 行脚 *angya* 'pilgrimage'.

1.3 TTS and TTS approaches

Text-to-speech synthesis (TTS) is a technology that allows written text to be output as speech. Because people are in fact very sensitive to both the words and the way they are spoken, the goals in building a high-quality TTS system should clearly get across the message and use a human-like voice. These two goals of TTS are called intelligibility and naturalness (Taylor, 2009: 2-3).

The TTS problem is traditionally split into front-end and back-end systems. As one of the front-end system problems, the TTS system must predict the pronunciations of the words. For the in-vocabulary words with a single pronunciation, this requires only dictionary lookup. But for other types of words, for instance, homographs, because polysemous words are pronounced differently depending on the intended sense, one must analyze the context in which a *kanji* character occurs to select a contextually appropriate pronunciation (Gorman et al., 2018). This problem has been studied as homograph disambiguation, e.g., in English and a few other languages. A number of methods have been tried for several disambiguation tasks in NLP, including part of speech (POS) tagging and decision lists. Sproat et al. (1992) propose statistics of POS bigram or trigram to solve the problem and improve the disambiguation performance with words that have different POS taggers. Yarowsky (1994, 1997) presents decision list algorithms that combine the strengths of n-gram taggers, Bayesian classifiers, and decision trees in a highly effective general-purpose decision procedure for lexical ambiguity resolution. Gorman et al. (2018) select a set of 163 homographs for the US English experiment and find that hybrid systems (making use of both rules and machine learning) are significantly more accurate than either hand-written rules or machine learning alone.

1.4 Japanese TTS homograph ambiguities

Japanese writing is a complex system, and a large part of the complexity resides in the reading of *kanji* characters. The trick in any case is to know which is the right reading, which makes reading Japanese text a challenge for the TTS system (Sproat, 2009: 47). As discussed in section 1.2.1, the *kanji* character 山 'mountain' could be pronounced either *san* or *yama*. The two pronunciations share the same meaning. However, the TTS system must do homograph disambiguation to find an appropriate pronunciation based on the contextual information of the *kanji* character.

Two features are also related to the Japanese homograph disambiguation performance: word boundaries and formality. Because there is no word-boundary delimiter in Japanese, it is hard to identify a word. In the word segmentation process, if word boundaries cannot be identified correctly, it may lead TTS to incorrectly pronounce a string (Olinsky, 2000; Ooyama et al., 1987; Tesprasit et al., 2003). Therefore, problems of word boundary ambiguity and homograph ambiguity always occur together. Additionally, because Japanese writing is a combination of different scripts, *kanji* is used primarily for stems and *hiragana* is used for most inflectional endings and grammatical devices, word boundary discrimination can be simplified by detecting the transitions of the two different scripts. For instance, the string "現代の行政区分" 'modern administrative divisions' can be segmented at least into three tokens with the intervention of the *hiragana* の 'possessive particle' between the two *kanji* clusters: "現代" 'modern time' and "行政区分" 'administrative divisions'. *Katakana*, on the other hand, is used primarily for phonetic renderings of foreign words, further reducing ambiguity. Thus, *kanji* can be considered the "harder" case for word segmentation (Olinsky, 2000). For instance, the *kanji* string "米国産業界" can be segmented into two separate ways. The first *kanji* character holds different meanings and pronunciations based on the different segmentations. The first segmentation is 米国 'America' 産業 'Industry' 界 'Realm', in which the first *kanji* character 米 is pronounced *Bei*; the second segmentation is 米 'Rice' 国産 'Domestic production' 業界 'Industry', in which the *kanji* character 米 is pronounced *Kome*. Taylor (2009: 46) discusses the homograph syntactic ambiguity using English sentence "Police help dog bite victim" which has at least two different possible syntactic patterns: (Police help dog) bite victim; and Police help (dog bite victim). The homograph syntactic ambiguities also exist in Japanese sentences. If not processed appropriately, it can hurt the performance of one of the TTS goals—intelligibility.

Japanese is famous for its politeness and formality. Some Japanese words have both informal and formal forms. Formal Japanese forms can additionally be divided into three categories: 丁寧語 *teinei-go* 'polite form', 尊敬語 *sonkei-go* 'honorific form', and 謙譲語 *kenjo-go* 'humble form'. The *kanji* word 今日 'today' has two pronunciations, the informal pronunciation is *kyo*, and the formal pronunciation is *konnichi*. Therefore, given the *kanji* word 今日, the system needs to analyze the formality based on the contextual information and select an appropriate pronunciation accordingly. Whether the system can do the contextual formality analysis perfectly or not will affect the achievement of the other TTS goal—naturalness.

In addition to its importance in TTS applications, homograph disambiguation is relevant to automatic speech recognition (ASR) and is also a subset of word sense disambiguation (WSD) (Seale, 2021). Therefore, the task of *kanji* homograph disambiguation is not only important in improving the Japanese TTS performance but is also a crucial part of gaining high ASR and WSD accuracy.

However, Japanese *kanji* homograph disambiguation, to the best of the author's knowledge, is not currently attested to in peer-reviewed literature or otherwise published online. Also, there does not exist a well-developed data set that can support the research.

1.5 Labeling in Japanese *kanji* homographs

In TTS synthesis, the selection of the correct pronunciation of a text string occurs when a homograph is encountered (Seale, 2021). Homographs are pronounced differently depending on the intended sense, and the context provides enough clues for a homograph to select a contextually appropriate pronunciation (Gorman et al., 2018; Hearst, 1991). Yarowsky (1997) describes the techniques of English homograph disambiguation where each homograph is labeled originally by hand and a collection of features such as nearby content words. We manually label the pronunciations for each *kanji* homograph given a context and use machine learning methods to test the performance of the Japanese *kanji* homograph disambiguation. The data is released to the public for further experimentation by the NLP research community.

1.6 Research contributions

This research serves as the first academic work focused on Japanese *kanji* homograph disambiguation. Its contributions include publicizing the first single *kanji* pronunciation annotated data set, a typology of homographs with implications for both labeling and modeling and offering substantial language-specific resources to do Japanese homograph disambiguation. The data is released to the public for further experimentation by the NLP research community.

2 Data-driven *kanji* homograph research

This chapter introduces the Japanese *kanji* homograph data collecting, labeling, and modeling. Although very well respected at the current time, this research determined that the part of speech (POS) method is not compatible with Japanese homograph disambiguation. An explanation will be presented at the beginning of the chapter.

2.1 The reason for not using POS

With the increasing availability of annotated language data, several statistical part of speech (POS) tags have been developed which achieve high accuracy. Many prior work (Asahara et al., 2000; Brants, 2000; Denis, 2009; Gorman et al., 2018; Manning, 2011; Ratnaparkhi, 1997; Seale, 2021; Toutanova et al., 2000) uses POS features for disambiguating words. However, unlike homographs in some languages, the readings of *kanji* are generally not disambiguated by POS tags: firstly, most readings of *kanji* characters correspond to the same parts of speech, for instance, the *kanji* character 山 is a noun whether it is read as *san* or *yama*; secondly, some *kanji* characters cannot be assigned part of speech, for instance, the *kanji* character 文 is a component of the nouns 文化 'culture', 文法 'grammar', and 文学 'literature', and the part of speech for 文 itself cannot be defined. Therefore, POS annotation was not adopted as an analyzer in this research. For more details, see Zhang (2023: 16f.).

2.2 *Kanji* homograph data

The goal of this research is to construct a way of determining an appropriate pronunciation for Japanese *kanji* homographs. For this purpose, a data set labeled the pronunciation of commonly used single *kanji* characters was constructed.

2.2.1 Data collection

The labeled single *kanji* homograph data set is constructed using the following data: Japanese dictionary Jiten[3] and Universal Dependencies (UD) Japanese-GSD.[4] Jiten is an online Japanese dictionary. According to Jiten, as of June 2023, the number of recorded *kanji* characters is 27,693, and the total number of commonly used *kanji* characters is 2,136. This research collected each commonly used *kanji* character readings, including *on* readings, *kun* readings, and personal name readings. In addition, sentences from UD Japanese-GSD were combed for the context of commonly used *kanji* characters. These *kanji* characters and their pronunciations were combined with the Jiten *kanji* characters. The UD Japanese-GSD resource consists of sentences from Wikipedia and sentences which have been automatically split into words by IBM's word segmenter (Asahara et al., 2018). The data set is segmented into 193,654 tokens and 8,100 sentences, and divided into training, development, and test sets. This research ignored the original splits for data collection.

2.2.2 *Kanji* homograph extractions

This research used Python libraries, data classes, and collections to extract the *kanji* homographs. The top 100 most commonly used *kanji* homographs in the combined UD Japanese-GSD data set were extracted. After this process, some kanji homographs were excluded. Firstly, it was determined that a *kanji* homograph with a frequency of 50 or more occurrences was optimal, because if there is not enough data for a given *kanji* homograph, we cannot build a good classifier. This resulted in 86 *kanji* homographs. Secondly, 18 semiotic classes were excluded. There are some semiotic classes, for instance, computer languages, email addresses, dates, times, telephone numbers, and postal addresses are much simpler than natural language, and problems will arise when we mix the natural language and those semiotic systems in the same signal and using the same characters to do so (Taylor, 2009: 33-34). In Japanese, the reading of a *kanji* character inside a number or date expression is different from reading a *kanji* character that is not a part of one of those expressions. For instance, the *kanji* homograph 一 'one' has multiple readings. When 一 stands alone, the reading is *ichi*; when 一 is one part of the semiotic classes, for example, *ichimai* 'one piece of', *ikko* 'one', and *hitotsu* 'one', the reading will be *ichi*, *itsu*, and *hito*, respectively, depending on the following characters. The third exclusion ensures that each pronunciation must occur more than once and be at least 2% overall of the annotated data. Therefore, *kanji* homographs with only one pronunciation were removed so as not to bolster model scores, as the models would correctly pick the only pronunciation class available, and 36 *kanji* homographs removed due to pronunciation invariance. Thus, there were 32 *kanji* homographs retained. 1 *kanji* homograph was excluded due to Japanese formality. The *kanji* character 私 is a first-person singular pronoun that has two pronunciations: *watashi* and *watakushi*. There is only a slight difference between the two pronunciations, and distinguishing the two pronunciations requires subtle context. Therefore, it was excluded to avoid confusing the system. 2 *kanji* homographs were removed due to automatic *kanji* homograph extraction errors.[5] Data for a further 3 *kanji* homographs were removed because the number of examples that can be labeled was very small.[6] For more details, see Zhang (2023: 18f.). After removing 74 *kanji* homographs, the remaining UD Japanese-GSD homograph data contains 26 unique homographs, and the 26 *kanji* homographs were modeled.

2.2.3 *Kanji* homograph pronunciation class size

Each *kanji* homograph in the data set has at least two pronunciations. 77% of the *kanji* homographs have two pronunciations, and 23% have three or four pronunciations. 70% of the *kanji* homographs with two pronunciations have one commonly used pronunciation, and the commonly used pronunciation is greater than or equal to 40% of the available data. One *kanji* homograph has the largest difference in pronunciation class size, with a ratio of 4:96, and one has a ratio of 49:51. On the other hand, four *kanji* homographs with more than two pronunciations have two commonly used pronunciations. Those two pronunciations accounted for around 90% of the available data and the ratio of the two is very close.

---

[3] `https://jitenon.com/cat/common_kanji.php`

[4] The treebank is licensed under the Creative Commons License Attribution-ShareAlike 4.0 International.

[5] The *kanji* homographs are 見 and 出.

[6] The *kanji* homographs are 名, 位, and 次.

いつ	も	、	人	が	沢山	い	ます。
	$t-2$	$t-1$	t	$t+1$	$t+2$		

Table 1: Example of n-gram features for the ambiguous *kanji* character 人 'people, person'.

2.2.4 Data split redistribution

The total number of examples for the 26 *kanji* homographs in the data set is 1,903. These samples were split into 80% train, 10% dev, and 10% test. Stratified sampling was used as the default to maintain pronunciation class distribution among the splits. The stratified sampling method could be advantageous to sample each *kanji* homograph pronunciation category independently.

2.2.5 Data release

The new data sets were released for general use with the hope of helping to advance future research in Japanese and cross-lingual homographs. The data sets were released in two parts. First, 2,136 commonly used *kanji* homographs with their readings and reading types were released in a tab-separated values (TSV) file.[7] Readings for each *kanji* homograph include *on* readings, *kun* readings, and personal name readings. An annotated UD Japanese-GSD—a data set of *kanji* homograph readings in context was also released.[8] It includes sentences in which the target *kanji* homograph has been found.

2.3 Modeling

As the task of homograph disambiguation is to select a contextually appropriate pronunciation for a homograph, a logistic regression classifier was developed to make pronunciation predictions, and a baseline was computed to compare it against. While a baseline makes predictions that ignore the input features, the logistic regression classifier derives the input features from the homographs and the context surrounding them.

2.3.1 Baseline

A baseline was computed using the most frequent class label for each homograph, and then it was compared to the logistic regression classifier accuracy.

2.3.2 Logistic regression classifier

As the main task of homograph disambiguation is to select an appropriate pronunciation for a homograph given the context, a logistic regression (henceforth, LR) classifier was developed which considers the contextual features. In the development of the LR classifier, one LR classifier per-*kanji* was trained with the following n-gram features: tokens indexed one and two before and behind the homograph token, bigrams indexed immediately before and after the homograph token, and a skip-gram, the constituents of which surround the homograph token.[9] Table 1 displays one example of the *kanji* homograph n-gram features: t shows the position of the target *kanji* homograph; t − 2 "も" and t − 1 "、" are the left two tokens, while t + 1 "が" and t + 2 "沢山" are the right two tokens. Each unigram t − 2, t − 1, t + 1, and t + 2; the previous bigram t − 2 and t − 1; the following bigram t + 1 and t + 2; and the skip-gram bigram t − 1 and t + 1 were extracted as the target token features.

2.4 Evaluation and analysis

Per-class accuracy of one of the models from the most performant model type is reviewed, and error analysis is done for all models.

[7] https://github.com/wenzhang0222/thesis

[8] https://github.com/wenzhang0222/thesis

[9] Writing script categories (*kanji*, *hiragana*, and *katakana*) for n-grams were also checked but not selected as one of the features because they did not help the overall performance.

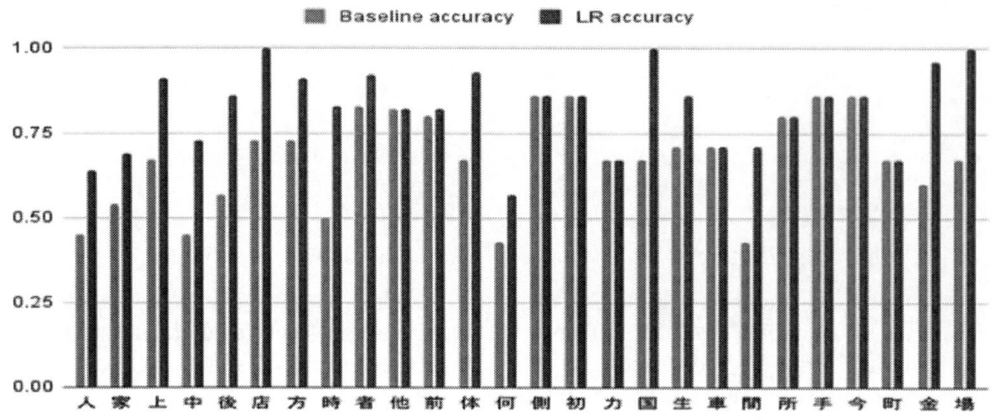

Figure 1: Baseline and LR accuracy for each *kanji* homograph.

Model	Micro acc.	Macro acc.
baseline	.67	.67
LR	.83	.83

Table 2: 26 *kanji* models' micro and macro accuracy.

2.4.1 Evaluation procedures

A baseline and LR classifier were trained and evaluated on the test set. Randomness can play a major role in the outcome of experiments and common sequence tagging tasks, the seed value for the random number generator can result in statistically significant differences for state-of-the-art systems (Reimers et al., 2017). Because randomness is inherent in the model, different results will be obtained if it is run multiple times. To protect against the human selection of metrics from a particularly good run, the reported metrics were taken from the model with the median balanced accuracy from each set of five models' performances. Hyperparameters were adjusted during training: L_1 regularization, LIBLINEAR solver, and hyperparameter C = 10. Separate models were trained for each *kanji* homograph. In addition, development of the models was done using the train and dev splits, and metrics were reported on the test split.

2.4.2 Metrics

The accuracy of a model provides a measure of its predictions' proximity to the correct values. Accuracy is determined in the range between 0 and 1. The performance of the models was evaluated using micro accuracy and macro accuracy.

2.4.3 Model performance

The micro and macro accuracies for the baseline and the LR classifier trained in this research are recorded in Table 2 — they show, on average, an increase between baseline and the non-baseline accuracies. The reasons are, firstly, logistic regression is famous for handling classification problems; secondly, L_1 regularization was applied in the LR classifier, and it can handle both dense and sparse input.

2.4.4 Per-*kanji* homograph performance

Figure 1 shows the accuracies for each *kanji* homograph: the baseline accuracy is represented by light blue histograms and the LR accuracy is shown in dark blue histograms. While the baseline accuracies range from .43 to .86, the LR accuracies range from 0.57 to 1.00. Overall, the LR accuracies outperform baseline accuracies. For more details, see Zhang (2023: 29f.).

2.4.5 Error analysis

The following sections report error analysis based on the errors made by the baseline and the LR classifier.

Kanji geographical feature error analysis

Reading a *kanji* character in some place names is a problem due to many *kanji* characters in those place names do not follow the default or general reading rules (Jones et al., 2022). Most parts of

Japan have their own dialects that can be used for colloquial interactions. As a result, *kanji* reading in place names are sometime following local traditions or dialects. In this research, there is one *kanji* character that reflects the Japanese *kanji* geographical features. The *kanji* character is 町 'town'. 町 has two pronunciations: the *on* reading *cho* and the *kun* reading *machi*. The reading of 町 seems casual and it is largely influenced by its geographical location. Both 町 's baseline and LR accuracy are .67. For more details, see Zhang (2023: 31f.).

Fixed expression error analysis

Most *kanji* characters have a commonly used *on* reading and a commonly used *kun* reading. Generally, when *on* reading and *kun* reading share the same meaning, the context will select a reading based on the n-gram features and sentential formality. While *kun* reading is casual, *on* reading is more formal. However, in some fixed expressions, due to history and/or geographical reasons, *on* reading and *kun* reading will no longer be distinguished, and there is only one reading. For instance, the *kanji* character 生 has two commonly used pronunciations: one is the *on* reading *sei*, the other is the *kun* reading *nama*. When 生 means 'live', it can only be read as *nama* instead of *sei*. The LR classifier predicts 50% incorrectly in this case. Other examples can be found in Zhang (2023: 34f.).

Formality error analysis

The Japanese honorific system is well-developed, ranging from pronouncing a single *kanji* character in a specific context to choosing sentence patterns and expressions. We retained a mild formality *kanji* homograph to test whether the model can learn, and to what extent formality can be learned during training. The *kanji* character is 他 'others'. 他 can combine with the *hiragana* phrase その 'that' to make a fixed expression その他 'the others', and it has two pronunciations in the combination: *hoka* and *ta*. The only difference between the pronunciations *sonohoka* and *sonota* is that *sonohoka* sounds more casual, which can be used in daily life conversations; *sonata* is formal, can be found in business expressions and official documents. The LR accuracy of the *kanji* character 他 is .82, and all the incorrect predictions are about the formality pronunciations of 他 in the combination その他. This indicates that the LR classifier was not able to differentiate the Japanese formality robustly.

Pronunciation class size imbalanced error analysis

There are two *kanji* characters that each of which has four pronunciations, one is the *kanji* character 家 'home, house, family' and one is the *kanji* character 後 'later, back'. The character 家 's pronunciations are: *ka*, *ke*, *ie*, and *ya*. Among the 105 examples of the *kanji* character 家, the pronunciation *ka* counts for 62%, *ke* is 19%, *ie* is 17%, and *ya* only counts for 2%. The LR classifier could not distinguish the two commonly used pronunciations: *ka* and *ke* and predicted all the *ke* to *ka*. LR also predicted *ya* to *ka*. Because the ratio of the pronunciation *ya* is very low, it can be assumed that features of the pronunciation *ya* were not fully learned by the LR classifier during training, and the LR classifier used the most frequent pronunciation *ka* to predict it. Other examples can be found in Zhang (2023: 35f.)

3 Discussion and conclusion

This research has been motivated by providing the first annotated Japanese single *kanji* pronunciation data set to solve Japanese *kanji* reading ambiguities. Although the pronunciation of Japanese *kanji* characters is a bottleneck on TTS performance, it has not been studied seriously due to the lack of reliable publicly available data. At the beginning of Chapter 2, this research addressed weaknesses in the use of part of speech (POS) as a mean of Japanese *kanji* homograph disambiguation and expounded on the source and methods of obtaining and processing the data. Some Japanese characteristics, for instance, *rendaku*, formality, and geographical features were taken in account when processing data.

Baseline and logistic regression (LR) classifier were used to examine the data performance. While the baseline can only obtain 67% prediction accuracy, the LR classifier, with the help of the n-gram feature extractions, effective statistical analysis and regularization, improved the prediction accuracy to 83%. The following sections provide information about the known limitations of this research and directions for future research.

3.1 Known limitations and future research

As mentioned in Chapter 2, since data is annotated by the author in person, it may include some human error in labeling. However, this can be resolved through a review of the labels and the publication of an amended version. In addition, the sentence data is obtained from the Universal Dependencies (UD) Japanese-GSD data set, this is just one of eight UD Japanese corpora and other ones could be used to expand the data set. Also, this research treats the single *kanji* homographs as the target, and the work could undoubtedly be improved by expanding the research to *kanji* combinations. As discussed in Chapter 1, Japanese is one of the languages that lack word boundaries. Therefore, the first interesting point will be that when a *kanji* homograph is in a *kanji* combination or phrase, which *kanji* homographs will tie together to make a word to create a word boundary with other *kanji* homographs. Then the second point is how the new *kanji* combination can affect the pronunciation selection of those *kanji* homographs.

An anonymous reviewer suggests that we compare against the *kanji* disambiguation system embedded in `MeCab`. However, we leave this comparison for future work.

Finally, due to time constraints, this research extracts n-gram features for the target *kanji* homographs. There will be other features that help analyze the context to improve the model performance.

3.2 Conclusion

This research has pioneered labeling for the task of Japanese *kanji* homograph disambiguation in text-to-speech applications. It contributes to providing the first public free *kanji* homograph annotated data. New data sets are offered to the research community to provide further research on this work. This research also provides a typology of homographs based on specific language features. The direction is set for future research in Japanese homograph studies and can be extended to research on the writing system of Chinese characters.

Acknowledgements

I would like to express my gratitude to my advisor, Dr. Kyle Gorman, for his generous and professional guidance on my studies at the Graduate Center, City University of New York, for helping me to shape and fine-tune this research, and for sharing his expertise and time with me throughout the paper. I deeply appreciate the opportunity to have worked together. I would also like to thank anonymous reviewers for their helpful feedback.

References

Aaron van den Oord, Sander Dieleman, Heiga Zen, Karen Simonyan, Oriol Vinyals, Alex Graves, Nal Kalchbrenner, Andrew Senior, and Koray Kavukcuoglu. 2016. WaveNet: A Genirative Model for Raw Audio. Proc. 9th ISCA Workshop on Speech Synthesis workshop (SSW9), 125.

Adwait Ratnaparkhi. 1997. A maximum entropy model for part-of-speech tagging. In *EMNLP*, pages 133–142. Reimers, N., and Gurevych, I. (2017). Optimal Hyperparameters for Deep LSTM-Networks for Sequence Labeling Tasks. In arXiv:1707.06799.

Anders Søgaard. 2010. Simple semi-supervised training of part-of-speech taggers. In *Proceedings of the ACL 2010 Conference Short Papers*, pages 205–208.

Christopher D. Manning. 2011. Part-of-speech tagging from 97% to 100%: is it time for some linguistics? In *CICLing*, pages 171–189.

Craig Olinsky and Alan W. Black. 2000. Non-Standard Word and Homograph Resolution for Asian Language Text Analysis. Sixth International Conference on Spoken Language Processing, ICSLP 2000 / INTERSPEECH 2000, pages 733-736.

Daniela Braga., Luís Coelho, and Fernando Gil V. Resende Jr. 2007. Homograph ambiguity resolution in front-end design for Portuguese TTS systems. In *INTERSPEECH*, pages 1761–1764.

David Yarowsky. 1994. Decision lists for lexical ambiguity resolution: Application to accent restoration in Spanish and French. *Proceedings of the 32nd Annual Meeting of the Association for Computational Linguistics*, pages 88-95.

David Yarowsky. 1997. Homograph disambiguation in text-to-speech synthesis. In *Jan P. H. van Santen, et al., editors, Progress in speech synthesis*, pages 157–172.

Denilson C. Silva, Daniela Braga, and Fernando Gil V. Resende Jr. 2012. A rule-based method for homograph disambiguation in Brazilian Portuguese text-to-speech. *Journal of Communications and Information Systems*, 27(1), pages 1–9.

Drahomíra "johanka" Spoustová, Jan Hajič, Jan Raab, and Miroslav Spousta. 2009. Semi-Supervised Training for the Averaged Perceptron POS Tagger. In *Proceedings of the 12th Conference of the European Chapter of the ACL (EACL 2009)*, pages 763–771.

Fabian Pedregosa, Gaël Varoquaux, Alexandre Gramfort, Vincent Michel, Bertrand Thirion, Olivier Grisel, Mathieu Blondel, Peter Prettenhofer, Ron Weiss, Vincent Dubourg, Jake Vanderplas, Alexandre Passos, David Cournapeau, Matthieu Brucher, Matthieu Perrot, and Édouard Duchesnay. 2011. Scikit-learn: Machine Learning in Python. *Journal of Machine Learning Research*, 12, pages 2825–2830.

Hang Li and Jun-ichi Takeuchi. 1997. Using Evidence that is both Strong and Reliable in Japanese Homograph Disambiguation. In *SIGNL*119-9, pages 53-59. IPSJ.

Honghui Dong, Jianhua Tao, and Bo Xu. 2004. Grapheme-to-phoneme conversion in Chinese TTS system. In *Proc.2004 International Symposium on Chinese Spoken Language Processing*, pages 165-168.

Jennifer M. Seale. 2021. Label imputation for homograph disambiguation: theoretical and practical approaches. Doctoral dissertation, The Graduate Center, City University of New York.

Junhui Zhang, Junjie Pan, Xiang Yin, Chen Li, Shichao Liu, Yang Zhang, Yuxuan Wang, and Zejun Ma. 2020. A hybrid text normalization system using multi-head self attention for mandarin. In *ICASSP 2020-2020 IEEE International Conference on Acoustics, Speech and Signal Processing (ICASSP)*, pages 6694–6698.

Junhui Zhang, Wudi Bao, Junjie Pan, Xiang Yin, and Zejun Ma. 2022. A Novel Chinese Dialect TTS Frontend with Non-Autoregressive Neural Machine Translation. In arXiv:2206.04922.

Junko Itô and Armin Mester. 1996. Rendaku I: Constraint Conjunction and the OCP. Kobe Phonology Forum 1996.

Kristina Toutanvoa and Christopher D. Manning. 2000. Enriching the knowledge sources used in a maximum entropy part-of-speech tagger. In *EMNLP*, pages 63–70.

Kristina Toutanova, Dan Klein, Christopher D. Manning, and Yoram Singer. 2003. Feature-rich part-of-speech tagging with a cyclic dependency network. In *NAACL* 3, pages 252–259.

Kyle Gorman, Gleb Mazovetskiy, and Vitaly Nikolaev. 2018. Improving homograph disambiguation with supervised machine learning. In chair), N. C. C., Choukri, K., Cieri, C., Declerck, T., Goggi, S., Hasida, K., Isahara, H., Maegaard, B., Mariani, J., Mazo, H., Moreno, A., Odijk, J., Piperidis, S., and Tokunaga, T., editors, *Proceedings of the Eleventh International Conference on Language Resources and Evaluation (LREC 2018)*. European Language Resources Association (ELRA).

Kyle Gorman, Lucas F.E. Ashby, Aaron Goyzueta, Arya D. McCarthy, Shijie Wu, and Daniel You. 2020. The SIGMORPHON 2020 shared task on multilingual grapheme-to-phoneme conversion. In *Proceedings of the 17th SIGMORPHON Workshop on Computational Research in Phonetics, Phonology, and Morphology*, pages 40–50. Association for Computational Linguistics.

Libin Shen, Giorgio Satta, and Aravind Joshi. 2007. Guided learning for bidirectional sequence classification. In *ACL 2007*.

Llion Jones, Richard Sproat, Haruko Ishikawa, and Alexander Gutkin. 2022. Helpful Neighbors: Leveraging Neighbors in Geographic Feature Pronunciation. In arXiv:2210.10200.

Lucas F.E. Ashby, Travis M. Bartley, Simon Clematide, Luca Del Signore, Cameron Gibson, Kyle Gorman, Yeonju Lee-Sikka, Peter Makarov, Aidan Malanoski, Sean Miller, Omar Ortiz, Reuben Raff, Arundhati Sengupta, Bora Seo, Yulia Spektor, and Winnie Yan. 2021. Results of the Second SIGMORPHON Shared Task on Multilingual Grapheme-to-Phoneme Conversion. *Proceedings of the 18th SIGMORPHON Workshop on Computational Research in Phonetics, Phonology, and Morphology*, pages 115–125.

Marti A. Hearst and Xerox Palo Alto Research Center. 1991. Noun homograph disambiguation using local context in large text corpora. In *Using Corpora*, pages 185-188.

Masayuki Asahara and Yuji Matsumoto. 2000. Extended models and tools for high-performance part-of-speech tagger. In *Proceedings of the 18th International Conference on Computational Linguistics*, pages 21–27.

Masayuki Asahara, Hiroshi Kanayama, Takaaki Tanaka, Yusuke Miyao, Sumire Uematsu, Shinsuke Mori, Yuji Matsumoto, Mai Omura, and Yugo Murawaki. 2018. Universal Dependencies Version 2 for Japanese. In *LREC*.

Nils Reimers and Iryna Gurevych. 2017. Reporting score distributions makes a difference: Performance study of LSTM-networks for sequence tagging. In *Proceedings of the 2017 Conference on Empirical Methods in Natural Language Processing*, pages 338–348. Association for Computational Linguistics.

Pascal Denis and Benoît Sagot. 2009. Coupling an annotated corpus and a morphosyntactic lexicon for state-of-the-art POS tagging with less human effort. In *Pacific Asia Conference on Language, Information and Computation*, pages 110–119.

Pual Taylor. 2009. *Text-to-speech synthesis*. Cambridge University Press, Cambridge.

Richard Sproat. 2009. *Language, Technology, and Society*. Oxford University Press.

Richard Sproat and Navdeeep Jaitly. 2016. RNN Approaches to Text Normalization: A Challenge. In arXiv:1611.00068.

Richard Sproat, Julia Hirschberg, and David Yarowsky. 1992. *A corpus-based synthesizer. In ICSLP*, pages 563–566.

Ryan McDonald, Joakim Nivre, Yvonne Quirmbach-Brundage, Yoav Goldberg, Dipanjan Das, Kuzman Ganchev, Keith Hall, Slav Petrov, Hao Zhang, Oscar Oscar Täckström, Claudia Bedini, Núria Bertomeu Castelló, Jungmee Lee. 2013. Universal Dependency Annotation for Multilingual Parsing. Proceedings of the 51st Annual Meeting of the Association for Computational Linguistics, pages 92-97. Association for Computational Linguistics.

Stalin Aguirre and Josaf́a de Jesus Aguiar Pontes. 2019. A Japanese Word Segmentation Proposal. In *Proceedings of the 57th Annual Meeting of the Association for Computational Linguistics: Student Research Workshop*, pages 429-435.

Stephen Mussmann, Robin Jia, Percy Liang. 2020. On the importance of adaptive data collection for extremely imbalanced pairwise tasks. In arXiv:2010.05103.

Takaaki Tanaka, Yusuke Miyao, Masayuki Asahara, Sumire Uematsu, Hiroshi Kanayama, Shinsuke Mori, and Yuji Matsumoto. 2016. Universal Dependencies for Japanese. In *LREC*.

1

Thorsten Brants. 2000. TnT - A Statistical Part-of-Speech Tagger. In *Proceedings of the Sixth Applied Natural Language Processing Conference (ANLP 2000)*, pages 224-231.

Virongrong Tesprasit, Paisarn Charoenpornsawat, and Virach Sornlertlamvanich. 2003. A context sensitive homograph disambiguation in Thai text-to-speech synthesis. In *Proc. HLT-NAACL'2003, short papers*, vol. 2.

Wen Zhang. 2023. Pronunciation ambiguities in Japanese *kanji*. Master's thesis, The Graduate Center, City University of New York.

William A. Gale, Kenneth W. Church, and David Yarowsky. 1992. Using bilingual materials to develop word sense disambiguation methods. In *Proceedings of the Fourth International Conference on Theoretical and Methodological Issues in Machine Translation*, volume 112. Citeseer.

Yoshihumi Ooyama, Miyazaki Masahiro, and Ikehara Satoru. 1987. Natural Language Processing in a Japanese text-to-speech system. In *Proceedings of the 15th annual conference on Computer Science*, pages: 44-47.

Zolzaya Byambador, Ryota Nishimura, Altangerel Ayush, Kengo Ohta, and Norihide Kitaoka. 2021. Text-to-speech system for low-resource language using cross-lingual transfer learning and data augmentation. In *EURASIP Journal on Audio, Speech, and Music Processing* 2021:42.

Lenient Evaluation of Japanese Speech Recognition: Modeling Naturally Occurring Spelling Inconsistency

Shigeki Karita and **Richard Sproat** and **Haruko Ishikawa**
Google DeepMind / Shibuya 3-21-3 Tokyo Japan
{karita,rws,ishikawa}@google.com

Abstract

Word error rate (WER) and *character error rate* (CER) are standard metrics in Speech Recognition (ASR), but one problem has always been *alternative spellings*: If one's system transcribes *adviser* whereas the ground truth has *advisor*, this will count as an error even though the two spellings really represent the same word.

Japanese is notorious for "lacking orthography": most words can be spelled in multiple ways, presenting a problem for accurate ASR evaluation. In this paper we propose a new *lenient* evaluation metric as a more defensible CER measure for Japanese ASR. We create a lattice of plausible respellings of the reference transcription, using a combination of lexical resources, a Japanese text-processing system, and a neural machine translation model for reconstructing kanji from hiragana or katakana. In a manual evaluation, raters rated 95.4% of the proposed spelling variants as plausible. ASR results show that our method, which does not penalize the system for choosing a valid alternate spelling of a word, affords a 2.4%–3.1% absolute reduction in CER depending on the task.

1 Introduction: "Word" error rate

For decades, a standard measure of performance in Automatic Speech Recognition (ASR) has been *word error rate* (WER), which gives a measure of how poorly a transcription hypothesized by the ASR system matches a reference transcription and which, while often criticized—e.g. (Wang et al., 2003)—is still widely used. While the expression *WER* uses the term *word*, it is important to note that what is matched is not really words, but rather *spelled forms*. To take a simple example from English, the reference transcription might have the token *advisor*, whereas the corresponding token in the hypothesis is *adviser*. Although these are variant spellings of the same word, the system would be assessed as getting the word wrong, since the spellings do not match. If one used instead *character error rate* (CER), the effect of the spelling discrepancy would be of course be less, but there would still be an error. Arguably this should really not count as an error, since the spelling alternates are both valid.

Orthographic variation (Meletis and Dürscheid, 2022, Section 4.6), is common in the world's writing systems, but for many systems the effect is a minor one. In English, for example, orthographic variation is of two main types: regional variation, in particular British versus American spelling (e.g. *neighbour* vs. *neighbor*); and more or less free variation within a regional variety such as the *advisor/adviser* example above, or issues such as whether to write a space in noun compounds (e.g. *doghouse* vs. *dog house*). In the former case, one can argue that a spelling discrepancy should count as an error since in contexts where, say, *flavour* would be an appropriate spelling, *neighbor* would not be, and vice versa. In the latter case, the variants should probably not be counted as errors, but a naive WER or CER computation would so count them. Still, since the amount of such spelling variation is relatively small, one can usually ignore this effect, or use cleanup scripts to handle the few cases that occur. WER is a fiction, but it is a fiction that can largely be ignored.

2 Japanese spelling inconsistency

In Japanese, unlike in English, spelling variation is rampant, and the fiction becomes too great to be ignored. Japanese spelling is very inconsistent, with many words that

Proceedings of the Workshop on Computation and Written Language (CAWL 2023), pages 61–70
July 14, 2023 ©2023 Association for Computational Linguistics

have kanji (Chinese character) spellings also appearing in text in hiragana (one of the two syllabaries used in Japanese), or even, for emphasis or other reasons, in katakana (the other syllabary). Thus common words like だめ (hiragana) *dame* 'not allowed' also frequently appear as ダメ (katakana) for emphasis, but there is also a somewhat infrequent but nonetheless occurring form in kanji, 駄目. ください *kudasai* 'please' also frequently appears as 下さい. うまい *umai* 'good' can also be written as 上手い. If one's reference transcription has ダメ *dame* and the ASR system hypothesizes だめ, a naive WER/CER computation would count this as an error, even though these are both valid variant spellings.

There are many reasons for the variation. Some of them have to do with style—on which see Section 6. Katakana is frequently used to mark *emphasis* so that in Japanese, orthographic variation is used to mark what in English would involve either, to adopt the terminology of Meletis and Dürscheid (2022), *graphetic* variation such as italics, or *graphemic* variation such as capitalization. Joyce and Masuda (2019) give the example of *mechamecha* 'absurdly', normally written in katakana メチャメチャ, being written in kanji as 目茶目茶 in a sentence with foreign words or emphasized words, both written in katakana. They suggest the reason for the kanji spelling in this case is to provide visual distinctiveness. Spelling variants may also be used for artistic reasons (Lowy, 2021). One would like to have a measure of error rate that takes these sorts of variation into account.

One could of course propose developing reference transcriptions that are highly standardized so that, e.g., *dame* is always written だめ, thus eliminating the problem. Indeed corpora such as the Corpus of Spontaneous Japanese[1] exist that have highly standardized orthographic transcriptions. But this is not a practical solution in general for a couple of reasons. First, a large amount of potential training data that comes with transcriptions—for example YouTube videos—will not have been subjected to rigorous transcription guidelines, and the cost of retranscribing such data would be prohibitive. Second, downstream applications cannot be expected to adhere to whatever guidelines have been adopted, and one would like the flexibility to provide transcriptions that can match what downstream applications expect. Over and above this, normalizing everything to a standard spelling misses the fact that variation is a normal part of Japanese spelling, and one can ignore this only by adopting an artificial standard. We propose therefore to try to model what every native speaker/reader of Japanese knows, namely that だめ, ダメ and 駄目 are all legal ways to write *dame* 'not allowed'.

At the same time, one cannot allow the system to be too loose. To return to an example cited above, for うまい *umai* 'good', one can also have 上手い, as above, but in addition another possible written form is 美味い. The second spelling, 上手い just means 'good' (i.e, good at something), whereas 美味い means 'good tasting'. These two senses are both available for うまい, but they are not interchangeable, and this issue comes up if the ground truth has a kana spelling, whereas the hypothesized form uses kanji. If ground truth has うまい, and the system transcribes 美味い 'delicious', whereas a native speaker could tell from context that what was intended was 上手い 'good', this should count as an error. In reconstructing spelling variants in kanji from reference forms in kana, the system therefore needs to do sense disambiguation.

3 Proposed method

Our method starts with the creation of a lattice of possible respellings, given a reference transcription for an utterance. In order to illustrate the method, we consider the hypothetical reference transcription

この	拉麺	は	うまい	。
kono	*rāmen*	*ha*	*umai*	.

'this ramen is delicious'. The first step involves computing hiragana transcriptions for kanji sequences, which in the case at hand will yield らーめん for *rāmen*. In general tokens written in kanji may have multiple readings, but usually only one reading is appropriate for a given context. For this conversion we use a proprietary Japanese

[1] https://clrd.ninjal.ac.jp/csj/en/data-index.html

lattice-based text normalization system that uses a large dictionary, annotated corpora, rules, and linear classifiers to determine the most likely readings of kanji sequences in context. The system has a roughly 97% token accuracy on held out data. As is well-known, Japanese text lacks word separators, but one side-effect of the text normalization system is to produce a word-segmentation of the sentence. These word segments are used as the tokens for subsequent processing in our lattice construction.

For each hiragana word, we also want a katakana equivalent—cf., the example of だめ/ダメ above. This is a fairly straightforward conversion and in the example at hand would produce ラーメン for *rāmen*, which also happens to be the way this word is normally written.

This completes the conversion of kanji tokens into kana, and the next step is to convert in the other direction. For example, the last non-punctuation token in the utterance うまい *umai* 'delicious', also has a common kanji spelling 旨い. However as noted above, in this as in many other cases, one needs to be careful, since another possible spelling for うまい is 上手い, which would not be appropriate in this instance since it means 'skillful'. For this conversion we train a transformer-based neural machine translation model (NMT)—e.g. (Tay et al., 2020)—on Japanese web text where we first converted successive kanji spellings into hiragana using the text normalization system previously described. For example, consider the input sentence:

再び、MTサミットが日本で
futatabi, MT samitto-ga nihon de
'Again, the MT Summit is in Japan'

which contains two words containing kanji 再び *futatabi* 'again' and 日本 *nihon* 'Japan'. Consider the second of these, which has the hiragana transcription にほん. We replace this into the sentence above and tag it with a special tag <to_kanji>...</to_kanji> so that the input appears as

再び、 MTサミットが <to_kanji> にほん </to_kanji> で

and we train the NMT system to predict 日本, given this context. We also need to train the model to predict cases where kana spellings should not be replaced by kanji: For example the final で does not have a kanji variant, and so in this case we would produce a variant of the input sentence with that token tagged with <to_kanji>...</to_kanji>, and the system would be trained to replace it with itself.

The NMT transformer is configured with 6 layers, 8 attention heads and a hidden-layer dimension of 2048, and trained on a web corpus of 7.3 billion tokens. At runtime the model is applied to each hiragana word in the sentence in turn to predict whether that token should be replaced with a word spelled in kanji, and if so which word. The token error rate for *kanji restoration* on a held out corpus is approximately 3.8%. In the case at hand, the system would correctly predict 旨い as an appropriate spelling of うまい.

Finally, 旨い has another possible kanji spelling, 美味い, which we have already seen in Section 2. To allow for these variants we use lexical resources licensed from the CJK Institute (`www.cjki.org`), in particular the Japanese Orthographic Dictionary, which lists spelling equivalence classes for several tens of thousands of Japanese words.[2] These equivalence classes are 'safe' in the sense that one can substitute any spelling in the class for any other without considering the context of the word. Thus 美味い and 旨い both mean 'delicious' and can be safely substituted for each other. To the CJKI institute data we have added additional equivalence classes mined from various data sources such as Wikipedia, for a total of about 54,200 equivalence classes.

Figure 1 shows the complete lattice that is reconstructed for the input sentence given above.

Lattices are implemented in OpenFst (Riley et al., 2009), with weights represented in the

[2]Public resources such as JMDict (Breen, 2004) also contain some information on spelling variants. However, as we note in the Limitations section, unlike the JOD, JMDict has not been curated with a view to marking which spellings are interchangeable. Nonetheless, we plan to investigate incorporating additional data from JMDict in future work.

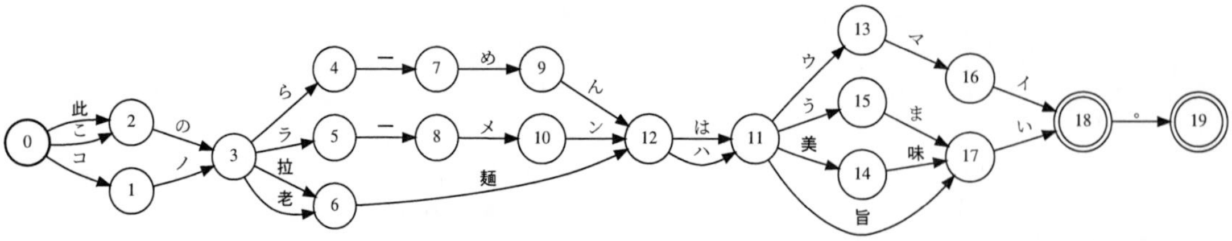

Figure 1: Final lattice computed for the reference transcription この拉麺はうまい。 'this ramen is delicious'.

Tropical semiring. During evaluation, the Levenshtein edit distance (Levenshtein, 1966) between the reference lattice and the hypothesized transcription is computed using the algorithm reported in Gorman and Sproat (2021), pp. 93–96.

As with standard CER, we define our lenient CER as the lattice edit distance—the sum of the substitution, insertion and deletion errors—divided by the number of characters in the best matching path in the reference lattice.

In future work (Section 6) we also wish to incorporate style/register language models to rank different transcriptions, and we will thus want to preserve language model weights for the various spelling alternatives. To that end, we first convert the Tropical weights into a <Tropical, Tropical> Lexicographic semiring (Sproat et al., 2014), where the first dimension is reserved for the edit distance weights, and the second dimension preserves the language model weights. This will guarantee that the path in the lattice closest to the hypothesized string is selected, with the language model score of that path preserved in the second dimension. After the shortest path has been computed, the result can be converted back to the Tropical semiring with just the (second-dimension) language model weights.

In the experiments reported in Section 5, we compare the results with multiple lattice variants, which are indicated with the terms boldfaced below:

1. The raw ground-truth transcription, represented as a trivial (single-path) lattice.
2. The lattice in (1) augmented with kana conversion via the text-normalization system (**+kana**).
3. The lattice in (2) augmented with the kanji restoration NMT model (**+kanji**).
4. The lattice in (3) augmented with the spelling equivalence classes (**+lexicon**).

4 Related Work

While the contribution of spelling variation to error rate computation for Japanese ASR has been noted—see Mishima et al. (2020), page 72—as far as we can tell, there has been no prior work that specifically addresses solutions to this problem. However, the problem of spelling variation in Japanese is similar to cases in other languages where no standardized spelling exists. For example, Ali et al. (2017)—and see also (Ali et al., 2019)—present an approach for ASR for Arabic dialects. Unlike Modern Standard Arabic, which has an official and standardized orthography, Arabic regional varieties such as Levantine, Gulf Arabic, or Maghrebi are spoken languages that have no generally agreed standard written form. Nonetheless, particularly with the advent of social media, people increasingly communicate in Arabic dialects in written form. But since there is no prescribed standard there is a substantial amount of variation in how words are spelled. Ali et al. (2017) propose the *WERd* ("word error rate for dialects") metric, which depends on a spelling variants table, which they construct from social media. Variants are collected by mining tokens that share the same context, occur a sufficient number of times, and are within a Levenshtein edit-distance bound of each other. This kind of approach for finding potentially intersubstitutable terms has been used in other applications: for example, Roark and Sproat (2014) propose a similar approach for finding potential pairs of words and novel abbreviations of those words. Once the spelling variants table is constructed, Ali et al. (2017) use it to match ASR candidates against the reference transcription similar to the way in which our lattice-based matching works. Related work includes Nigmatulina et al. (2020), who report on an ASR system for Swiss German, which like dialectal Arabic, has no standard orthography, but where spellings are loosely based on pronunciation.

Another case of spelling variation can be found with transliteration, say when someone whose native language is Hindi using the Devanagari script, transliterates a Hindi word into English. As Roark et al. (2020) discuss, this problem has a practical application, since while keyboards for Devanagari and other South Asian scripts exist, they tend to be difficult to use, whereas many users are used to typing in English. Therefore many users prefer to type in Latin script transliteration, and have the system automatically convert to the native script. But this introduces a problem since, while there are standards for transliteration of South Asian languages into Latin script, few people adhere to them. The result is that one can find quite a large amount of variation in how to spell words in Latin script, whereas there is generally one way to correctly write a given word in the native script. Roark et al. (2020) investigated a variety of methods including both neural and pair n-gram methods, and found that they got the best performance with a pair 6-gram model using a Katz-smoothed trigram language model for the output.

While the above cases are similar to the problem with Japanese spelling variation, there is also an important difference. For dialectal Arabic, and transliterated South Asian languages, there is no standard, and so long as the message can be communicated, users are more or less unconstrained in how they will spell words. In the case of Japanese, spelling variation is not completely unconstrained: there are definitely *wrong* spellings for words, even if there is in any given case no *single* right spelling. While this does not dictate a particular approach to the problem, it does mean that the variation needs to be constrained by lexical knowledge implemented in some fashion.

Our use of Neural MT models for kanji restoration is related to the similar use of NMT models for transliteration: see, e.g., Grundkiewicz and Heafield (2018) and Kundu et al. (2018).

Finally, we note that the problem of lenient evaluation comes up in other domains, for example in evaluation of MT systems. For example, Bouamor et al. (2014) argue that the rich morphology of Arabic has a negative impact on BLEU scores in that a naive application of BLEU can rank correct translations lower than incorrect ones. They propose a lenient metric they term "AL-BLEU", which takes morphological variation into account. They argue that this metric provides a more defensible evaluation metric.

5 Experiments

We investigated our proposed evaluation metrics on several Japanese ASR tasks. Using large-scale multiple domain datasets, we calculated error reductions from conventional naive CER, using lattices that incorporate the additional resources discussed in the last section. We also conducted human evaluations to validate the generated spelling alternatives.

5.1 ASR datasets

We evaluated on proprietary Japanese datasets in three domains: *Farfield*, *Voice-Search* (VS), and *YouTube* (YT)— respectively, domains involving far-field speech, voice search, and YouTube video segments, (Narayanan et al., 2019). These datasets contain anonymized and hand-transcribed utterances. The numbers of evaluated utterances were 15,693 (161,174 characters) for Farfield; 9,440 (78,606 characters) for VS; and 17,780 (238,662 characters) for YT.

5.2 ASR models

Our Japanese ASR models are Conformer-based Recurrent Neural Network Transducers (RNN-T) (Gulati et al., 2020). For the YT domain evaluation, we trained the ASR model only with a YT training set of 2,000 hours using a 17-layer, 512-dimensional, 8-attention-head, non-causal encoder, and a 5000-class character vocabulary. Apart from YT, our model was trained with all the multi-domain training sets of 25,000 hours using a 12-layer,

1024-dimensional, 8-attention-head, causal encoder, with a 6400-class *wordpiece* model vocabulary (Schuster and Nakajima, 2012).

5.3 Results with ASR tasks

Table 1 shows conventional WER and CER using the raw ground truth text, and CERs using our proposed target lattices for each ASR domain evaluation, as discussed in Section 3. In addition to the average error rates, we also computed ±95% confidence interval following Vilar (2008).

First, comparing WER and CER with the raw reference text, CERs were always lower than WERs in every domain. This is largely because WER depends on word boundaries estimated by a word segmenter, which can often lead to artificial mismatches between reference and transcription. CER, obviously, does not require word segmentation. For this reason, we evaluated our evaluation method by comparing baseline CER rates against the lenient CER lattice-based scoring.

When we added alternative kana spellings into the reference lattice (**+kana**), CERs were decreased by at least 2% absolute for all domains. More spellings from the kanji-restoration NMT (**+kanji**) and the lexicon (**+lexicon**) further reduced CERs to 2.4%–3.1% absolute depending on the domain. For example, VS was the most impacted domain, with a 25.16% relative error reduction.

A manual examination of cases of mismatch between the reference transcription and the hypothesized transcription in YT revealed many cases where one had kanji spellings and the other kana, or where one had hiragana and the other katakana, as one would expect given the discussion in Section 2. For example, the following pairs show, (1) kana-kana, (2) kana-kanji, (3) kanji-kana, and (4) kanji-kanji (false) errors between the ASR hypothesis (hyp) and reference ground truth (ref). Also given are romaji and a translation:

1. hyp: イナバのチュールかな
   ref: いなばのちゅーるかな
   rom: *inaba no chūru-ka-na*
   tra: Inaba Churu (dog treats)...

2. hyp: 皆さんご機嫌よう
   ref: みなさんごきげんよう
   rom: *minasan gokigenyō*
   tra: hello everyone

3. hyp: がんばれ
   ref: 頑張れ
   rom: *ganbare*
   tra: do your best

4. hyp: 柔らかい設定になってます
   ref: 軟らかい設定になってます
   rom: *yawarakai settei ni nattemasu*
   tra: it has a soft setting

The proposed system correctly produces these alternative spellings in the lattices created from the reference ground truth.

5.4 Manual evaluation of spelling variants

We evaluated spelling variants of 913 phrases generated by the model against the original spellings from the YT domain. More specifically, we evaluated phrases extracted from the transcription in the reference lattice that had the best edit-distance score when matched against the ASR hypothesis. The phrases varied in length from 1 to 93 characters, where 80% are 2 to 15 characters. Three trained raters were asked to assign each variant to one of the following bins:

- **Acceptable**: Spelling variants are without errors and acceptable.
- **Acceptable (Depending on the context)**: Acceptable in the context of a given phrase.
- **Great**: Great or better than the original spellings. Note that 'great' means that the selected alternate spellings are indeed commonly used valid spellings for the intended term, and 'better' means that the alternative spelling is even more natural, and easier and clearer for native speakers to read.
- **Great (Depending on the context)**: Great in the context of a given phrase.
- **Wrong**: Spelling contains errors.

	Farfield	**VoiceSearch**	**YouTube**
WER	12.74 ± 0.49	11.58 ± 0.52	22.58 ± 0.42
CER	12.53 ± 0.49	9.62 ± 0.47	18.36 ± 0.38
+kana	9.93 ± 0.42	7.68 ± 0.40	16.67 ± 0.35
+kanji	9.59 ± 0.42	7.45 ± 0.39	16.18 ± 0.35
+lexicon	9.46 ± 0.41	7.20 ± 0.39	15.84 ± 0.35

Table 1: Multi-domain ASR evaluation results with ±95% confidence interval. For "WER" and "CER", we used raw ground truth texts as reference targets. Other results show CERs using additional reference lattices augmented with alternative spellings of **+kana**, (kana)**+kanji**, and (kana+kanji)**+lexicon**, respectively. See Section 3 for details on what each of these augmentations means.

- **Wrong (Depending on the context)**: Spellings are inappropriate and considered as errors in the context of a given phrase.

Consolidated results show that over 95.4% of spelling variants are valid, and 16% are great or better than the original transcripts.

6 Conclusions and Future Work

In this paper we have proposed a lattice-based lenient evaluation method applied to computing character error rate in Japanese ASR. The method combines lexical resources, a Japanese text-processing system, and a neural MT system to reconstruct kanji from kana spellings in context. We evaluated on three different commercial Japanese ASR domains, and demonstrated a 2.4%–3.1% absolute reduction of CER—translating into an over 25% relative error reduction for the Voice Search domain.

Obviously these reductions in CER are not due to any improvement in the ASR method itself, but rather reflect a more defensible measure than naive comparison to a single reference transcription. This in turn points to the importance of taking spelling variation into account when evaluating systems on languages where such variation is simply a fact of life.

As noted in Section 3, we plan in future work to address another issue, namely style and register. While it is true that one often sees spelling variation for words even within the same text, it is also the case that style and register are important factors in deciding which spellings are felicitous in any given context. Thus while the word *kawaii* 'cute', has a kanji spelling 可愛い, that spelling would not usually be found in social media where the hiragana かわいい or katakana カワイイ variants would be more expected, especially if the goal is to communicate a more "friendly" message. We are currently experimenting with using style/register language models that are trained on different genres of text ranging from (informal) social media texts scraped from the Web to (formal) official Japanese government documents. In the context of the system described in this paper, the language models will be used to rank alternative spellings. Thus, a hypothesized spelling for a sentence may be a technically valid variant for a given reference transcription, but may also not be the most consistent in terms of style, and thus should be evaluated somewhat worse than a transcription that is more consistent. This would involve not only considering the edit distance measure—first dimension of the lexicographic semiring described in Section 3, but also the language-model cost in the second dimension.

We are also investigating using the spelling-variant-augmented reference lattices during training of the ASR system rather than just evaluation. Currently the ASR systems are trained with a single ground truth, which means that the ASR systems themselves are not sensitive to spelling variation. To this end, we are developing lattice-based loss functions that can be used during ASR training.

In addition to the above, we will continue to improve the system in various ways. We plan to include more lexical resources, such as publicly available resources like JMDict (see footnote 2), as well as improve the NMT-based kanji restoration model, with a goal to reducing human-judged unacceptable substitutions below the current 4.6%. An open question is whether large language models such as GPT-4 or Bard can be induced to provide judgments on whether two Japanese spellings are inter-

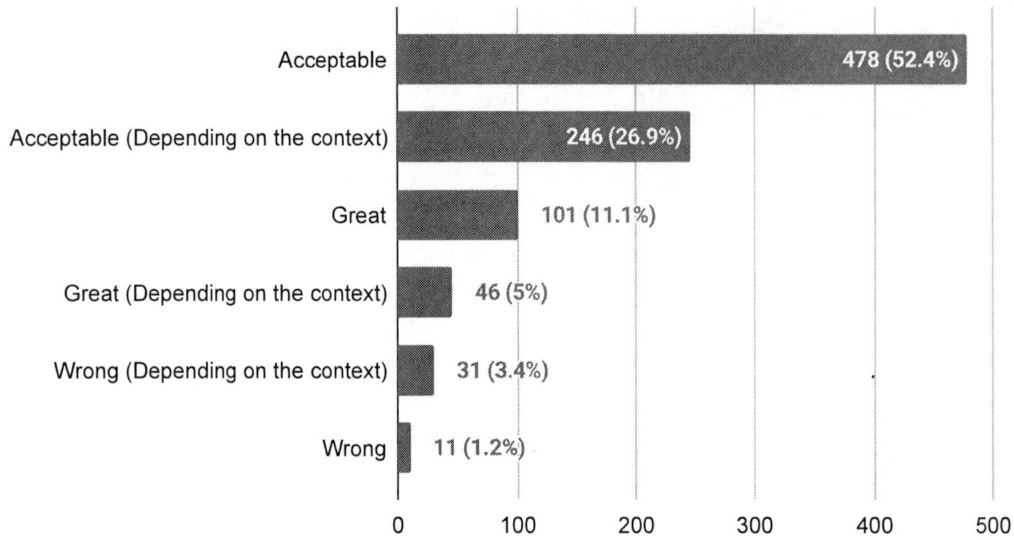

Figure 2: Manual evaluation results on spelling variants quality of 913 phrase pairs.

substitable in a given context, and we also plan to investigate this in future work.

Finally, while Japanese provides a particularly rich example of spelling variation compared to other modern writing systems, as discussed in Section 4, there are many languages that are primarily oral, and for which there no accepted written standard. In such languages, one can expect a fair amount of variation in spelling when people attempt to write them, and the methods proposed in this paper could be applicable to such cases.

Limitations

Our work focuses on the problem of spelling variation in Japanese. The Japanese writing system is the most complex of any modern writing system (to find anything of comparable complexity, one would have to go back to cuneiform Akkadian or Hittite) and presents a unique range of issues that impact speech and language technology, one of which is the spelling variation discussed in this paper.

Nonetheless, as also noted in Section 6, we believe that the approach here should be applicable, perhaps with less dramatic results, to other cases where spelling variation occurs. This may be particularly an issue in languages that do not have a standardized writing system—e.g. Colloquial Arabic dialects—and where a large amount of spelling variation is often observed. However we have not evaluated the approach on this sort of data.

Our evaluation system is not open-sourced due to the propriety lexical resources, text normalizer and kana/kanji translators. The text normalizer could probably be replaced with, e.g., the open-source Mecab (Kudo, 2006) system, though we expect that performance would be degraded. Similarly our lexical resources could potentially be replaced with publicly available Japanese dictionaries such as JMDict (Breen, 2004), but again performance would probably suffer. Note in particular that unlike CJKI's Japanese Orthographic Dictionary, JMDict entries have not been carefully curated to indicate which spellings are interchangeable, and which are, rather, words with the same reading but distinct meanings. An informal manual evaluation we performed on potential spelling variant pairs that were extracted from JMDict entries nominally representing the same word sense, revealed that about 92% were valid variant spellings, but that the rest were either wrong, or at least unclear.

Ethics Statement

The work reported in this paper relates to the impact of Japanese spelling inconsistency on the development and evaluation of Automatic Speech Recognition systems. The data used for our experiments is from a variety of sources and includes data from users, but it contains no Personal Identifiable Information. While it is possible that some of the data (especially data from YouTube) includes content that may have ethical concerns (e.g. hate speech, hurtful terminology, intentional or unintentional bias), the algorithms presented here are neutral with respect to these issues.

As discussed in Section 5.4, a subset of data was manually verified by human raters, all of whom were paid linguistic consultants hired through a third-party vendor.

Acknowledgments

We thank our colleagues, in particular Yuma Koizumi, Llion Jones and Michiel Bacchiani for discussion and feedback. We also thank three reviewers for useful comments.

References

Ahmed Ali, Salam Khalifa, and Nizar Habash. 2019. Towards variability resistant dialectal speech evaluation. In *Interspeech*, pages 336–340, Graz. ISCA.

Ahmed M. Ali, Preslav Nakov, Peter Bell, and Steve Renals. 2017. WERd: Using social text spelling variants for evaluating dialectal speech recognition. *CoRR*, abs/1709.07484.

Houda Bouamor, Hanan Alshikhabobakr, Behrang Mohit, and Kemal Oflazer. 2014. A human judgment corpus and a metric for Arabic MT evaluation. In *Proceedings of the 2014 Conference on Empirical Methods in Natural Language Processing (EMNLP)*, pages 207–213, Doha, Qatar.

Jim Breen. 2004. JMdict: a Japanese-multilingual dictionary. In *Proceedings of the Workshop on Multilingual Linguistic Resources*, pages 65–72, Geneva, Switzerland. COLING.

Kyle Gorman and Richard Sproat. 2021. *Finite-State Text Processing.* Number 50 in Synthesis Lectures on Human Language Processing. Springer, Heidelberg.

Roman Grundkiewicz and Kenneth Heafield. 2018. Neural machine translation techniques for named entity transliteration. In *Proceedings of the Seventh Named Entities Workshop*, pages 89–94, Melbourne, Australia. Association for Computational Linguistics.

Anmol Gulati, James Qin, Chung-Cheng Chiu, Niki Parmar, Yu Zhang, Jiahui Yu, Wei Han, Shibo Wang, Zhengdong Zhang, Yonghui Wu, and Ruoming Pang. 2020. Conformer: Convolution-augmented Transformer for Speech Recognition. In *Interspeech*, pages 5036–5040.

Terry Joyce and Hisashi Masuda. 2019. On the notions of graphematic representation and orthography from the perspective of the Japanese writing system. *Written Language and Literacy*, 22(2):248–280. Special issue: Writing Systems: Past, present (...and future?).

Taku Kudo. 2006. MeCab: Yet another part-of-speech and morphological analyzer.

Soumyadeep Kundu, Sayantan Paul, and Santanu Pal. 2018. A deep learning based approach to transliteration. In *Proceedings of the Seventh Named Entities Workshop*, pages 79–83, Melbourne, Australia. Association for Computational Linguistics.

Vladimir I. Levenshtein. 1966. Binary codes capable of correcting deletions, insertions, and reversals. *Soviet Physics Doklady*, 10(8):707–710.

Christopher Lowy. 2021. *At the Intersection of Script and Literature: Writing as Aesthetic in Modern and Contemporary Japanese-language Literature.* Ph.D. thesis, University of Washington.

Dimitrios Meletis and Christa Dürscheid. 2022. *Writing Systems and Their Use: An Overview of Grapholinguistics.* De Gruyter Mouton, Berlin and Boston.

Takeshi Mishima, Aiko Hagiwara, Hitoshi Ito, Tomoyasu Komori, Daisuke Horikawa, Naoya Kawase, and Shoei Sato. 2020. Development of transcription system using speech recognition for program production. *The Journal of The Institute of Image Information and Television Engineers*, 75(1):118–124. In Japanese.

Arun Narayanan, Rohit Prabhavalkar, Chung-Cheng Chiu, David Rybach, Tara N. Sainath, and Trevor Strohman. 2019. Recognizing long-form speech using streaming end-to-end models. In *2019 IEEE Automatic Speech Recognition and Understanding Workshop (ASRU)*, pages 920–927.

Iuliia Nigmatulina, Tannon Kew, and Tanja Samardzic. 2020. ASR for non-standardised languages with dialectal variation: the case of Swiss German. In *Proceedings of the 7th Workshop on NLP for Similar Languages, Varieties and Dialects*, pages 15–24, Barcelona, Spain (Online). International Committee on Computational Linguistics (ICCL).

Michael Riley, Cyril Allauzen, and Martin Jansche. 2009. OpenFst: An open-source, weighted finite-state transducer library and its applications to speech and language. In *Proceedings of Human Language Technologies: The 2009 Annual Conference of the North American Chapter of the Association for Computational Linguistics, Companion Volume: Tutorial Abstracts*, pages 9–10, Boulder, Colorado. Association for Computational Linguistics.

Brian Roark and Richard Sproat. 2014. Hippocratic abbreviation expansion. In *Proceedings of the 52nd Annual Meeting of the Association for Computational Linguistics (Volume 2: Short Papers)*, pages 364–369, Baltimore, Maryland. Association for Computational Linguistics.

Brian Roark, Lawrence Wolf-Sonkin, Christo Kirov, Sabrina J. Mielke, Cibu Johny, Isin Demirsahin, and Keith Hall. 2020. Processing South Asian languages written in the Latin script: the Dakshina dataset. In *Proceedings of the Twelfth Language Resources and Evaluation Conference*, pages 2413–2423, Marseille, France. European Language Resources Association.

Mike Schuster and Kaisuke Nakajima. 2012. Japanese and Korean voice search. In *2012 IEEE International Conference on Acoustics, Speech and Signal Processing (ICASSP)*, pages 5149–5152.

Richard Sproat, Mahsa Yarmohammadi, Izhak Shafran, and Brian Roark. 2014. Applications of lexicographic semirings to problems in speech and language processing. *Computational Linguistics*, 40(4):733761.

Yi Tay, Mostafa Dehghani, Dara Bahri, and Donald Metzler. 2020. Efficient transformers: A survey. *CoRR*, abs/2009.06732.

Juan Miguel Vilar. 2008. Efficient computation of confidence intervals for word error rates. In *2008 IEEE International Conference on Acoustics, Speech and Signal Processing*, pages 5101–5104.

Ye-Yi Wang, Alex Acero, and Ciprian Chelba. 2003. Is word error rate a good indicator for spoken language understanding accuracy. In *2003 IEEE Automatic Speech Recognition and Understanding Workshop (ASRU)*, pages 577–582, St Thomas, VI, USA.

Disambiguating Numeral Sequences to Decipher Ancient Accounting Corpora

Logan Born[1] loborn@sfu.ca

M. Willis Monroe[2] willis.monroe@ubc.ca

Kathryn Kelley[3] kathrynerin.kelley@unibo.it

Anoop Sarkar[1] anoop@cs.sfu.ca

[1]Simon Fraser University
School of Computing Science

[2]University of British Columbia
Department of Philosophy

[3]Università di Bologna
Dipartimento di Filologia Classica e Italianistica

Abstract

A *numeration system* encodes abstract numeric quantities as concrete strings of written characters. The numeration systems used by modern scripts tend to be precise and unambiguous, but this was not so for the ancient and partially-deciphered proto-Elamite (PE) script, where written numerals can have up to four distinct readings depending on the system that is used to read them. We consider the task of disambiguating between these readings in order to determine the values of the numeric quantities recorded in this corpus. We algorithmically extract a list of possible readings for each PE numeral notation, and contribute two disambiguation techniques based on structural properties of the original documents and classifiers learned with the bootstrapping algorithm. We also contribute a test set for evaluating disambiguation techniques, as well as a novel approach to cautious rule selection for bootstrapped classifiers. Our analysis confirms existing intuitions about this script and reveals previously-unknown correlations between tablet content and numeral magnitude. This work is crucial to understanding and deciphering PE, as the corpus is heavily accounting-focused and contains many more numeric tokens than tokens of text.

1 Introduction

Proto-Elamite (PE) is a partially-deciphered script unearthed at early 3rd millennium BCE sites across the Iranian plateau. This script was exclusively used to record spreadsheet-style administrative accounts, and well over half of the attested glyphs are known to be digits. Despite this abundance of numeric notations, no large-scale quantitative analysis of PE numerals has ever been undertaken, and most prior work has focused on the adjoining *text*. This is likely because the script employs multiple distinct number systems, which use partially-overlapping sets of digits and occasionally assign distinct values to identical-looking sign shapes (Figure 1). Many numerals can be read according to two or more of these systems, and represent different values depending on the system used.

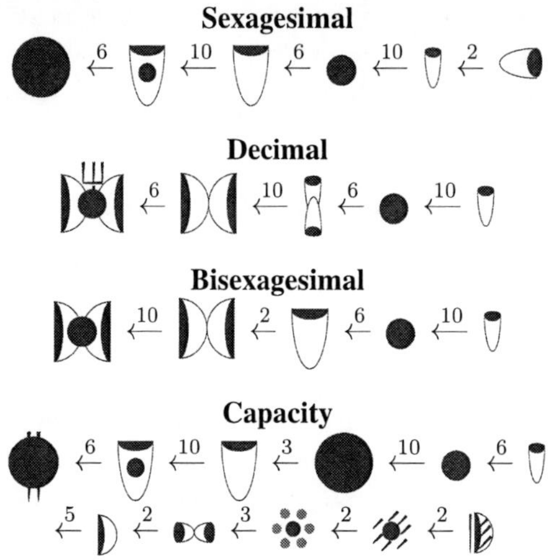

Figure 1: Relative values of digits in the main proto-Elamite number systems. $X \overset{n}{\leftarrow} Y$ means that one X has the same value as n Ys.

Some PE signs have been given tentative readings in prior work, and on the basis of these readings there appears to be a regular relationship between the kind of object recorded and the number system used to count it (in a manner not entirely dissimilar to the measure words found across East Asian languages). Knowing which system is in use for a given numeral therefore increases the possibility of understanding what category of object is recorded in the adjoining text, and thus opens new avenues for the ongoing decipherment of this script.

In this work, we consider the task of disambiguating which systems are used in ambiguous PE numeral notations in order that the values of these numerals may be determined. We describe a simple rule-based technique to extract lists of possible readings from PE numeral notations, which allows

Proceedings of the Workshop on Computation and Written Language (CAWL 2023), pages 71–81
July 14, 2023 ©2023 Association for Computational Linguistics

us to give the first large-scale survey of PE numerals since Friberg 1978 (whose manual analysis occurred at a time when fewer texts were known). We then propose two disambiguation techniques, one based on the subset-sum problem and another which uses a bootstrap classifier (Yarowsky, 1995). We describe the construction of a test set for evaluating PE numeral disambiguation models, and propose a novel approach to cautious rule selection which significantly improves the performance of a bootstrap classifier on our data. Our analysis shows how these techniques lead to a deeper understanding of this ancient and undeciphered writing system.

2 Data & Background

We base our analysis off the transliterated PE corpus hosted by the CDLI.[1] Each text in this corpus contains an optional header, followed by a series of "entries" written one per line of the transliterated file. Each entry contains a (possibly empty) span of text, a comma delimiter, and a (possibly empty) numeral notation. The transliterations use a work-in-progress signlist that reflects experts' current understanding of the texts, but which may not exactly match the true character inventory of the underlying script. In this signlist, characters that are believed to represent text are transliterated with labels beginning in "M" (e.g. M001, after Meriggi who pioneered the study of this script), and those representing digits are labeled with "N" (e.g. N01). The notation `n(N00)` means that the digit `N00` is written down n times. Figure 2 shows an example of a tablet alongside its transliteration.

Most proto-Elamite numerals are written using one of four[2] number systems, which are called *decimal* (D), *sexagesimal* (S), *bisexagesimal* (B), and *capacity* (C). In spite of their names, all of these systems use mixed radices. Figure 1 shows the relative values of the digits in each of these systems, as derived through prior manual analyses (Friberg, 1978; Damerow and Englund, 1989; Dahl, 2019). Unlike Hindu-Arabic notation, where the value of a digit depends on its position, the values

Text	Numeral
`M056~f`	`1(N34) 5(N14) 1(N01) 1(N8B)` $= 111.5 \times$ `N01`^{S}
`M341 M288`	`7(N14) 2(N01) 3(N39B)` $= 44.6 \times$ `N01`^{C}

Figure 2: Proto-Elamite tablet MDP 26, 177 (Scheil 1935; P008805) alongside its transliteration and converted readings for both numerals. The tablet is read right-to-left: M056~f is the sign in the top-right corner. Observe that 111.5/44.6 equals the 2.5:1 ratio noted in Section 4.1.2.

of proto-Elamite digits are fixed, and larger values are denoted by repeating a digit multiple times.

Note that some digits can be used with distinct values in multiple systems (e.g. `N14` equals $10\times$`N01` in S, but only $6\times$`N01` in C): this means that it can sometimes be impossible to determine the absolute value of a numeral unless context makes clear which system it employs.

Since `N01` occurs as part of every number system, we use this sign as a standard unit and report values as multiples of `N01` whenever we convert to Hindu-Arabic notation. The S, D, and B systems are understood to represent unitless cardinal numbers, while C records unit*ful* measures of volume. When it is necessary to emphasize that these systems are not commensurable, we add a superscript to denote the system in use: e.g. $12 \times$ `N01`^{C} is a measure of volume which is not equivalent to $12 \times$ `N01`^{D}, despite having identical magnitude.

We summarize the above points with an illustrative example. The following notation (read from right-to-left)

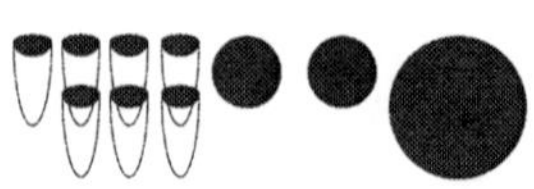

would be transliterated as `1(N45) 2(N14) 7(N01)`. This numeral must use either the S or C system, as

[1] Cuneiform Digital Library Initiative, `https://cdli.mpiwg-berlin.mpg.de`; corpus downloaded 3 Oct 2022.

[2] Additionally, there are marginal systems (labeled B#, C#, and C") which appear to be derived from one of the four main systems by the addition of hatch marks or boxes drawn around the digits. These systems are rare, and the extra hatching or boxing makes them trivial to identify, so we ignore them for the remainder of this work.

the large circle N45 only occurs in these systems (Figure 1). Using the readings from the S system, this notation encodes a value of

$$3627 \times \texttt{N01} = (1 \times 3600 + 2 \times 10 + 7 \times 1) \times \texttt{N01}$$

Using the C system, it instead encodes

$$79 \times \texttt{N01} \quad = (1 \times 60 \quad + 2 \times 6 \quad + 7 \times 1) \times \texttt{N01}$$

Of these, we know that the S reading must be the correct one, since 7(N01) should never occur in the C system (every 6 N01 would be bundled into an N14, so the actual notation for $79 \times \texttt{N01}^C$ would be 1(N45) 3(N14) 1(N01)).

It is not clear whether these notations would have been considered ambiguous at the time they were written. It is very plausible that the original scribes would have been able to infer the correct reading for a numeral based on contextual information which is not salient to the modern reader (for example, by knowing that certain items are consistently counted with a particular number system, a possibility discussed by Englund 2004, 2011). There is equally the possibility that these notations were ambiguous even to their authors, but that this ambiguity did not interfere with their intended use, for example if the PE texts were intended for short-term use when the scribes would still recall which system they intended at the time of writing.

3 Methodology

3.1 Automated Conversion

We extract all of the numeral notations from the transliterated corpus by using a regular expression to find every contiguous sequence of N-signs; we discard sequences which are damaged, which we identify as being immediately adjacent to a transliterated X or .... Algorithm 1 uses the relative values from Figure 1 to automatically extract a dictionary of possible readings for each of these numerals.

Of the 8011 intact numerals which we have extracted, there are 7954 for which this conversion returns at least one reading. Of these, only 1919 unambiguously belong to a particular number system: the remainder are ambiguous between two, three, or even all four systems (Table 1). The following sections outline two proposals for disambiguating the ambiguous cases. Section 4.1.1 discusses the 57 cases for which there is no valid reading in any system.

Algorithm 1 PE Numeral Readings

Input: $digits = [(n_1, sign_1), ..., (n_k, sign_k)]$
▷ A list of signs and num. times each one occurs.
Returns: A map from number systems to possible readings for this digit list.

for $sys \in \{S, D, B, C\}$ **do**
    $value_{sys} \leftarrow 0$
for $(n, sign) \in digits$ **do**
    for $sys \in \{S, D, B, C\}$ **do**
        if $sign \notin signs\_used\_by(sys)$ **then**
            $value_{sys} \leftarrow \bot$
            ▷ $\bot$ means there is no valid reading in this system.
            continue
        if $n > max\_count(sign, sys)$ **then**
            ▷ max_count returns the max num. of times this digit can occur before it would carry over to a higher value digit.
            $value_{sys} \leftarrow \bot$
        $v \leftarrow$ value of $sign$ in sys
        $value_{sys} \leftarrow value_{sys} + n \times v$
        ▷ $\bot$ plus anything equals $\bot$.
return $\{sys \mapsto value_{sys} \forall sys \in \{S, D, B, C\}\}$

3.2 Subset-Sum Analysis

Our first approach to disambiguation relies on the fact that some PE documents end in a summary line, which records the total sum of the preceding entries. Although the entries themselves may be ambiguous, the sums naturally record larger amounts and are therefore more likely to use high-magnitude digits that unambiguously belong to a particular system. When a tablet records values from multiple number systems, they are summarized separately; thus if we can identify unambiguous summaries, we can infer that all of the entries which they sum must belong to the same system.

To achieve this, we filter the corpus to find texts with one or two entries on the reverse, as current understandings of the corpus suggest that these are likely to be summaries.[3] For each of these texts, we solve an instance of the subset-sum problem to identify whether any combination of readings from the obverse adds up to the same value as any reading of the reverse.

[3]Some transliterations include an annotation which explicitly labels a particular entry as a summary. However, not all summaries are labeled in this way, so we rely on automatic detection of summaries to expand the number of texts available for this analysis.

Possible Readings	Number of Numerals
none	57
B	19
C	1727
D	66
S	107
B or D	21
B or S	5
C or S	143
B, C, or S	185
B, D, or S	292
B, C, D, or S	5389

Table 1: Distribution of readings produced by our automated conversion. A majority of numerals in the corpus can be read using *any one* of the four number systems.

Feature	Description of Value(s)
TABLET	The tablet where this numeral occurs.
FIRST_SIGN	The first sign of the tablet where this numeral occurs (where we may expect to find a header).
SAME_ENTRY	Bag of signs which occur in the entry preceding this numeral.
SAME_TABLET	Bag of signs which occur anywhere on the same tablet as this numeral.
OBJECT	The sign immediately preceding this numeral (where we may expect to find a counted object).
IMPLICIT_OBJECT	The last sign in the first entry of the text where this numeral occurs (where we may expect to find an implicit object).

Table 2: Each numeral is associated with a set of features from this list, which we use to train our bootstrap classifiers.

If an accurate summation is found, and any of the component terms has an unambiguous number system, we use this as evidence to disambiguate the entire text to that system. We manually evaluate this approach by confirming with domain experts whether the resulting disambiguations are correct.

3.3 Bootstrapping

Some of the PE numeral notations are inherently unambiguous, either because they use a digit which only occurs in a single system, or because they contain more instances of a digit than would be allowed by some systems. We propose to use these cases as seed rules to train a bootstrap classifier (Yarowsky, 1995) for disambiguation.

We choose bootstrapping because it requires only a small number of seed labels, and as seen in Table 1 some systems have few unambiguous attestations. Moreover, bootstrapping yields interpretable results which can be understood by examining the label distribution associated with each input feature. This helps to legitimize model outputs to domain experts, and to situate model predictions relative to prior manual analyses.

Table 2 lists the features used by our classifier. A numeral's initial label distribution is uniform over every system for which our automated conversion returns a valid reading, and zero elsewhere. We use the DL-2-ML algorithm (Haffari and Sarkar, 2007; Abney, 2002), which models $\pi_x(j)$ (the likelihood that sample x belongs to class j) as

$$\pi_x(j) \propto \prod_{f \in F_x} \theta_{fj}$$

where F_x is the set of features associated with sample x, and θ_{fj} is a learnable parameter which measures the association between feature f and class j. We apply the "cautious" approach from Collins and Singer 1999, which limits the number of rules that can be added to the decision list at each iteration of training. Specifically, candidate rules are sorted according to the number of labeled examples that support them, and only the n with the largest support are added to the decision list.[4] n starts at 5 and increases by 5 each iteration.

The cautious algorithm was motivated by the observation that "the highest frequency rules [are] much 'safer' [than low-frequency rules], as they tend to be very accurate" (Collins and Singer, 1999). This observation does not seem to hold for our data, where many of the most frequent features barely meet the confidence threshold to be added to the decision list and, impressionistically, do not appear to be any more accurate than those with lower frequency. We therefore propose a novel approach to cautious rule selection whereby θ_f is

[4]Whitney and Sarkar 2012 note that many details are omitted from the description of the cautious algorithm in Collins and Singer 1999. We follow Whitney and Sarkar in assuming that confidence thresholding is performed using unsmoothed label counts. However, we differ from their approach by selecting the top n rules overall (not the top n for each label) as this yields stronger results on our data.

only updated if the update increases $\max_j \theta_{fj}$, i.e. if it increases the confidence of the label distribution associated with feature f. In this setting we visit the features in a random order each iteration, to prevent a degenerate outcome whereby endless incremental updates are made only to the first rules visited.

System	Number of Test Items
B	3
C	18
D	14
S	13

Table 3: Distribution of target classes in our numeral disambiguation test set. This set contains every instance of the B class which we were able to manually disambiguate with the help of domain experts; the other classes are kept small to maintain as balanced a distribution as possible.

Prior to training, we upsample seeds with rare labels to obtain an equal number for each class. We evaluate our classifiers on a test set which we construct by manually disambiguating some of the ambiguous notations in the corpus. We endeavoured to keep this set as balanced as possible, but some systems (particularly B) can only be confidently identified in a few texts. This means the test set cannot contain every numeral for which we know the target label, as doing so would yield too great an imbalance between classes. Appendix A describes what evidence was used to disambiguate each numeral in the set, and Table 3 summarizes the overall class distribution. All of the labels in the test set have been verified by domain experts.

4 Results

4.1 Automated Conversion

4.1.1 Invalid Notations

There are 57 intact numerals for which our automated conversion does not return a valid reading according to any number system. The vast majority of these violate the bundling principles established in prior work and shown in Figure 1. For example, the notation `11(N01)` in P008043 should not be attested in any system, as every system carries over to a higher digit after at most ten `N01`s.

Some of these illegal notations may reflect errors on the part of the original scribes. For example, in P008844, the sum of the D values on the obverse equals `9(N23) 3(N14) 3(N01)`, or 573; the scribe has actually written `9(N23) 7(N14) 3(N01)`, which violates the usual principle that 6 `N14`s carry over to one `N23`. This suggests that the scribe may have conceived of the D system as a truly decimal notation (in which case the least significant digits would be written as 7 tens and 3 ones, exactly as we find on the tablet), forgetting that `N23` uses a different radix. Several of the other aberrant notations lend credence to this view, such as P008788 which apparently records 88 M367s (likely goats, usually counted with D) as `8(N14) 8(N01)`. These cases suggest a lack of standardisation across scribes or across documents, which is consistent with the longstanding view that the writing system never achieved a significant degree of standardisation (Dahl, 2019).

Systems Used	Number of Tablets
C and S	12
C and D	15
C and B	4
S and D	1

Table 4: Number of tablets which unambiguously use more than one number system.

4.1.2 Mixed Systems

Our automated conversion reveals numerous accounts (Table 4) which unambiguously use two different number systems (no tablets unambiguously use more than two systems). In all but one of these, the C system occurs alongside one of the "integer" systems S, D, or B. This suggests a general pattern of accounts which record capacities of goods received/disbursed from/to individual people, animals, households, or other entities also counted in whole numbers on the tablet. The text P009383 is unique in that it unambiguously uses two of the "integer" systems S and D. On close inspection, however, the original tablet is heavily abraded where the putative S notation occurs, and the sign which forces this notation to be read as S (`N08`) is almost entirely unreadable. Given the otherwise total absence of texts which mix integer systems, we posit that this text may contain a transliteration error and that the broken sign is not in fact an `N08`.

Several texts which mix the S and C systems also have other features in common. P008796, P008798, and P008805 are exemplary of this group, which are all two-entry texts where the first entry is an S-denominated amount of M056∼f (possibly a plow), and the second is a C-denominated amount of M288. In all of these texts, there are exactly $2.5 \times$ `N01`^{S} per `N01`^{C}: this ratio was previously identified and discussed by Damerow and Englund (1989); Englund (2004). P008791 appears to belong to this same class of texts, and given that the first entry records $128 \times$ `N01`^{S} M056∼f we should expect $51.2 \times$ `N01`^{C} in the final entry (or `8(N14) 3(N01) 1(N39B)`). We actually find $52 \times$ `N01`^{C}, or `8(N14) 4(N01)`. Close inspection of the tablet, however, reveals that there has been a transliteration error, and that the final sign, although mostly broken, is recognizably an `N39B`. The text yields the expected ratio when this mistake is corrected. Errors such as these are much easier to identify when dealing in converted Arabic numerals, which modern readers can understand and manipulate more quickly and intuitively than the original PE notations.

Out of 244 signs which precede at least two unambiguous notations, only 11 occur next to notations from distinct systems. These 11 (M001, M056∼f, M059, M096, M124, M218, M305, M327, M371, M387, M388) include signs which have been speculated (Dahl, 2019) to represent human laborers or overseers (M388, M124), signs with possible syllabic values (M001, M096, M218, M387, M371), and headers or account owners (M059, M305, M327). In other words, these are signs which we expect to qualify or describe an object being counted, and not to be counted themselves. It therefore appears that, while counted objects are consistently recorded using one particular number system, these qualifying signs can potentially be used to qualify objects from several different systems. This suggests a novel approach to determine the function of signs with unknown meanings, by looking at the variety of number systems they occur beside.

4.2 Subset-Sum Analysis

Our subset-sum analysis identifies 24 texts which, upon manual inspection, can be fully or partially disambiguated based on their summary line(s). We highlight one which is of particular interest. In P008014, all entries must use the C system in order to equal the same value as the unambiguous C summary on the reverse. The text of the summary contains only the "grain container" sign M288, implying that the entire tablet should record amounts of M288. However, on the obverse of the tablet, M288 only occurs as the final sign of the very first entry. This suggests that the scribe has only explicitly marked the counted object in the first entry, and left it implicit in the following entries (this is in keeping with known practices from other ancient Mesopotamian accounting corpora; Nissen et al. 1993, pp. 37–38, Englund 2001). This means that there exist long-distance dependencies between the entries in some texts, which need to be accounted for if these texts are to be fully understood.

4.3 Bootstrapping

Figure 3 and Table 5 compare results from our two approaches to bootstrapping. The baseline, vanilla bootstrapping algorithm achieves a mediocre 0.60 F1. Recall of the B and S classes is perfect, but only half of the instances of the C class are correctly labeled. This classifier does not seem to have uncovered any clear signals to identify the D system: 3 instances of this class remain unlabeled (none of their associated features ever attained the required confidence to be added to the decision list), and those which are labeled are distributed uniformly across all of the possible classes.

Model	4-way			2-way		
	prec.	rec.	F1	prec.	rec.	F1
Baseline	0.64	0.56	0.60	0.74	0.65	0.69
Ours	**0.88**	**0.88**	**0.88**	**0.90**	**0.90**	**0.90**

Table 5: Numeral disambiguation results. In the 4-way setting, we seek to identify exactly which number system is in use for each numeral. In the 2-way setting, we only seek to distinguish C notations from everything else.

By contrast, our proposed approach to cautious rule selection yields 0.88 F1, with significantly better recall of both the C and D classes than the baseline. This suggests that frequency-based caution may be ill-suited for bootstrapping on some datasets, and that, in settings where bootstrap classifiers remain viable, it may be worthwhile to explore alternative approaches to cautious rule selection.

Note from Figure 1 that ambiguities between the S, D, and B systems primarily come from the digits `N01` and `N14`, which have the same relative values across all three systems. S and B further overlap in the sign `N34`, which also maintains the

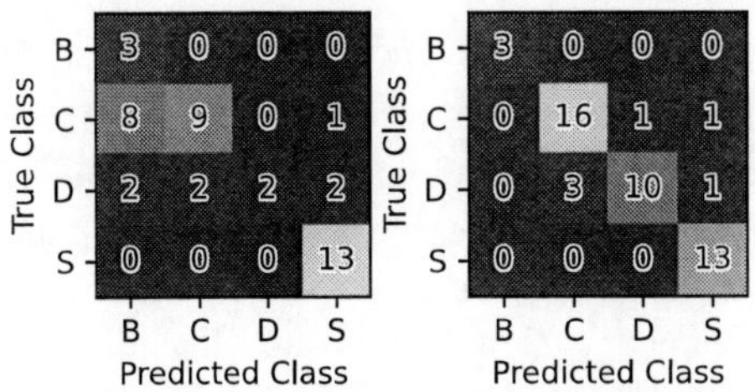

Figure 3: Confusion matrices from classifiers trained using the vanilla bootstrap algorithm (left) and our proposed variant (right).

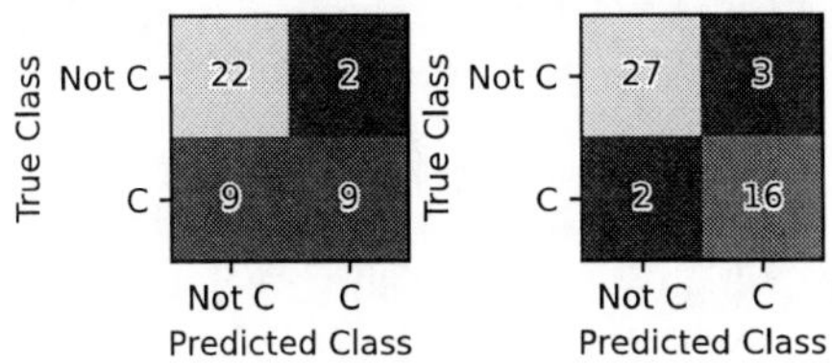

Figure 4: 2-way disambiguation results. Confusion matrices from vanilla bootstrapping (left) and our proposed variant (right).

same value across both systems. Thus many numerals which are technically ambiguous between these *systems* nonetheless have unambiguous *values*.[5] In settings where the absolute value of a numeral is all that matters, it is therefore usually sufficient to distinguish these systems from C without distinguishing them from one another. In this two-way setting, our model achieves 0.90 F1, versus 0.69 F1 from the vanilla baseline (Figure 4).

We emphasize that our test set only contains numerals which domain experts were able to disambiguate based on manual inspection. Easy cases may therefore be over-represented, and we expect our results to be an upper bound on the classifier's accuracy across the whole corpus. Despite this, the results are strong enough to suggest that a majority of the ambiguous numerals in the corpus can be disambiguated with some certainty.

5 Analysis

In this section, we investigate how the features from our bootstrap classifier relate to known or hypothesized properties of the script.

A number of signs have been suggested as indicating types of livestock (sheep, goats, etc.); these include M346, M362, M367, and M417 (Dahl, 2005). In our analysis, all of these signs also predict the decimal system, which suggests that they were typically used to count flock sizes.

M376 has been suggested as either a "high-status human" (Dahl, 2005, p. 95) or livestock (Kelley, 2018, p. 165); it is strongly predicative of the sexigesimal system in our analysis. Other objects associated with this system include M056~f (a plow), M219, M371 and M296 (very speculatively, syllables used to write personal names), M059, M145, and M365 ("owners", possibly persons or institutions to whom these accounts belonged), and M269~c (a vessel?). This may cast some doubt on the livestock reading for M376, in favor of the high-status human reading which is a more natural fit among the owner signs and possible personal names in this collection.

We note one text, P008212, which may exhibit a consistent ratio related to M376. P008212 alternates between entries ending in M288 and entries ending in M376 or M367~i. The magnitude of the numeral in an M288 entry is always exactly 4 times as large as the magnitude of an adjacent M376 entry, or 2 times as large as an adjacent M367~i entry. This pattern is very unlikely to be due to chance, as it holds across 44 total entries. Whatever the meaning of M376, on the basis of this text we can assert that it is associated with amounts of M288 that are exactly twice as large as those associated with M367~i. To our knowledge this ratio has not yet been noted in previous publications.

After disambiguating every numeral in the corpus to the most likely system according to our bootstrap classifier, we measure the average magnitude of counts associated with each feature. We observe that certain features accompany significantly higher or lower counts than others. Entries ending in M288 have the largest capacity magnitudes on average, while those ending in M263 are among the smallest. Both signs have been speculated to represent containers; from our results one might further speculate that M263 is a container of smaller dimension, or one that was never dealt with in bulk quantities. Entries ending in M297~b also accompany unusually large capacity measures, though the visually-similar M297 does not stand out as unusually large or small. This may point towards these signs having distinct meanings or uses despite sharing a visual resemblance.

The numerical systems of proto-Elamite have been proposed to have functional uses relating to

[5] Here we assume that the *absolute* value of `N01` is the same across all three systems, and not just its value relative to the other digits. Current understandings suggest that this is the case, but the undeciphered nature of the script means this is technically not certain.

cultural practices in 3rd millennium south-western Iran. For instance, the capacity system (C) is suggested to be used for counting rations disbursed to households or workers (Kelley, 2018, pgs. 153-155). Among the recipients of these rations are M388 and M124, parallel "worker categories" which may represent the heads of work teams. We find that entries beginning in M388 accompany significantly larger capacity measures on average than those in M124, which may point towards M388 individuals heading teams of larger sizes or comprising workers of higher status.

6 Related Work

Naik et al. (2019) demonstrate that word embedding models fail to capture magnitude and numeration (i.e. the equivalence between *3* and *three*), and suggest the need for dedicated representations of numerals in NLP models. Sundararaman et al. (2020) follow up with DICE embeddings designed to explicitly capture both magnitude and numeration, and demonstrate improved results on numeracy tests introduced by Wallace et al. (2019). Spithourakis and Riedel (2018) describe a GMM-based approach to numeral embedding for language models, which also incorporates explicit representations of magnitude. These models assume that the magnitudes in question are known and must simply be encoded; they do not consider the task of *determining* magnitude from ambiguous notations.

While introducing a benchmark to test LM numeracy, Shi et al. (2022) note that numeral representations can vary across scripts; however, they assume a setting where the conversion to Hindu-Arabic notation is straightforward, and do not discuss ambiguities which may result from this conversion.

One approach to handling numeric values in word problems is to replace them with variables $v_1, v_2, ...$, generate the solution as an equation in terms of these variables, and substitute the original values back to obtain a concrete solution. Wu et al. (2021) note that the choice of equation can sometimes depend on whether the original quantities were absolute values or percentages, and therefore this replacement can introduce ambiguities which make some problems unsolvable. They introduce a magnitude-aware encoding for digit sequences, and describe a numerical properties prediction mechanism which estimates whether a numeral is an integer, fraction, percentage, etc. This mirrors our attempt to predict an underlying number system.

Berg-Kirkpatrick and Spokoyny (2020) investigate the task of predicting a numeric value given surrounding text as context. They find that models which implicitly separate a value's mantissa from its exponent achieve better results than those which predict the value directly, and that context from large pretrained text encoders is useful even when the pretraining task was not focused on promoting numeracy. As we are dealing with an undeciphered corpus, our models are unfortunately unable to rely on pretrained embeddings for context.

Friberg (1978) is responsible for early analyses of proto-Elamite and proto-cuneiform (a related script which is also partially deciphered) which helped to establish the relative values of the digits in these corpora. Nissen et al. (1994) perform what is possibly the earliest computer-assisted analysis of bookkeeping practices in proto-cuneiform, while Damerow and Englund (1989) and Englund (2011) discuss accounting practices in proto-cuneiform and proto-Elamite and the relationships between the two.

7 Conclusion

We have automated the process of extracting candidate readings for ancient proto-Elamite numeral notations, and have described ambiguities in the original script which make this extraction challenging. We present two approaches for disambiguating these ambiguous notations: one exploits a common structural property of proto-Elamite accounts to look for unambiguous summations, and the other exploits the few unambiguous notations to train a bootstrap classifier. We create a test set for the disambiguation task by manually disambiguating a subset of the corpus, and we describe a novel variant of cautious rule selection which significantly improves bootstrapping performance on this test set. As a result of this work, we are able to assign confident values to a majority of the numeral notations in proto-Elamite, to identify and correct a number of transliteration errors in the proto-Elamite corpus, and to shed new light on existing hypotheses about the meanings of some signs in this partially-deciphered script. As the proto-Elamite script was fundamentally an accounting technology, we believe that this work represents a crucial step towards deepening our understanding of this ancient corpus.

Limitations

As PE remains largely undeciphered, our results can only be evaluated on the small subset of numerals which we have manually disambiguated. As noted in the paper, these may be easier than the rest of the corpus, meaning our evaluation can only give an upper bound on model performance.

We use a feature-based classifier to give interpretable results which can more easily be shared and discussed with non-technical experts in Assyriology. A limitation of this approach is that model performance depends on the choice of input features, and features which are effective can sometimes seem arbitrary. We attempt to justify the features used by our model by explaining in Table 2 which aspects of the script each is intended to capture.

Lastly, PE numerals are just one aspect of a complex and multifarious decipherment problem. Our results alone cannot paint a complete picture of this script, and must be interpreted in relation to results from outside of computer science.

References

Steven P. Abney. 2002. Bootstrapping. In *Proceedings of the 40th Annual Meeting of the Association for Computational Linguistics, July 6-12, 2002, Philadelphia, PA, USA*, pages 360–367. ACL.

Taylor Berg-Kirkpatrick and Daniel Spokoyny. 2020. An empirical investigation of contextualized number prediction. In *Proceedings of the 2020 Conference on Empirical Methods in Natural Language Processing (EMNLP)*, pages 4754–4764, Online. Association for Computational Linguistics.

Michael Collins and Yoram Singer. 1999. Unsupervised models for named entity classification. In *1999 Joint SIGDAT Conference on Empirical Methods in Natural Language Processing and Very Large Corpora*.

Jacob L. Dahl. 2005. Animal husbandry in Susa during the proto-Elamite period. *Studi Micenei ed Egeo-Anatolici*, 47:81–134.

Jacob L. Dahl. 2019. *Tablettes et fragments Proto-élamites / Proto-Elamite Tablets and Fragments*. Départment des Antiquités Orientales.

Peter Damerow and Robert K. Englund. 1989. *The proto-Elamite texts from Tepe Yahya*, volume 39 of *American School of Prehistoric Research: Bulletin*. Peabody Museum, Cambridge, Massachusetts.

Robert K. Englund. 2001. Grain accounting practices in archaic Mesopotamia. In J. Høyrup and Peter Damerow, editors, *Changing Views on Ancient Near Eastern Mathematics*, pages 1–35.

Robert K. Englund. 2004. The state of decipherment of proto-Elamite. *The First Writing: Script Invention as History and Process*, pages 100–149.

Robert K. Englund. 2011. Accounting in proto-cuneiform. In K. Radner and E. Robson, editors, *The Oxford Handbook of Cuneiform Culture*, pages 32–50.

Jöran Friberg. 1978. *The Third Millennium Roots of Babylonian Mathematics I-II*. Göteborg Dept. of Mathematics, Chalmers University of Technology, Göteborg, Sweden.

Gholamreza Haffari and Anoop Sarkar. 2007. Analysis of semi-supervised learning with the Yarowsky algorithm. In *Uncertainty in Artificial Intelligence (UAI 2007)*, pages 159 – 166. AUAI Press. Conference in Uncertainty in Artificial Intelligence 2007, UAI 2007 ; Conference date: 19-07-2007 Through 22-07-2007.

Kathryn Kelley. 2018. *Gender, Age, and Labour Organization in the Earliest Texts from Mesopotamia and Iran (c. 3300–2900 BC)*. Doctoral dissertation, University of Oxford.

Piero Meriggi. 1971. *La scrittura proto-elamica. Parte Ia: La scrittura e il contenuto dei testi*. Accademia Nazionale dei Lincei, Rome.

Aakanksha Naik, Abhilasha Ravichander, Carolyn Rose, and Eduard Hovy. 2019. Exploring numeracy in word embeddings. In *Proceedings of the 57th Annual Meeting of the Association for Computational Linguistics*, pages 3374–3380, Florence, Italy. Association for Computational Linguistics.

Hans J. Nissen, Peter Damerow, and Robert K. Englund. 1994. *Archaic Bookkeeping: Writing and Techniques of Economic Administration in the Ancient Near East*. University of Chicago Press.

H.J. Nissen, P. Damerow, and R.K. Englund. 1993. *Archaic Bookkeeping: Early Writing and Techniques of Economic Administration in the Ancient Near East*. University of Chicago Press.

Vincent Scheil. 1935. *Texte de comptabilité Proto-Élamite (Troisième Série)*, volume 26 of *Mémoires de la Mission Archaéologique de Perse*. Paris: Librairie Ernest Leroux.

Freda Shi, Mirac Suzgun, Markus Freitag, Xuezhi Wang, Suraj Srivats, Soroush Vosoughi, Hyung Won Chung, Yi Tay, Sebastian Ruder, Denny Zhou, Dipanjan Das, and Jason Wei. 2022. Language models are multilingual chain-of-thought reasoners. *CoRR*, abs/2210.03057.

Georgios Spithourakis and Sebastian Riedel. 2018. Numeracy for language models: Evaluating and improving their ability to predict numbers. In *Proceedings of the 56th Annual Meeting of the Association for Computational Linguistics (Volume 1: Long Papers)*, pages 2104–2115, Melbourne, Australia. Association for Computational Linguistics.

Dhanasekar Sundararaman, Shijing Si, Vivek Subramanian, Guoyin Wang, Devamanyu Hazarika, and Lawrence Carin. 2020. Methods for numeracy-preserving word embeddings. In *Proceedings of the 2020 Conference on Empirical Methods in Natural Language Processing (EMNLP)*, pages 4742–4753, Online. Association for Computational Linguistics.

Eric Wallace, Yizhong Wang, Sujian Li, Sameer Singh, and Matt Gardner. 2019. Do NLP models know numbers? probing numeracy in embeddings. In *Proceedings of the 2019 Conference on Empirical Methods in Natural Language Processing and the 9th International Joint Conference on Natural Language Processing (EMNLP-IJCNLP)*, pages 5307–5315, Hong Kong, China. Association for Computational Linguistics.

Max Whitney and Anoop Sarkar. 2012. Bootstrapping via graph propagation. In *Proceedings of the 50th Annual Meeting of the Association for Computational Linguistics (Volume 1: Long Papers)*, pages 620–628, Jeju Island, Korea. Association for Computational Linguistics.

Qinzhuo Wu, Qi Zhang, Zhongyu Wei, and Xuanjing Huang. 2021. Math word problem solving with explicit numerical values. In *Proceedings of the 59th Annual Meeting of the Association for Computational Linguistics and the 11th International Joint Conference on Natural Language Processing (Volume 1: Long Papers)*, pages 5859–5869, Online. Association for Computational Linguistics.

David Yarowsky. 1995. Unsupervised word sense disambiguation rivaling supervised methods. In *33rd Annual Meeting of the Association for Computational Linguistics*, pages 189–196, Cambridge, Massachusetts, USA. Association for Computational Linguistics.

A Constructing a Test Set for Numeral Disambiguation

This appendix describes a set of ambiguous numerals which we believe can be confidently disambiguated. Together, these numerals comprise the test set which we use to evaluate automated disambiguation via bootstrapping.

A.1 Capacity Measures

P008014 Our subset-sum analysis (Section 3.2) reveals that the sole entry on the reverse of this tablet (P008014:18:num) exactly equals the sum of the entries on the obverse, provided the whole tablet is read in the capacity system. This is consistent with the fact that four of the entries on the text are unambiguously capacity measures (P008014:11:num, P008014:14:num, P008014:15:num, and P008014:18:num; the other entries are SDBC-ambiguous). Moreover, the apparent summary line has an M288 object, and the first entry on the obverse ends in M288. This suggests that the entire text may record amounts of M288 (which is strongly associated with the capacity system), but that this object has been left implicit in all but the first and last entries.

On the basis of this evidence, we disambiguate the seven ambiguous entries in this text (P008014:6:num, P008014:7:num, P008014:8:num, P008014:9:num, P008014:10:num, P008014:12:num, P008014:15:num) to the capacity system.

A.2 Sexagesimal Measures

P008173 Our subset-sum analysis reveals that the first entry on the reverse (P008173:13:num), which is an unambiguous sexagesimal notation counting $7.5\times$ `N01`^{S} instances of M376, exactly equals the sum of the M376 entries on the obverse (P008173:5:num, P008173:7, P008173:8) if these entries are read in the sexagesimal system. On the basis of this evidence we disambiguate these entries to the sexagesimal system.

M056∼f/M288 Texts P008798 is exemplary of a set of two-entry texts of comparable physical dimensions (approx. 43mm x 31mm x 18mm) which count M056∼f in the first entry and M288 in the second. In many of these texts, the first entry is unambiguously sexagesimal and the second is unambiguously capacity; in these cases the amount of M056∼f is always exactly 2.5 times the amount of M288.

If P008797:6:num is read as a sexagesimal notation, then this text follows the same pattern as these other texts, and exhibits the expected 2.5:1 ratio of M056∼f to M288. On the basis of this evidence we disambiguate this entry to the sexagesimal system.

By the same argument, we also disambiguate P008791:6, P008799:6, P008800:6, P008801:6, P008802:6, P008804:4 and P008810:7 to the sexagesimal system.

A.3 Decimal Measures

P008179 This tablet is broken: a fracture on the obverse renders one digit partially unreadable. The broken digit has been restored as `2(N23)`, but we propose that the correct reading should in fact be `1(N23)`.

To see that this should be the case, notice that the first entry on the reverse (P008179:14:num) unambiguously equals $852\times$ `N01`^{D}; this is exactly the same sum obtained by reading the obverse entries in the decimal system, provided one uses our restoration instead of the current transliteration.

This reading is consistent with the fact that some entries (P008179:8:num, P008179:9:num, P008179:14:num) are already unambiguous decimal counts. Moreover, all but one of the entries on the obverse count the same object (M388), which further points towards their likely using the same number system. On the basis of this evidence, we disambiguate P008179:10 and P008179:11 to the decimal system.

The original restoration (`2(N23)`) presumably arose from the observation that the lacuna is wide enough to span two signs. The last visible sign before the lacuna is M388, which only occurs at the very end of entries elsewhere in this text, implying that all of the missing signs are likely digits. Our proposed reading requires that the `N23` in the lacuna occupy a slightly wider space than would be typical, or perhaps that some of the lacuna be occupied by an erasure. If the original restoration is correct, there must instead be an arithmetic error in the summary line (which in this case differs from the true sum by `1(N23)`).

P008012 Following the claim that sheep and goats are counted decimally in proto-Elamite (Englund, 2011), the entirety of this text should be expected to use the decimal system. Our subset-sum analysis confirms that the entry on the reverse (P008012:16) equals the sum of the entries on the obverse when read in this system, though in this case that would also be true for sexagesimal and bisexagesimal readings. Notably, the summation does *not* work out if the summary is read as a capacity measure. Thus, while we may confidently say that this text does not contain capacity measures, we can only tentatively assign it to the decimal system in particular.

P008243 Kelley (2018) observes that this is a decimally-counted roster. We follow this author in disambiguating all ambiguous numerals in this text to the decimal system.

A.4 Bisexagesimal Measures

P009048 This text contains a large number of unambiguous bisexagesimal notations. Of these, P009048:16:num counts the same object (M352∼h) as P009048:19, on the basis of which we propose that P009048:19 is also a bisexagesimal notation. Similarly, the unambiguous entries P009048:10 and P009048:15 count the same objects (M351+X and M354, respectively) as P009048:13 and P009048:7, respectively, on the basis of which we also disambiguate these entries to B.

Decipherment of Lost Ancient Scripts as Combinatorial Optimisation using Coupled Simulated Annealing

Fabio Tamburini
FICLIT, University of Bologna, Italy
fabio.tamburini@unibo.it

Abstract

This paper presents a new approach to the ancient scripts decipherment problem based on combinatorial optimisation and coupled simulated annealing, an advanced non-convex optimisation procedure. Solutions are encoded by using k-permutations allowing for null, one-to-many, and many-to-one mappings between signs. The proposed system is able to produce enhanced results in cognate identification when compared to the state-of-the-art systems on standard evaluation benchmarks used in literature.

1 Introduction

There are still a number of undeciphered scripts in the world and most of them date back thousands of years. The lack of an appropriate amount of inscriptions, the lack of known language descendants written using these scripts or even any certainty whether the symbols actually constitute a writing system made the decipherment of such scripts really challenging. In the Aegean area, for example, we can count at least three syllabic scripts that have not been deciphered yet, namely the Linear A script, Cretan Hieroglyphs and the Cypro-Minoan script. They are scripts strictly connected from a historical point of view, but no one has yet been able to solve these decipherment puzzles. In this work we deal with general decipherment problems, but we are mainly interested in investigating these undeciphered scripts from the Aegean area.

Deciphering an ancient script is, in general, a very complex task; the solution of this problem has been often split into different subproblems in order to obtain specific answers or to simplify the task by decomposing it into simpler problems. In the literature, we can find various contributions dealing with all these subproblems and propose computational methods for solving them in some way, often in relation to one specific script. In order, we have to (a) decide if a set of symbols actually represent a writing system, then (b) we have to devise appropriate procedures to isolate or segment the stream of symbols into a sequence of single signs and then (c) reduce the set of signs to the minimal set for the given writing system forming the alphabet (or syllabary, or whatever inventory of signs), identifying all the allographs. Once we have such a minimal, but complete, set of symbols, we can start (d) assigning to them phonetic/orthographic values and, finally, (e) trying to match phonetic/orthographic transcriptions to a specific language. Here we are interested in studying and discussing steps (d) and (e).

2 Related Works

Any modern attempt to decipher lost scripts using computational tools, a field that has been gaining more and more interest in NLP in the last years (Knight and Sproat, 2009), is based on the comparison of a lost script/language wordlist with words of a known deciphered script/language. These computational approaches have to address two main problems: the first regards the possibility that the two scripts do not correspond. In this case the phonological values of the lost symbols could also be unknown and the matching between the two wordlists must be preceded by some matching between scripts; then, the two wordlists must be matched in some way searching for "cognate" words, i.e. words in different languages that can share an etymological ancestor in a common parent language.

Some scholarly works focus only on cognate detection within the same script (Bouchard-Côté et al., 2009) or directly using the International Phonetic Alphabet sound representations (Hall and Klein, 2010). In both cases the tested languages were typologically very similar.

Conversely, the most advanced recent studies on the automatic decipherment of lost languages proposed systems producing both signs mappings be-

Proceedings of the Workshop on Computation and Written Language (CAWL 2023), pages 82–91
July 14, 2023 ©2023 Association for Computational Linguistics

tween different scripts and mapping of words into their corresponding cognates (e.g. Snyder et al., 2010; Berg-Kirkpatrick and Klein, 2011; Luo et al., 2019, 2021). These studies share a common view on the computational approach: they structured the algorithm as a two-step procedure, taking inspiration from the Expectation–Maximization (EM) algorithm. The first step proposes a temporary matching between the two "alphabets"[1], and the second step, by relying on the script-matching, tries to match the two word lists proposing possible cognates. At the beginning of the process the scripts matching will be almost random, and so will the cognate matching, but, after several iterations the whole process should converge proposing both a script-matching and a list of possible cognates. The key point hinges on finding an appropriate function, to be optimised by this iterative process, representing in an optimal way the concept of matching between words, including also some linguistic constraints regarding scripts, words and possibly sounds. Let us review the most recent and relevant analyses, in our view, which tackle the decipherment problem in an automatic way, all following the general scheme just discussed.

Snyder et al. (2010) presented the first paper which adopts the modern approach to the computational decipherment problem: their method requires a non-parallel corpus in a known related language and produces both alphabetic mappings and translations of words into their corresponding cognates, employing a non-parametric Bayesian framework to simultaneously capture both low-level sign mappings and high-level morphemic correspondences. They tested this method on Ugaritic, an ancient Semitic language, comparing it with old Hebrew: the model correctly maps 29 of 30 signs to their old Hebrew counterparts, and deduces the correct Hebrew cognate for 60% of the Ugaritic words that have cognates in Old Hebrew.

Berg-Kirkpatrick and Klein (2011) took a different approach: they devised an objective function that, when optimised, yields accurate solutions to both decipherment and cognate pair identification problems. Their system requires only a list of words in both languages as input. The proposed solution is both simple and elegant: binary variables govern both the matching between signs in the two scripts and the matching between the two lexica. By applying an integer combinatorial optimisation procedure, their system was able to obtain good results on the same problem introduced by Snyder et al. (2010) and on a new matching task on Romance languages.

Luo et al. (2019) present a novel neural approach that defines the state-of-the-art for the automatic decipherment of lost languages producing the highest matching performance. To compensate for the lack of strong supervision information, their model is designed to include known patterns in language change documented by historical linguistics. The mapping between signs is carried out by a bidirectional recurrent neural network while the procedure for matching cognates is formalised as a minimum-cost flow problem. They applied this method to the same problem presented in Snyder et al. (2010), a sort of benchmark in this field, and on a brand new dataset that included Linear B and ancient Mycenaean Greek lexica obtaining very good mapping results.

In a subsequent paper by Luo et al. (2021), the authors faced a more difficult hurdle considering scripts that are not fully segmented into words and contexts in which the closest known language is not determined. By building on rich linguistic constraints reflecting consistent patterns in historical sound change, they were able to capture natural phonetic geometry by learning character embeddings based on the International Phonetic Alphabet. The resulting generative framework jointly models word segmentation and cognate alignment, informed by phonetic/phonological constraints. They tested their method on both deciphered languages, namely Gothic and Ugaritic, and on an undeciphered one, Iberian, showing that incorporating phonetic geometry leads to consistent gains.

The two studies from Berg-Kirkpatrick and Klein (2011) and Luo et al. (2019) are the main works with which to compare our proposal.

Berg-Kirkpatrick and Klein (2011) proposed an approach that inspires our work, namely the possibility of tackling the decipherment problem as a pure function optimisation problem, but their results do not represent the state-of-the-art because they have been superseded by subsequent works.

The work from Luo et al. (2019), on the contrary, presents a system able to obtain very good results, but it is not as flexible as we need. With this respect, the mapping between lost and known signs is realised by a recurrent neural network (NN)

[1]With the term "alphabet", we indicate a generic notion of inventory of signs, glyphs, etc. used as a writing system.

and, despite the positive facts that context could be taken into account, it does not allow any further flexibility. In practical decipherment situations we have to face two problems that cannot be easily solved by the approach from Luo et al. (2019): the first regards the fact that very often paleographers have a partial knowledge about the mapping of some signs and this information must be injected into the system and taken into account; the second problem concerns the fact that very often real inscriptions are broken or damaged and some signs cannot be read, thus some kind of uncertainty must be included into the system, for example by using wildcards or other special symbols. These special treatments are very hard to implement into a recurrent NN. Moreover, deep NNs typically require a lot of data in order to be properly trained and this is often not the case in real situations.

As we said before, we are interested in studying some undeciphered scripts from Aegean and we definitely need a more flexible system that allows partial readings and fixed knowledge to be included as well as being able to work on limited amounts of data.

3 Reference Benchmarks and other Datasets

Various datasets have been used in past studies and became standard benchmarks for evaluating the performance of any computational tool aiming at helping scholars in the decipherment process.

3.1 Ugaritic/Old Hebrew - U/OH

Ugaritic is an ancient Semitic language closely related to Old Hebrew. This dataset has been introduced by Snyder et al. (2010) for testing their system and became a common benchmark in the field. Following Berg-Kirkpatrick and Klein (2011), we evaluate our system on 2214 cognates pairs in the two lexica.

3.2 Linear B/Mycenaean Greek - LB/MG

Linear B is a syllabic writing system used to write Mycenaean Greek dating back to around 1450BC. Luo et al. (2019) introduced a new dataset extracting pairs of Linear B and Greek words from a compiled lexicon and removing some uncertain translations obtaining 919 pairs of cognates. This is a very interesting benchmark for us as we are primarily interested in working on syllabic scripts from the Aegean area. On the LB side, we defined the signs inventory as the original set of signs defined in LB while for Greek, given the syllabic nature of the mapping, we included complex signs formed by all open syllables excluding those marking vowel quantity (syllables ending in η or ω) to reduce the signs inventory dimension on the Greek side.

The same authors introduced also a more challenging benchmark, more realistic from the paleographic point of view, considering the same LB lexicon and compare it with a reduced Greek lexicon containing only proper nouns (LB/MG-names).

3.3 Cypriot Syllabary/Arcadocypriot Greek - CS/AG

Given our primary interests, it seemed reasonable to introduce a new dataset to be used as reference for the decipherment of syllabic scripts from the same area. The Cypriot Syllabary is a right-to-left syllabic script used in Iron Age Cyprus. It is descended from the Cypro-Minoan syllabary, in turn, a derivative of Linear A. Most texts using this script are in the Arcadocypriot dialect of Greek.

Relying on the alphabetic-syllabic index in Hintze (1993), we compiled a new dataset consisting of 693 pairs of cognates, the first written using the CS and the second the Greek alphabet from which we removed any diacritic following the same procedure applied in Luo et al. (2019) for creating the LB/MG dataset. With regard to Greek, we considered only the open syllables as for the previous dataset.

4 The Proposed Method

The proposed approach to the decipherment problem is configured as a global optimisation procedure taking inspiration from the work proposed in Berg-Kirkpatrick and Klein (2011). We will introduce a flexible encoding of possible solutions and an 'energy function' able to capture the goodness of a single solution, both from the point of view of signs matching and lexica matchings; by minimising the energy function, we will search for suitable solutions to a decipherment problem.

Let us introduce some notation useful in the next sections: L_s and K_s are two linearly ordered sets[2] containing respectively the signs in the lost and known languages (with $|L_s|$ and $|K_s|$ their cardinality and l^i, k^j respectively the i-th and j-th element in the ordered sets), while L_{lex} and K_{lex} are

[2]A linearly ordered set is a set with a total order on it. Here, it is useful only for indexing the set elements.

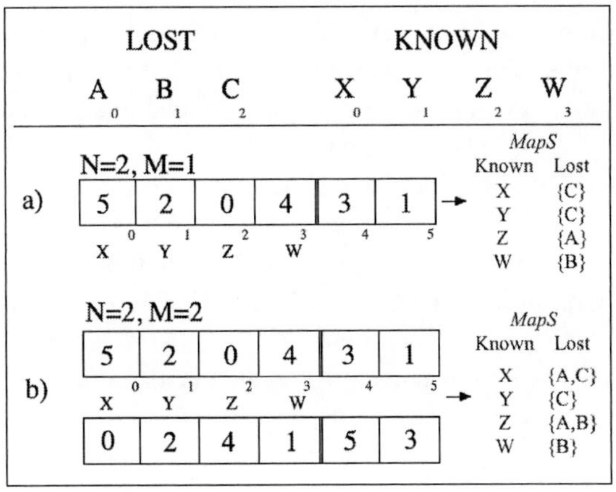

Figure 1: Two simple examples of solution coding. a) $M = 1$ then the first $|K_s|$ cells contain the mapping $MapS$ (shown on the right) for the known signs to the lost signs. Note that using k-permutations of size $N \cdot |L_s|$ allows for one-to-many mappings from lost to known signs (see also the definition $MapS$ in 4.1). b) $M = 2$, then we have two k-permutations allowing for one-to-many assignments from known to lost signs. In both cases it could happen that a lost sign does not receive any assignment (not shown in the picture).

the two lexica and $|L_{lex}|$ and $|K_{lex}|$ their respective number of words.

4.1 Solution Coding

The basic tool for encoding a problem solution is the k-permutation without repetition. Let $p_1, ..., p_n$ be n objects. Let s_1,...,s_k be k (where $k \leq n$) slots to which k of the n objects can be assigned. A k-permutation of n objects is one of the possible ways to choose k objects and place them into the k slots respecting the order. Each object can be chosen only once. The number of possible k-permutations is $P_{n,k} = n!/(n-k)!$. Here we consider the k-permutation of the first n integer numbers.

In order to find a suitable sign assignment between lost language and known language, a generic solution σ must have the possibility to express multiple assignments in both directions but paying attention to the combinatorial explosion problem.

Let us start considering the case $|L_s| \leq |K_s|$: in this situation some lost signs must be mapped to more than one known sign and we can easily encode this fact with a single k-permutation σ with $n = N \cdot |L_s|$ and $k = |K_s|$, $N = 2, 3, ...$ Each known sign k_j being in position j, with $j \leq k$, of the k-permutation $\sigma = \langle \sigma_1, ..., \sigma_k, ..., \sigma_n \rangle$ is then mapped to a set of lost signs by the function

$$MapS^{\sigma}: K_s \to \mathcal{P}(L_s),$$

$$MapS^{\sigma}(k_j) = l_{\sigma_j \bmod |L_s|}$$

where $\mathcal{P}(L_s)$ is the power set of L_s.

In the other case with $|L_s| > |K_s|$ we can define a solution σ formed by M k-permutations, $M = 2, 3, ...$, concatenated one after the others, each managed exactly in the same way as before, but now N can also be equal to 1.

By defining the structure of possible solutions σ in this way, each sign in the lost language can receive from 0 to a maximum of $N \times M$ possible assignments of known signs, allowing a very high level of flexibility in signs matching. Given that in the definition of k-permutations $k \leq n$, N controls the well-formedness of the basic structure supporting solution definition ensuring that every known sign will be assigned to at least one lost sign and managing the different situations that occur when $|L_s| \leq |K_s|$. Moreover, M controls the number of times a known sign will be assigned to a lost sign. N and M are not completely independent parameters as they interact in a complex way for governing the number of multiple assignments in both directions.

Figure 1 shows two small examples of the proposed schema for encoding solutions.

As an added value, k-permutations exhibit an interesting property: we can build an isomorphism between k-permutations and the natural numbers (Patel, 2022), thus each solution encoded by using our schema can be mapped into M integers and, for reasonable problems with $M \leq 2$, fragments of the search space can be visualised and inspected using a 2D/3D graph.

4.2 Energy function

The second fundamental ingredient used in the proposed method regards the design of an appropriate energy function able to measure the goodness of a given solution for a decipherment problem.

As we said before, Luo et al. (2019) broke the optimisation process into two separate steps repeated iteratively: the first computes the best match between signs given a lexicon match and, after having fixed the signs match, the second computes the best match between lexica. We adopted a different approach taking inspiration from Berg-Kirkpatrick and Klein (2011) and designed an energy function that measures the goodness of both aspects together.

4.2.1 Lost Words Expansion and Transliteration

In order to transliterate the lost lexicon we need to define the inverse function of $MapS$, $invMapS^{\sigma}: L_s \rightarrow \mathcal{P}(K_s)$, that associates each lost sign to the set of known signs mapped to it, as

$$invMapS^{\sigma}(l_i) = \{k_j | l_i \in MapS^{\sigma}(k_j)\} .$$

By building on this definition, we can introduce the transliteration and expansion function $TrExp^{\sigma}$ for a given lost word $lW = \langle lW_1, ..., lW_n \rangle$, with $lW_1, ..., lW_n$ the sequence of signs forming lW, as

$$TrExp^{\sigma}(lW) = \{ \, tW \mid \quad tW = \langle q_1, ..., q_n \rangle, \quad q_j \in invMapS^{\sigma}(lW_j) \, \}.$$

$TrExp$ transliterates each lost word into the known alphabet and associates to it a set of transliterated words formed by any combination of known signs allowed by the mapping $invMapS$. This way of proceeding could potentially produce a combinatorial explosion, but, given that N and M are typically very small integers (almost always ≤ 3), this problem will not be particularly severe. Table 1 shows an example of this process.

l_i	$invMapS^{\sigma}(l_i)$	lW	$TrExp^{\sigma}(lW)$
A	{Z,X}	AA	{ZZ,ZX,XZ,XX}
B	{W,Z}	BC	{WX,WY,ZX,ZY}
C	{X,Y}	ABC	{ZWX,ZWY,ZZX, ZZY,XWX,XWY, XZX,XZY}

Table 1: Transliteration and expansion example over the same sets of signs used in Figure 1 (b).

4.2.2 Word Matching

A standard way to compare strings makes use of the so called *edit distance* - ED (a.k.a. Levenshtein distance). We used this measure to compare the expanded transliterations of lost words to known words. The standard definition of the ED involves counting the number of sign insertions, deletions and substitutions to transform the first string into the second. We modified the standard definition, following the ideas in Wang et al. (2021), for adding two wildcards that could be very useful in real settings. Very often real inscriptions are broken and/or some signs cannot be reliably distinguished; in these situation it might be preferable to process these data maintaining the reading problems. For these reasons, we included the special sign '?' to indicate a single unreadable sign and '*' to indicate multiple unreadable signs both allowed only in lost words. Let $X = \langle x_1, ...x_n \rangle$ and $Y = \langle y_1, ...y_m \rangle$ two words to be compared, with n and m their respective lengths, then the ED with wildcards used in this study, $EDW_{X,Y}(n, m)$, has been defined as in Figure 2.

The edit distance in general, and also our variation including wildcards, does not take into account word lengths and it is not suitable for comparing the distance between sets of words. For this reason, most studies introduced a kind of normalisation for ED values. Given the interesting properties (Fisman et al., 2022) of the *Generalised Edit Distance* proposed by Li and Liu (2007)[3], we normalised EDW as

$$\overline{EDW}_{X,Y} = \frac{2 \cdot EDW_{X,Y}}{|X| + |Y| + EDW_{X,Y}}$$

where $|\cdot|$ represents the word length.

We used $\overline{EDW}$ to compare the transliterated and expanded lost lexicon, created by applying the $TrExp$ function to every word in L_{lex}, with the known words in K_{lex} (see next Section).

We implemented the $\overline{EDW}$ function in a fast code that also works on GPUs[4].

4.2.3 Lexica Matching

The datasets presented in Section 3, as produced by the cited works, associate each lost word with one or more cognates in the known language. In order to adhere to this view and to perform a correct evaluation, we introduced a specific variant of the standard Linear Sum Assignment - LSA - problem (a.k.a. Hungarian algorithm) for matching lexica: instead of matching single words, we match groups of words both on the lost side and on the known side. On the lost language side, this accounts for different transliteration of the same lost word due to multiple assignments to the same lost sign (see the definitions of functions $invMapS$ and $TrExp$), while, on the known language side, this accounts for the sets of cognates considered in the cited benchmarks.

In order to introduce our modified version of the LSA algorithm, let us define a partition

[3]Generalised Edit Distance is a metric, its upper bound is 1 and it does not escalate repetitions remaining simple and quick to calculate.

[4]https://github.com/ftamburin/EditDistanceWild

$$EDW_{X,Y}(i,j) = \begin{cases} \max(i,j), & min(i,j) = 0 \\ \min \begin{cases} EDW_{X,Y}(i-1,j) + wD \\ EDW_{X,Y}(i,j-1) + wI \\ EDW_{X,Y}(i-1,j-1) + S(x_i,y_j) \cdot wS \end{cases} & min(i,j) \neq 0, x_i \neq \text{'*'} \\ \min \begin{cases} EDW_{X,Y}(i-1,j) \\ EDW_{X,Y}(i,j-1) \\ EDW_{X,Y}(i-1,j-1) \end{cases} & min(i,j) \neq 0, x_i = \text{'*'} \end{cases}$$

$$S(x,y) = \begin{cases} 0 & x = y \text{ or } x = \text{'?'} \\ 1 & \text{otherwise} \end{cases}$$

Figure 2: Edit Distance with Wildcards definition. wD, wI and wS represents the weight penalisations respectively for sign deletion, insertion and substitution and, for this study, they have been all fixed to 1.

$K_{lexG} = K^1_{lexG}, ..., K^G_{lexG}$ of K_{lex} where K^j_{lexG} represents a set of known cognates in the dataset; we can then introduce the variables $A_{i,j} \in \{0,1\}$ representing the lexica alignment obtained by the LSA algorithm (with $A_{i,j} = 1$ iff lW^i is assigned to K^j_{lexG}), configure the LSA problem to be solved as

$$\min \sum_{i=1}^{|L_{lex}|} \sum_{j=1}^{|K_{lexG}|} A_{i,j} \cdot \left[\min_{\substack{X \in TrExp^\sigma(lW^i) \\ Y \in K^j_{lexG}}} \overline{EDW}_{X,Y} \right]$$

$$\text{s.t.} \quad \sum_i A_{i,j} = 1, \quad j = 1, 2, ..., |K_{lexG}|$$

$$\sum_j A_{i,j} = 1, \quad i = 1, 2, ..., |L_{lex}|$$

and, once solved the LSA and fixed the values for the As matching variables, we can define the Energy function E for a given problem solution σ as

$$E(\sigma) = \sum_{i=1}^{|L_{lex}|} \sum_{j=1}^{|K_{lexG}|} A_{i,j} \cdot \left[\min_{\substack{X \in TrExp^\sigma(lW^i) \\ Y \in K^j_{lexG}}} \overline{EDW}_{X,Y} \right] \tag{1}$$

See Figure 3 for an example of the lexica matching process.

It seems important to note that the computation of the energy function E for a given solution σ strictly derives from the solution itself, first by converting the solution coding into signs assignments by using the function $TrExp$ and then matching the two lexica by the LSA procedure described above.

4.2.4 Penalty factors

In order to regularise the entire process and help the optimisation procedure to find reliable solutions, we introduced some regularisation factors into the energy function E. Given that our method relies on a flexible assignment schema allowing no assignments to lost signs and multiple assignments of known signs, we have to guarantee that the optimisation procedure does not abuse of these instruments. In general, no assignments to lost signs rarely produces a good solution as well as exaggerating in including multiple assignments of known signs. In order to discourage solutions with these characteristics, we introduced two penalisation factors: if we define $\#UA(\sigma)$ the number of lost signs without any assignment and $\#MA(\sigma)$ the number of known signs with multiple assignments for a given solution σ, then the final energy function to be minimised is

$$E'(\sigma) = E(\sigma) + \lambda \cdot (\#UA(\sigma) + \#MA(\sigma)) \, . \tag{2}$$

To strongly discourage these potentially degenerate solutions we set $\lambda = 4$.

4.3 Energy Optimisation using Coupled Simulated Annealing

Having configured our problem as a general global optimisation procedure led us to minimise the energy function E' defined before by using any metaheuristic proposed in the literature, e.g. tabu-search, genetic and evolutionary methods, ant colony optimisation, simulated annealing, etc.

Coupled Simulated Annealing - CSA (de Souza et al., 2010) is a method for global optimisation

L_{lex}		K_{lex}				
lW	$TrExp$	WX	WW	XX	XWY	XWZ
AA	ZZ	2	2	2	3	2
	ZX	**1**	2	1	3	3
	XZ	2	2	1	2	**1**
	XX	1	2	**0**	2	2
BC	WX	**0**	1	**1**	2	2
	WY	1	1	2	**1**	2
	ZX	1	2	1	3	3
	ZY	2	2	2	2	3
ABC	ZWX	**1**	2	2	2	2
	ZWY	2	2	3	1	2
	ZZX	2	3	2	3	3
	ZZY	3	3	3	2	3
	XWX	1	2	**1**	1	1
	XWY	2	2	2	**0**	1
	XZX	2	3	1	2	2
	XZY	3	3	2	1	2

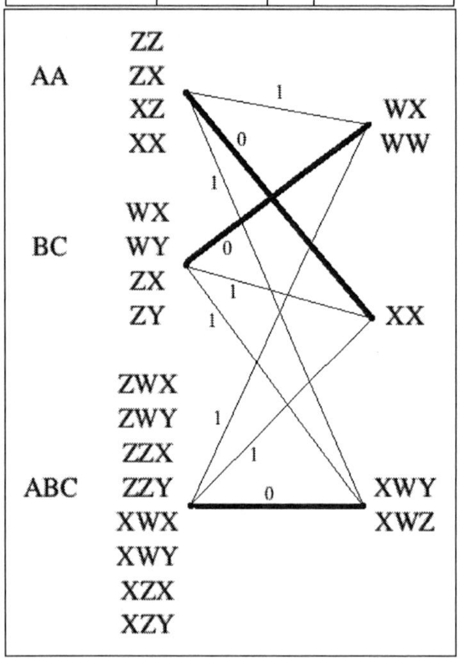

Figure 3: A simple example of the lexica matching process. The lost lexicon is identical to that in Table 1, while the known lexicon is formed by five words grouped into three set of cognates. On the top, we have the cost matrix computed by using the edit distance (we did not use the normalised version for readability) and the values surrounded by a box indicate the minimum considering two respective groups. At the bottom, these minimal values represent the costs for a LSA problem that finds the min-cost matching (thick lines) between the two lexica respecting the groupings in the lost and known lexica.

based on Simulated Annealing (SA). CSA is characterised by a set of parallel standard SA processes (with $\#Anns$ defining the number of annealers) coupled by their acceptance probabilities. The coupling is performed by a term in the acceptance probability function that is a function of the energies of the current states of all SA processes creating a cooperative behaviour via information exchange between the parallel annealing processes. Coupling can also provide information that can be used to drive the overall optimisation process towards the global optimum. The authors of the original work present a system able to use the acceptance temperature to control the variance of the acceptance probabilities with a simple control scheme (called 'CSA-MwVC' in the original paper). This leads to a much better optimisation efficiency because it reduces the sensitivity of the algorithm to initialisation parameters while guiding the optimisation process towards quasi-optimal states.

After some attempt with other techniques, we decided to adopt CSA mainly for two reasons: (a) it is a method that can be easily parallelised on a multicore CPU allowing for heavily parallel computations with a minimal exchange of information and (b) the control mechanism over the variance of the acceptance probabilities automatically governs the annealing process avoiding the introduction of complex annealing schemas that often have to be tuned for a specific dataset.

For the implementation of CSA we relied on a code specifically developed for problems based on permutations[5] configuring it to employ 16 parallel annealers.

The generic SA algorithm is quite simple: given a solution, we have to perturb it obtaining a new solution in its neighbourhood that is accepted, or not, depending on a stochastic decision based on the new solution energy and the global current system temperature. Selecting a neighbouring solution perturbing the current is a delicate step as we have to ensure an appropriate sampling of the solution space. Luckily, Tian et al. (1999) made an in depth study regarding the most promising 'moves' for solutions based on permutations and the swapping of two items in the permutation is considered the best move for assignment problems. In order to help the system to avoid getting stuck in a local minimum, we further introduced a random k-swap perturbation with probability 0.1 with k decaying

[5] `https://github.com/structurely/csa`.

Algorithm 1 *CSA_OptMatcher*

Data: $L_s, K_s, L_{lex}, K_{lex}, N, M, \#Anns$
Result: the optimised solution $best\_\sigma$
• Init one solution σ_j for each annealer j
• Init annealing and generation temperatures T_a and T_g
for $iter = 1, \ldots$ **do**
  • Generate $\#Anns$ perturbed solutions σ'_j by swapping two indices in each of them
  • Compute $E'(\sigma'_j), j = 1, ..., \#Anns$ using equations (1) and (2)
  for $j = 1, ..., \#Anns$ **do**
    if $E'(\sigma'_j) \leq E'(\sigma_j)$ **then**
      • $\sigma_j = \sigma'_j$
    else
      • Accept σ'_j following the CSA-MwVC algorithm
    end if
  end for
  • Decrease T_a and T_g according to CSA-MwVC temperature schedules
  • $best\_\sigma = min_j \; E'(\sigma_j)$
end for

with the generation temperature governed by the CSA schedule.

See Algorithm 1 for a general picture of the entire optimisation process.

4.4 Evaluation

With regard to evaluation, we stick to the same procedure introduced in previous literature and, in particular, in Luo et al. (2019) and measured the system Accuracy in finding pairs of lost and known cognates as listed in the considered dataset.

The influential paper from Reimers and Gurevych (2017) makes clear to the community that reporting a single score for each session could be heavily affected by the system random initialisation and we should instead report the mean and standard deviation of various runs, with the same setting, in order to get a more accurate picture of the real systems performance and make more reliable comparisons between them. For these reasons, any new result proposed in this paper is presented as the mean and standard deviation of system Accuracy over 4 runs with different random initialisations. In this way, we should give a real picture of our system performances.

5 Results

The two parameters N and M for solution shaping described in Section 4.1 could be considered hyperparameters for the proposed method as they can give more power to the possible solutions at the price of more parameters to be fixed and thus slower convergence. We decided to avoid any optimisation of these parameters in our experiments and fix them using a very simple rule: $N = 1$, $M = 2$ if $|L_s| > |K_s|$ and $N = 2$, $M = 1$ otherwise.

Table 2 shows the results of our experiments compared with the reference literature. Our system is able to produce better Accuracy than any other work on all considered benchmark datasets with a large margin. If we consider the fact that our results are presented as the mean and std. deviation of more runs and not as the maximum Accuracy achieved by the system, the results are even more relevant.

6 Discussion and Conclusions

We presented a new approach to the ancient scripts decipherment able to produce very good results in cognate identification w.r.t. the state-of-the-art. All the hyperparameters were not optimised at all and it seems reasonable that increasing N and/or M even better results can be reached. We plan to perform more experiments in that direction.

Another system feature worth of mention regards its ability to converge to reasonable solution for any simulation; even during the development phase, the proposed system never got trapped into very poor sub-optimal solutions. Simulations took a relevant time to converge, but they always converged without any need to restart the process, a common technique for this kind of methods (see e.g. Berg-Kirkpatrick and Klein 2013), confirming the strength of CSA as a function optimisation technique.

There are other approaches to the problem in the literature that we have not explicitly discussed in Section 2 because not strictly devoted to the decipherment of ancient scripts, but address the problem of deciphering substitution or homophonic codes like the famous Zodiac-408 cipher or the Beale cipher (e.g. Ravi and Knight, 2011; Nuhn et al., 2013, 2014). For example Ravi and Knight (2011) proposed a stochastic model taking into account both token n-grams and dictionaries. Knowing for certain the target language, they can esti-

System	Benchmark Dataset			
	U/OH	LB/MG	LB/MG names	CS/AG
(Berg-Kirkpatrick and Klein, 2011)	90.4	-	-	-
(Luo et al., 2019)	93.5	84.7	67.3	-
This work (*CSA_OptMatcher*)	**95.5**±0.83 max **96.3**	**89.4**±1.81 max **91.0**	**83.4**±2.50 max **87.0**	**86.3**±1.73 max **87.9**

Table 2: Accuracy results in cognate identification compared with the reference literature.

mate a language model (LM) using a large set of data, even artificially generated, and can take advantage of complete lexica and frequency information for the known language. Unfortunately, when using these methods to solve the decipherment problems on ancient languages often the target language is not known for certain, maybe it is a language from the same area sharing the same data scarcity as the lost one and thus it is not possible to build useful LMs or rely on a complete dictionary. On the contrary, everything is only partially known or unreliable: phonetic values, signs mappings, frequency information and the true underlying language. This facts make it very difficult to use methods like the one proposed by these authors.

Our very promising results in the decipherment of ancient scripts might suggest that these tools can solve all the unsolved problems, of palaeographic, epigraphic and linguistic nature, debated for years by experts. This is naturally not the case. These techniques, even if very promising, also present a large number of problems when applied in real decipherment attempts: (a) first of all, segmented and clean corpora are needed. Building a corpus for an ancient undeciphered script, even in the case where we have already solved the segmentation problems and were able to collect single sign images and sign/word sequences, is not an easy task. Most inscriptions are damaged and many signs are not readable. Broken words and/or partial sentences are also frequent; (b) an extensive cognate list must be available, but in most real cases we only have two word lists that must be matched without any guarantee that lost language cognates are really present in the known language lexicon; (c) in NLP we have to make evaluation on well-known test beds and all the studies we discussed before worked on well known correspondences to prove the system effectiveness. It is an entirely different matter to test the same systems on real cases when we have to deal with unknown writing systems and their corresponding languages.

In the light of these considerations, we agree with Sproat (2020) who suggested that these tools can help paleographers shed light on the decipherment process, but we cannot rely on them only for providing a complete solution to our real problems without any human intervention for guiding the process and interpreting the results. However, our future plans regard the application of the proposed system to undeciphered scripts from the Aegean area, hoping to shed some light on problems unresolved for centuries.

Codes and all datasets for reproducing the experiments are available on github[6].

Acknowledgements

We would like to thank Silvia Ferrara for her help in defining Ancient Greek syllables and the reviewers for their valuable suggestions for improving the final version of the manuscript.

References

Taylor Berg-Kirkpatrick and Dan Klein. 2011. Simple effective decipherment via combinatorial optimization. In *Proceedings of the 2011 Conference on Empirical Methods in Natural Language Processing*, pages 313–321, Edinburgh, Scotland, UK. Association for Computational Linguistics.

Taylor Berg-Kirkpatrick and Dan Klein. 2013. Decipherment with a million random restarts. In *Proceedings of the 2013 Conference on Empirical Methods in Natural Language Processing*, pages 874–878, Seattle, Washington, USA. Association for Computational Linguistics.

Alexandre Bouchard-Côté, Thomas L. Griffiths, and Dan Klein. 2009. Improved reconstruction of protolanguage word forms. In *Proceedings of Human Language Technologies: The 2009 Annual Conference of the North American Chapter of the Association for Computational Linguistics*, pages 65–73,

[6]https://github.com/ftamburin/CSA_OptMatcher

Boulder, Colorado. Association for Computational Linguistics.

Samuel Xavier de Souza, Johan A. K. Suykens, Joos Vandewalle, and Désiré Bollé. 2010. Coupled simulated annealing. *IEEE Trans. Syst. Man Cybern. Part B*, 40(2):320–335.

Dana Fisman, Joshua Grogin, Oded Margalit, and Gera Weiss. 2022. The normalized edit distance with uniform operation costs is a metric. In *33rd Annual Symposium on Combinatorial Pattern Matching, CPM 2022, June 27-29, 2022, Prague, Czech Republic*, volume 223 of *LIPIcs*, pages 17:1–17:17. Schloss Dagstuhl - Leibniz-Zentrum für Informatik.

David Hall and Dan Klein. 2010. Finding cognate groups using phylogenies. In *Proceedings of the 48th Annual Meeting of the Association for Computational Linguistics*, pages 1030–1039, Uppsala, Sweden. Association for Computational Linguistics.

Almut Hintze. 1993. *A lexicon to the Cyprian syllabic inscriptions*. Buske, Hamburg.

Kevin Knight and Richard Sproat. 2009. Writing systems, transliteration and decipherment. In *Proceedings of Human Language Technologies: The 2009 Annual Conference of the North American Chapter of the Association for Computational Linguistics, Companion Volume: Tutorial Abstracts*, pages 15–16, Boulder, Colorado. Association for Computational Linguistics.

Yujian Li and Bo Liu. 2007. A normalized levenshtein distance metric. *IEEE Transactions on Pattern Analysis and Machine Intelligence*, 29(6):1091–1095.

Jiaming Luo, Yuan Cao, and Regina Barzilay. 2019. Neural decipherment via minimum-cost flow: From Ugaritic to Linear B. In *Proceedings of the 57th Annual Meeting of the Association for Computational Linguistics*, pages 3146–3155, Florence, Italy. Association for Computational Linguistics.

Jiaming Luo, Frederik Hartmann, Enrico Santus, Regina Barzilay, and Yuan Cao. 2021. Deciphering undersegmented ancient scripts using phonetic prior. *Transactions of the Association for Computational Linguistics*, 9:69–81.

Malte Nuhn, Julian Schamper, and Hermann Ney. 2013. Beam search for solving substitution ciphers. In *Proceedings of the 51st Annual Meeting of the Association for Computational Linguistics (Volume 1: Long Papers)*, pages 1568–1576, Sofia, Bulgaria.

Malte Nuhn, Julian Schamper, and Hermann Ney. 2014. Improved decipherment of homophonic ciphers. In *Proceedings of the 2014 Conference on Empirical Methods in Natural Language Processing (EMNLP)*, pages 1764–1768, Doha, Qatar.

Deepesh Patel. 2022. Generating the nth lexicographical element of a mathematical k-permutation using permutational number system. *SSRN*, http://dx.doi.org/10.2139/ssrn.4174035.

Sujith Ravi and Kevin Knight. 2011. Bayesian inference for zodiac and other homophonic ciphers. In *Proceedings of the 49th Annual Meeting of the Association for Computational Linguistics: Human Language Technologies*, pages 239–247, Portland, Oregon, USA.

Nils Reimers and Iryna Gurevych. 2017. Reporting Score Distributions Makes a Difference: Performance Study of LSTM-networks for Sequence Tagging. In *Proceedings of the 2017 Conference on Empirical Methods in Natural Language Processing*, pages 338–348, Copenhagen, Denmark. ACL.

Benjamin Snyder, Regina Barzilay, and Kevin Knight. 2010. A statistical model for lost language decipherment. In *Proceedings of the 48th Annual Meeting of the Association for Computational Linguistics*, pages 1048–1057, Uppsala, Sweden. Association for Computational Linguistics.

Richard William Sproat. 2020. Translating lost languages using machine learning? Wellformedness, http://www.wellformedness.com/blog/translating-lost-languages-machine-learning/.

Peng Tian, Jian Ma, and Dong-Mo Zhang. 1999. Application of the simulated annealing algorithm to the combinatorial optimisation problem with permutation property: An investigation of generation mechanism. *European Journal of Operational Research*, 118(1):81–94.

Yuanhao Wang, Qiong Huang, Hongbo Li, Meiyan Xiao, Huang Jianye, and Guomin Yang. 2021. Public key encryption with fuzzy matching. In *Provable and Practical Security, LNCS 13059*, pages 39–62. Springer.

Learning the Character Inventories of Undeciphered Scripts Using Unsupervised Deep Clustering

Logan Born[1] **M. Willis Monroe**[2] **Kathryn Kelley**[3] **Anoop Sarkar**[1]
loborn@sfu.ca willis.monroe@ubc.ca kathrynerin.kelley@unibo.it anoop@cs.sfu.ca

[1]Simon Fraser University
School of Computing Science

[2]University of British Columbia
Department of Philosophy

[3]Università di Bologna
Dipartimento di Filologia Classica e Italianistica

Abstract

A crucial step in deciphering a text is to identify what set of characters were used to write it. This requires grouping character tokens according to visual and contextual features, which can be challenging for human analysts when the number of tokens or underlying types is large. Prior work has shown that this process can be automated by clustering dense representations of character images, in a task which we call "script clustering". In this work, we present novel architectures which exploit varying degrees of contextual and visual information to learn representations for use in script clustering. We evaluate on a range of modern and ancient scripts, and find that our models produce representations which are more effective for script recovery than the current state-of-the-art, despite using just 2% as many parameters. Our analysis fruitfully applies these models to assess hypotheses about the character inventory of the partially-deciphered proto-Elamite script.

1 Introduction

One of the first tasks in decipherment is to solve an instance of the token-to-type problem by recognizing which tokens represent the same underlying character, and thereby to construct a list of every character used in the script (cf. Gelb and Whiting 1975). Accurate character inventories are important for decipherment, as they indicate patterns of frequency and adjacency which can reveal information about the underlying message. However, it can be challenging for human annotators to determine which characters are truly distinct: tokens with different appearances can represent the same underlying character (such as English 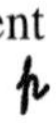 and 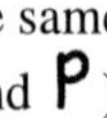), while visually-similar tokens can represent distinct characters (such as  and  or ß and B).

This work introduces novel, VAE-based techniques for learning the character inventory of an unknown script by clustering images of character tokens. We show, through a range of experiments on deciphered and undeciphered scripts from modern and ancient corpora, how the complexity and number of characters in a script impact our models' ability to learn the underlying character inventory. On the ancient Cypro-Greek syllabary, our models outperform the recent Sign2Vec architecture (Corazza et al., 2022a) despite using just $\sim$2% as many parameters. We also apply these models to the undeciphered proto-Elamite script (PE; Dahl 2019), and find that they independently replicate expert intuitions about the underlying character inventory and suggest new relationships between signs which have not yet been noted in prior work.

2 Methodology

Corazza et al. 2022a and Corazza et al. 2022b outline a two-step procedure for learning the character inventory of an unknown script by clustering images of character tokens. They first train an unsupervised neural encoder to learn vector representations for images of the characters in question. After training, they cluster these representations: the resulting clusters serve as an estimate for the script's underlying character inventory. The authors demonstrate good performance on the ancient Cypro-Greek script, and fruitfully apply this technique to the study of a related, undeciphered script called Cypro-Minoan.

Our work follows the same overall approach, and investigates how changes to the encoder architecture, data quality, and training process can affect the final clustering.

2.1 Motivation

Sign2Vec (Corazza et al., 2022a) uses the ResNet18 encoder (He et al., 2016), which is an 18-layer convolutional stack with residual connections. ResNet was originally developed for object detection and segmentation on the ImageNet (Deng et al., 2009) and COCO (Lin et al., 2014) datasets, which in-

Proceedings of the Workshop on Computation and Written Language (CAWL 2023), pages 92–104
July 14, 2023 ©2023 Association for Computational Linguistics

clude photorealistic depictions of complex scenes. In this setting, very deep networks are necessary to capture the full range of visual information present in the input images (He et al., 2016). By contrast, images of written characters tend to be visually simple: they often read clearly in greyscale or black-and-white, and can generally be broken down into simple lines, curves, or wedges against a uniform background. In light of this, we hypothesize that the ResNet encoder may be significantly over-parameterized for the task of script clustering. This may lead to longer training times than necessary, more expensive compute costs, and increased risk of overfitting when applied to low-resource decipherment corpora.

Additionally, one of the tasks used to train the Sign2Vec encoder is a masked prediction task, where information about a character must be recovered given the representations of the characters to its immediate left and right. This provides the model with a very narrow context window, which is sufficient for the experiments in the original work (Corazza et al., 2022a), but which we hypothesize may hamper the model's performance in settings where wider context is available.

2.2 Model Architectures

In light of these limitations, we propose to compare four architectures which reduce the size of the encoder relative to Sign2Vec and incorporate varying degrees of context.[1]

VAE All of our models are built around a variational autoencoder (VAE; Kingma and Welling 2014) with a convolutional encoder and a deconvolutional decoder (Figure 1). This architecture uses three stacked convolutional layers to learn vector representations $\mu, \sigma \in \mathbb{R}^d$ from an input image $\mathbf{x} \in \mathbb{R}^{n \times n}$. These are used to sample a "code" $\mathbf{z} \sim \mathcal{N}(\mu, \sigma)$. A stack of transposed convolutional layers decodes $\mathbf{z}$ to an image $\tilde{\mathbf{x}} \in \mathbb{R}^{n \times n}$. This model is trained to minimize the reconstruction error of $\tilde{\mathbf{x}}$ with respect to the input $\mathbf{x}$:

$$\mathcal{L} = \mathrm{BCE}(\tilde{x}, x) \quad (1)$$

where BCE is binary cross-entropy.

VAE+Neighbors Our second model adds an auxiliary masked prediction task (Figure 2). Let $\mathbf{z}_{i-1}$ and $\mathbf{z}_{i+1}$ be the encodings of the images to the

[1]Code to be released at https://github.com/MrLogarithm/cawl-clustering

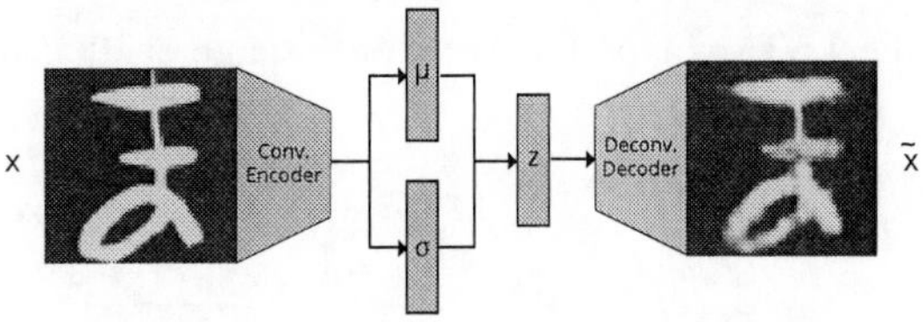

Figure 1: VAE architecture. This model reconstructs its input from a dense vector encoding.

direct left and right of a token $\mathbf{x}_i$. We learn a projection $M \in \mathbb{R}^{2d \times d}$ and decode $M(\mathbf{z}_{i-1} \oplus \mathbf{z}_{i+1})$ to produce an image $\tilde{\mathbf{x}}'_i$. We add a new loss term to Equation (1) to minimize the reconstruction error of $\tilde{\mathbf{x}}'_i$ with respect to $\mathbf{x}_i$:

$$\mathcal{L}_{\text{Neighbor}} = \mathrm{BCE}(\tilde{\mathbf{x}}'_i, \mathbf{x}_i)$$

This is similar to the auxiliary task in Sign2Vec (Corazza et al., 2022a), with the difference that our model *draws* the masked sign, whereas Sign2Vec was trained to predict a property called its "pseudolabel" (see Section 2.3).

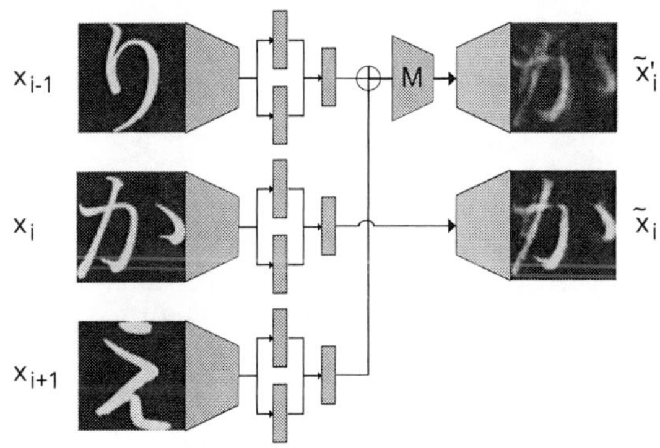

Figure 2: VAE+Neighbor architecture. This model adds the auxiliary task of reconstructing a character image given the encodings of the adjacent characters.

VAE+LSTM To include wider context, we propose a third architecture incorporating an autoregressive LSTM (Hochreiter and Schmidhuber, 1997) language model. The input to this model is a sequence of character images $\{\mathbf{x}_1, ..., \mathbf{x}_n\}$. We encode each image using convolutional encoders with tied parameters to produce a sequence of codes $\{\mathbf{z}_1, ..., \mathbf{z}_n\}$, and decode these using tied decoders to produce a sequence of images $\{\tilde{\mathbf{x}}_1, ..., \tilde{\mathbf{x}}_n\}$. Up to this point, the model is equivalent to a batched version of the basic VAE model. To incorporate context, we pass $\{\mathbf{z}_1, ..., \mathbf{z}_n\}$ to a unidirectional LSTM, and use our VAE decoder to decode the LSTM outputs to a second image sequence $\{\tilde{\mathbf{x}}'_1, ..., \tilde{\mathbf{x}}'_n\}$.

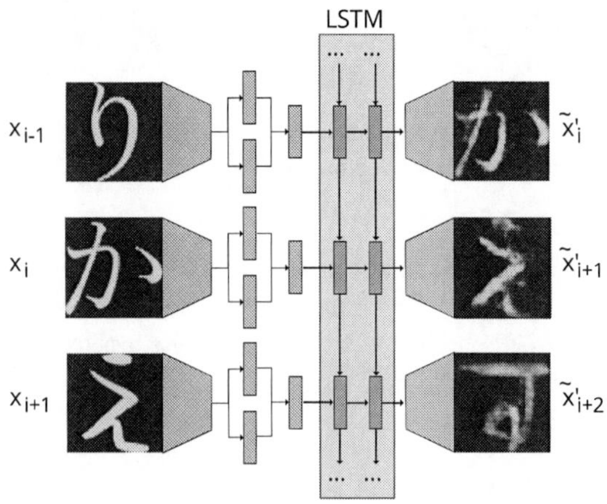

Figure 3: VAE+LSTM architecture. This model adds the auxiliary task of drawing the next token given a sequence of encodings for the preceding tokens.

We add the following loss term to Equation (1) to minimize the reconstruction error of this image sequence:

$$\mathcal{L}_{\text{LSTM}} = \sum_{i=1}^{n-1} \text{BCE}(\tilde{\mathbf{x}}'_i, \mathbf{x}_{i+1})$$

This can be viewed as an autoregressive character-level language modeling objective, where we wish to draw the image of the next character $\mathbf{x}_{i+1}$ given all of the preceding characters $\mathbf{x}_1, ..., \mathbf{x}_i$.

VAE+Transformer Our final model replaces the LSTM component from the previous model with a Transformer encoder stack (Vaswani et al., 2017); we obtain the output image sequence $\{\tilde{\mathbf{x}}'_1, ..., \tilde{\mathbf{x}}'_n\}$ by decoding the top layer of this Transformer. We train this model on a masked language modeling task: we mask input tokens at random by replacing their images with standard Gaussian noise, and train the model to recover the unmasked image sequence by adding the following term to Equation (1):

$$\mathcal{L}_{\text{Transformer}} = \sum_{i=1}^{n} \text{BCE}(\tilde{\mathbf{x}}'_i, \mathbf{x}_i)$$

2.3 Training Details

At training time, we use a denoising technique (Vincent et al., 2008, 2010) to regularize

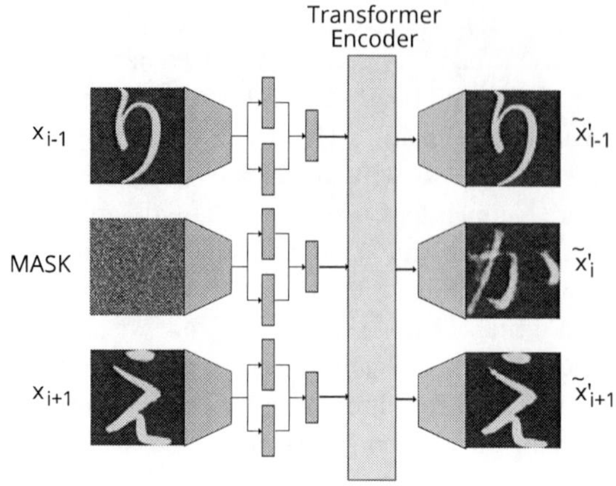

Figure 4: VAE+Transformer architecture. This model adds the auxiliary task of reconstructing characters which have been masked by random Gaussian noise.

our models: we apply a random transformation (rotation of up to 45 degrees, shear of up to 25 degrees, and a random scale factor between 0.4 and 1) to each input image, while keeping the target of the reconstruction loss unchanged.

All of our models are trained using stochastic gradient descent (SGD) to minimize Eq. (1), plus the appropriate model-specific auxiliary loss ($\mathcal{L}_{\text{Neighbor}}$, $\mathcal{L}_{\text{LSTM}}$, or $\mathcal{L}_{\text{Transformer}}$), plus a *pseudolabel* loss term $\mathcal{L}_\Psi$ which we describe below. We jointly minimize the sum of all of the relevant loss terms in a single pass, with no pretraining and no warmup steps.

Pseudolabels We follow Corazza et al. 2022a in using a soft, unsupervised technique to organize our models' encodings into loose clusters. This technique, inspired by the neural clustering algorithm DeepCluster-v2 (Caron et al., 2018), begins by clustering the encodings using K-Means with an **arbitrary** number of clusters k. Let C be a matrix with columns corresponding to the K-Means centroids (normalized to unit length). Let $\mathbf{z}_i$ be an arbitrary encoding, let C_j be the centroid which is closest to $\mathbf{z}_i$, and let $\mathbf{y}_i$ be a one-hot vector with a one in the jth position. The pseudolabel loss is then given by:

$$\mathcal{L}_\Psi = \sum_{i=1}^{n} \text{CCE}(\frac{\mathbf{z}_i}{||\mathbf{z}_i||}C, \mathbf{y}_i) \quad (2)$$

where CCE is categorical cross-entropy. For each $\mathbf{z}_i$, this constructs a probability distribution $\frac{\mathbf{z}_i}{||\mathbf{z}_i||}C$ over k categories, where the mass in each category is proportional to the similarity between $\mathbf{z}_i$ and the corresponding centroid. Minimizing this loss concentrates the mass of the distribution into a single term; in other words, this performs a soft clustering by pulling each $\mathbf{z}_i$ towards the nearest centroid in the embedding space.

We follow Corazza et al. 2022a in using a pseudolabel loss with 100 centroids, which we recompute using K-Means at the beginning of each training epoch.

3 Data

We aim to apply these models to the study of the undeciphered proto-Elamite script, which is attested across ca. 1581 clay tablets recovered from the ancient city of Susa and other parts of the Iranian plateau. These texts have been transliterated by domain experts using a work-in-progress list of about 1500 distinct signs;[2] the most complete and up-to-date transliterations are hosted by the Cuneiform Digital Library Initiative[3] and described in a recent survey by J. Dahl (2019). Each sign has an accompanying digital image, also produced by Dahl, depicting its "archetypal" form. These images smooth over many of the irregularities of the original shapes drawn on clay, while still preserving slight visual differences between tokens which may actually represent the same underlying character (such as and). They therefore represent an intermediate level of detail that is cleaner than segmented images of the original texts, yet still faithful to the original hand. We convert the entire transliterated proto-Elamite corpus[4] into a set of image sequences by replacing each transliterated sign name with the corresponding sign image (Figure 5). Table 1 summarizes the token count for the resulting dataset.

We evaluate our models on their ability to recover three scripts whose character inventories are already known (English, Japanese, and Cypro-Greek). We construct an English dataset by extracting the first 33k alphanumeric tokens (approximately the same number of tokens as are attested in

Figure 5: Samples of image sequences from our PE (top), En (middle) and Jp (bottom) datasets.

Language	# Characters	#Tokens	# Images
EN	62	33k	3410
JP	938	33k	1607
CG	55	3k	3005
PE	—	35k	1319

Table 1: Size and character inventories of scripts used for training. PE is undeciphered, and the size of its character inventory remains unknown.

proto-Elamite) from the WikiText-2 corpus (Merity et al., 2016). We convert this text into image sequences by replacing each character token with a handwritten image of that character. We use images from de Campos et al. 2009, who provide 55 handwritten instances of all 62 upper- and lowercase English letters and digits: one of these 55 images is chosen at random each time a character occurs. The resulting sequences (Figure 5) imitate the level of detail in our proto-Elamite data, in that each letter is attested by multiple distinct images, and the same image can be used for multiple tokens.

We construct a Japanese dataset according to the same procedure, using the first 33k tokens from the Japanese Tatoeba corpus (Artetxe and Schwenk, 2018; Tiedemann, 2012). As we do not have handwritten character images for Japanese, we instead extract the glyphs from two Japanese fonts (Yuji Boku and Zen Old Mincho). The Japanese writing system uses three scripts: *kanji* which are highly logographic, and two syllabaries called *hiragana* and *katakana*. Similarly, proto-Elamite has been speculated to contain a set of possibly-syllabic signs, together with a large number of logograms (Dahl, 2019). Syllabic signs convey phonetic information that can provide crucial insights for decipherment, and are therefore a major focus of decipherment efforts on this script. In our Japanese experiments (see Section 4), we therefore train on the entire script, but only evaluate the model's ability to recover the two syllabaries.

We use the same Cypro-Greek data as Corazza et al. 2022a. Unlike the other datasets, this uses manually-segmented images from hand-drawn

[2]Different sign-counting methodologies can yield sign counts as low as 287 or as high as 1623 (Born et al., 2019), depending on whether numerals, tilde-variants, complex graphemes, and other categories of grapheme are included. To further complicate matters, the signlist continues to vary as transliterations are updated and sign names are revised. At the time of publication, a list of sign names which are currently in use can be found at `https://cdli.mpiwg-berlin.mpg.de/resources/token-lists`

[3]`https://cdli.mpiwg-berlin.mpg.de/`

[4]`https://cdli.mpiwg-berlin.mpg.de/search?period=proto-elamite&genre=administrative`

copies of artifacts bearing the Cypro-Greek script. There is therefore a greater degree of variation between the character shapes in this data, and no two tokens ever have identical images. This means that our three datasets fall along a cline from fully naturalistic, handwritten sequences (Cypro-Greek), to synthetic sequences derived from handwritten images (English), to synthetic sequences derived from digital fonts (Japanese).

We trim extraneous whitespace from all character images and resize them to 64×64 pixels with a single grayscale color channel before training.[5]

4 Experiments

We train each of the models from Section 2.2 on the four corpora detailed above (see Appendix B for hyperparameters and additional training details). After training, we encode each image using the trained encoder and cluster the resulting encodings using (i) agglomerative clustering with varying numbers of clusters (English, Japanese, proto-Elamite) or (ii) DBSCAN (Ester et al., 1996) with varying ε (Cypro-Greek). We use DBSCAN for Cypro-Greek to enable a fair comparison against the results in Corazza et al. 2022a; however, we find that DBSCAN is generally not effective when clustering the other scripts. When clustering with DBSCAN, we follow Corazza et al. 2022a in using a minimum cluster size of 2, to imitate a decipherment setting where the true number and frequency of characters is unknown; for the other scripts we vary the number of clusters for the same reason.[6]

For English, Japanese, and Cypro-Greek, we report homogeneity, completeness, and V-measure (Rosenberg and Hirschberg, 2007) relative to the gold labels. Homogeneity ranges from 0 to 1, where 1 means that each cluster contains instances from just one of the underlying characters, and smaller values imply that some clusters combine instances of two or more distinct characters. Similarly, a completeness of 1 means that each of the underlying characters is represented by a single cluster, while smaller values mean that some characters have been divided across multiple clusters. Intuitively, low homogeneity scores mean that a clustering merges together characters which are actually distinct, while low completeness means that it splits some characters into subgroups that are not underlyingly distinct. V-Measure is the harmonic mean of homogeneity and completeness.

DBSCAN can label samples as outliers (and thus, not part of any cluster): we only evaluate on tokens which it assigns to a cluster.

In our Japanese experiments, we only evaluate on hiragana and katakana, in imitation of the proto-Elamite setting where we eventually aim to understand the divisions of a putative syllabary comprising only a subset of the overall script.

In our Cypro-Greek experiments, we compare against the Sign2Vec and DeepCluster-v2 results reported in Corazza et al. 2022a. For the other scripts, we compare against agglomerative clusterings over the input images.

In proto-Elamite, where the ground truth is not known, we perform a qualitative evaluation in collaboration with domain experts. We look for sets of tokens which are assigned to the same cluster by our VAE+Neighbor, VAE+LSTM, or VAE+Transformer model, but belong to *different* clusters in the vanilla VAE model. The vanilla VAE differs from the other models in that it lacks contextual information; therefore, any groupings which are absent from this model's output likely reflect primarily contextual similarities. Contextual resemblances are harder for human annotators to notice than visual resemblances, and so we expect these groupings to reflect similarities which may have been overlooked in prior work. We collaborate with domain experts to assess how these token groupings relate to their intuitions about this script.

5 Results

5.1 Modern Scripts

Figure 6 plots V-Measure from agglomerative clusterings over our models' representations of handwritten English letters (Appendix A shows the breakdown into homogeneity and completeness scores). The curve for the baseline is obtained by clustering the raw character images, rather than their encodings.

All four of our proposed models are able to recover the underlying script more accurately than the baseline. When the number of clusters is close

[5]Rescaling the images to a fixed size obscures the height of the original character (see Fig. 5, where って is indistinguishable from つて). For this reason, our Japanese evaluation only tests the model's ability to recover the gojūon, dakuon, and handakuon, ignoring the yōon, sokuon, and small vowels which are distinguished only by size.

[6]The present work will otherwise ignore the problem of selecting the correct number of clusters, for which a variety of heuristics have been proposed in prior work (Rousseeuw 1987; Thorndike 1953; Sugar and James 2003; Honarkhah and Caers 2010; Tibshirani et al. 2002 i.a.).

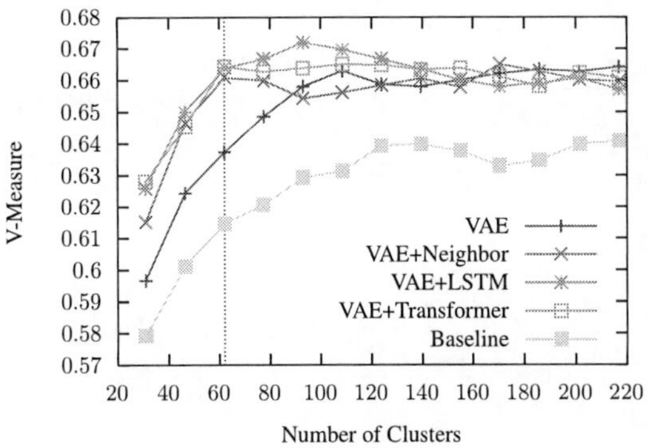

Figure 6: V-Measure on handwritten English. The true character inventory comprises 52 upper- and lowercase letters plus 10 digits.

to the true size of the alphabet, our LSTM and Transformer-based models achieve the highest performance, which supports our hypothesis that wider context windows allow for more accurate script recovery.

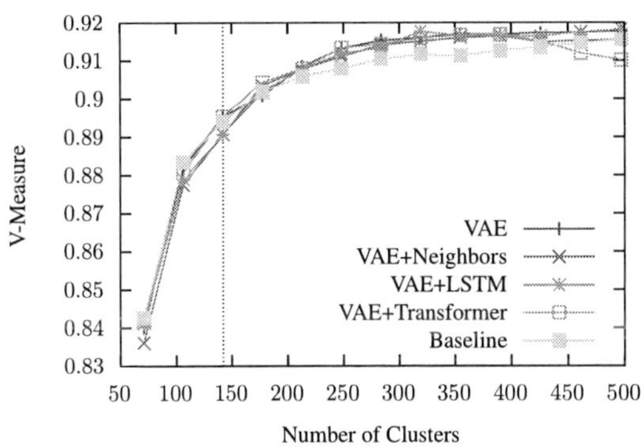

Figure 7: V-Measure on a synthetic mixture of Japanese fonts. The target character inventory comprises 142 hiragana and katakana (46 gojūon, 20 dakuon, and 5 handakuon each).

Figure 7 plots the same metrics for our synthetic Japanese dataset. In this setting, the differences between models are much less pronounced: the context-aware models do not exhibit the same advantage as in English, and in fact the VAE+LSTM model fails to outperform the naive baseline when the number of clusters exactly matches the true number of underlying characters. When the number of clusters is much larger than the true number of signs, our models do outperform the baseline, however, the contextual models continue to slightly underperform the contextless VAE on average. Regardless of the number of clusters chosen, the V-Measure for Japanese is always much higher than for English.

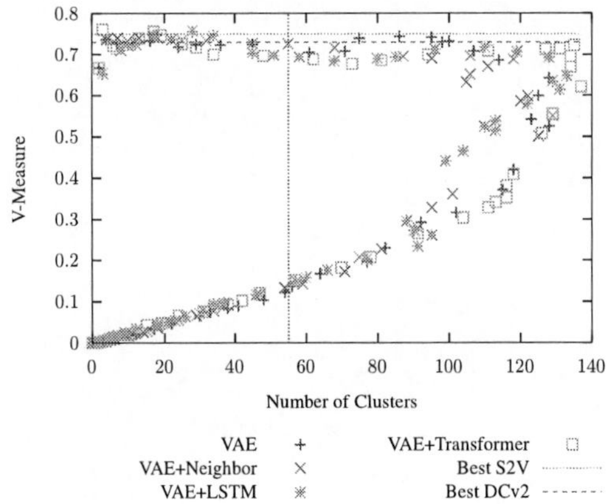

Figure 8: V-measure vs number of clusters for DBSCAN clusterings on Cypro-Greek. We evaluate over the interval $0.1 \leq \varepsilon < 8$ in steps of 0.1. The dotted line represents the true number of signs in the script.

These differences between English and Japanese are likely due, in part, to the fact that there are only two distinct images per character in the Japanese data, compared to 55 in English. The Japanese data are also fully synthetic, whereas the English is handwritten. This may make the Japanese task too easy (despite covering a much larger number of unique characters) to the point that contextual models are not needed. This is nevertheless a useful result, as it suggests that the difficulty of script clustering depends less on the number of graphemes than on the degree of variation between allographs.

5.2 Cypro-Greek

Table 2 compares the best result from each of our models against the best results reported in Corazza et al. 2022a; Figure 8 shows our full results for different values of DBSCAN's ε parameter. Our best models (VAE+LSTM and VAE+Transformer) outperform the Sign2Vec baseline, and all of our models outperform DeepCluster-v2 (Caron et al., 2018) which was the inspiration for Sign2Vec. Although our V-measure gains are modest, we emphasize that our models use **$\sim$98% fewer parameters than Sign2Vec**, and **$\sim$99% fewer than DeepCluster-v2**. This supports our hypothesis that the ResNet encoder is over-parameterized for the task of script clustering, and demonstrates that accurate script recovery is clearly possible even with much more lightweight architectures.

Figure 9 plots homogeneity and completeness vs number of clusters for each of our CG models. Each model exhibits a unique trend: the

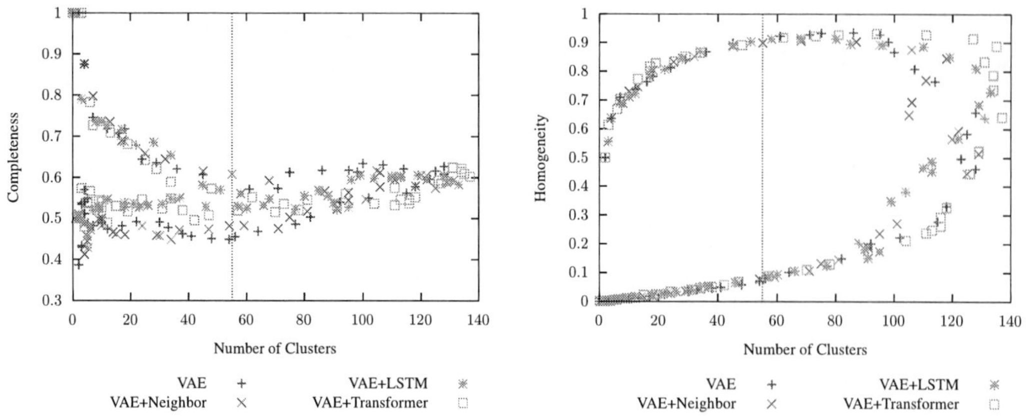

Figure 9: Completeness (left) and homogeneity (right) vs number of clusters for DBSCAN clusterings on Cypro-Greek. We evaluate over the interval $0.1 \leq \varepsilon < 8$ in steps of 0.1. The dotted line represents the true number of signs in the script.

	$V \uparrow$	Parameters$\downarrow$
DeepCluster-v2 (Corazza et al., 2022a)	0.73	> 23M
Sign2Vec (Corazza et al., 2022a)	0.75	> 11M
VAE (Ours)	0.75	**0.215M**
VAE+Neighbor (Ours)	0.74	0.215M
VAE+LSTM (Ours)	**0.76**	0.218M
VAE+Transformer (Ours)	**0.76**	0.227M

Table 2: V-measure (V) and parameter counts for Cypro-Greek. Best results for each model from Figure 8 and Corazza et al. 2022a.

VAE+Transformer exhibits less variation in its completeness scores across a range of clustering sizes, while the other models exhibit a more pronounced fall and rise as the number of clusters increases. All models are capable of achieving comparable homogeneity in the neighborhood surrounding the true number of clusters, but the VAE+Transformer maintains high homogeneity up to a much higher number of clusters than the other models. Geshkovski et al. 2023 have argued that self-attention mechanisms cause tokens to cluster around certain attracting states in the representation space; pseudolabeling (Caron et al., 2018) is intended to have the same effect. We speculate that the VAE+Transformer's strong performance may result in part from these behaviours reinforcing one another to perform a more effective soft clustering at training time.

5.3 Proto-Elamite

Table 3 shows pairs and triplets of proto-Elamite characters which have distinct labels in the working signlist and VAE clustering, yet occupy the same cluster in the VAE+Neighbor, VAE+LSTM, or VAE+Transformer clusterings.[7]

The VAE+Neighbor model differs from the working signlist and VAE clustering in only two places, merging M332~g with M297~B and M356~B with M327~N. Neither merger appears to reflect any known similarities in how these signs are used.

By contrast, the 6 mergers proposed by the VAE+LSTM model appear much more plausible. One cluster combines tokens which are currently labeled as M362 and M362~a, which adds hatching to the central circle in a manner resembling "gunuification" in early cuneiform. The ~ notation in the working sign name explicitly acknowledges that experts believe M362~a may[8] be a graphic variant of M362; both signs have been glossed as 'nanny goat' (Dahl, 2005), and previous scholarship has already acknowledged a likely equivalence between M362~a and another hatched variant called M362~b (Dahl, 2005).

The output from our VAE+Transformer differs the most from the working signlist, suggesting 17 sets of shapes which may represent the same

[7] For the VAE model, we use 1306 clusters, which equals the number of unique sign images available at the time we created our training data. We cluster the other models using $3.5\times$ this many clusters; using such a large number helps to guarantee that the observed groupings reflect legitimate similarities and are not simply a side effect of compressing too many tokens into too few groups.

[8] Specifically, ~ followed by a number marks one sign as a graphic variant of another; ~ followed by a letter means that the sign *may* be a variant of another, but experts remain agnostic in the absence of further evidence.

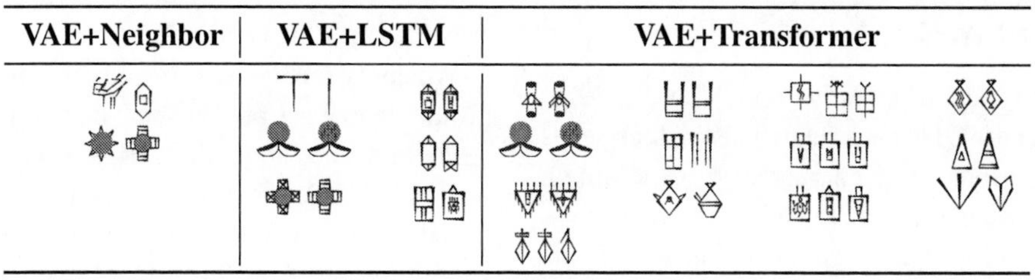

Table 3: Pairs/triplets of character images which have distinct labels in the working signlist, but which our models merge into single clusters.

underlying character. A significant number of these are *complex graphemes*, where one glyph has been drawn inside the whitespace at the center of another. Previous work has suggested that the meaning of a complex grapheme is principally determined by its outer component (Born et al., 2021), and indeed most of the merges proposed by the VAE+Transformer occur between complex graphemes with the same outer part. This suggests that the model has rediscovered the same pattern identified in prior work, and that these particular merges do reflect plausible groupings on the part of our model. Many of the other mergers occur between signs which are already labeled as possible variants in the working signlist (such as M029∼a and M029∼b, or the possible syllables M387∼h and M387∼ca) and thus appear similarly plausible.

Of greater interest are cases such as M209∼a, M210∼f, and M195+M057. The working signlist labels these as wholly distinct characters, and no explicit relationship between these signs has been proposed in prior work. However, the visual resemblance between M209∼a and M210∼f is undeniable; both signs occur in texts which contain the "yoke" character M054, and both occur in texts which appear to record amounts of grain (M209∼a appears with the speculative grain capacity sign M354, while M210∼f occurs with the more common container sign M288). Moreover, in one text M209∼a is attested alongside a related variant of M210, labeled M210∼d. Given these signs' visual resemblance to a plant sprouting from a field, and their association with yokes and grain accounts, we believe it is reasonable for the model to have grouped these characters under the same umbrella. M195+M057 is also attested in texts alongside both M288 and M354; although it does not occur next to the yoke sign M054, it often occurs near the sign M003∼b, which is speculated to be another field utensil and which experts note is "related to M054" (Dahl, 2007). Both M195+M057 and M209∼a are also attested as "headers", the first sign of a document which is believed to offer global context for interpreting the following text (Damerow and Englund, 1989; Born et al., 2022). While we are skeptical that M195+M057 is truly the same underlying character as M209∼a and M210∼f, they clearly share contextual similarities and are attested in comparable, apparently agricultural, contexts. This demonstrates our proposed model's ability to detect contextual parallels which are helpful for understanding the possible relationships between signs in this script.

By reducing the number of clusters to force additional merges, we can obtain yet more groupings of the sort reported in Table 3. For example, when we reduce the number of clusters in the VAE+Transformer model by a factor of $\frac{1}{7}$, a new merger appears between M175+M131∼d and M157+M131∼d. The outer components M157 and M175 differ only in the shape of the protrusion at the top of the box, and a merger between these signs is tentatively expected based on current understandings of the corpus. Other mergers which appear, and which are also expected based on current understandings of the corpus, include M056∼f with M056∼e, both signs being understood to depict a plow; M075∼ff, M075∼g, M075∼h, and M075∼o apparently depicting minor variations on a sprouting plant; and M111∼c, M111∼d, and M111∼e which differ only in the direction of the internal hatching. Such cases serve as useful confirmations of experts' current understanding of sign use in this script.

The cases reported so far represent only a small fraction of the candidate mergers which can be extracted from our models, and we are optimistic that this work will continue to give rise to useful insights as experts take the opportunity to investigate this space more fully.

6 Related Work

Scribal hand identification (Popović et al., 2021; Srivatsan et al., 2021) is a related task which seeks to cluster instances of characters from a known script according to the hand which wrote them.

Yin et al. (2019) describe a system for segmenting, transliterating, and deciphering images of historical manuscripts. In the transliteration step, their model implicitly learns an underlying script by clustering character representations obtained from a Siamese neural network trained to discriminate between characters from known scripts. This network learns character representations without access to context, similarly to our vanilla VAE and the DeepCluster-v2 baseline in Corazza et al. 2022a.

In a setting where the underlying script is already known, Dencker et al. (2020) and Gordin et al. (2020) also describe systems for automated transliteration from images of cuneiform text.

Kelley et al. (2022) study the character inventory of proto-Elamite using a model similar to our VAE+LSTM. Their model is not variational; it uses softmax decoding over a fixed vocabulary initialized to match the working signlist, which biases it towards recovering the same divisions speculated by experts. Our models use a deconvolutional decoder, which sidesteps this bias by allowing an open vocabulary. Their evaluation does not test on any known scripts, which makes it challenging to determine the accuracy of the clusters their model produces.

7 Conclusion

We have described four models which add varying degrees of contextual information to a VAE, and have shown how these can be used to cluster token images to recover a script's character inventory. On the ancient Cypro-Greek script, our best models meet or outperform the state-of-the-art Sign2Vec baseline using just $\sim$2% as many parameters, which supports our claim that written text lacks the visual complexity to warrant models of the depth used in other image processing applications. Our English and Cypro-Greek experiments also demonstrate that contextual models are more effective for script recovery than contextless models. On synthetic Japanese data, which contains many distinct graphemes but little variation between allographs, our models achieve extremely high V-Measure (>0.91), suggesting that they handle large character inventories more easily than they handle allography.

We apply our models to study the undeciphered proto-Elamite script, and show that they capture existing intuitions about this script as well as suggest new parallels between signs which have never been noted in prior work. Our best insights for proto-Elamite come from the LSTM and Transformer models, while for Cypro-Greek our VAE+Neighbor model is the only one which produces a clustering with precisely the same number of clusters as there are signs in the underlying script. This indicates that it is useful to consider models with varying access to contextual information according to the number of long-distance contextual dependencies the input script is expected to exhibit.

Limitations

Proto-Elamite is undeciphered, which means that our results on this script cannot be compared to any known ground truth. We attempt to ground our results by situating them relative to current Assyriological scholarship instead.

Writing systems exhibit considerable variation in terms of the number of characters used, the visual complexity of those characters, and the degree to which they represent phonetic information. Although we try to cover a range of alphabetic and non-alphabetic scripts in our evaluations, we cannot cover all possible cases, and focus on those which have some similarity to the proto-Elamite script which is the main concern of our work.

References

Mikel Artetxe and Holger Schwenk. 2018. Massively multilingual sentence embeddings for zero-shot cross-lingual transfer and beyond. *arXiv:1812.10464v2*.

Logan Born, Kate Kelley, Nishant Kambhatla, Carolyn Chen, and Anoop Sarkar. 2019. Sign clustering and topic extraction in Proto-Elamite. In *Proceedings of the 3rd Joint SIGHUM Workshop on Computational Linguistics for Cultural Heritage, Social Sciences, Humanities and Literature*, pages 122–132, Minneapolis, USA. Association for Computational Linguistics.

Logan Born, Kathryn Kelley, M. Willis Monroe, and Anoop Sarkar. 2021. Compositionality of complex graphemes in the undeciphered Proto-Elamite script using image and text embedding models. In *Findings of the Association for Computational Linguistics: ACL-IJCNLP 2021*, pages 4136–4146, Online. Association for Computational Linguistics.

Logan Born, M. Monroe, Kathryn Kelley, and Anoop Sarkar. 2022. Sequence models for document structure identification in an undeciphered script. In *Proceedings of the 2022 Conference on Empirical Methods in Natural Language Processing*, pages 9111–9121, Abu Dhabi, United Arab Emirates. Association for Computational Linguistics.

Mathilde Caron, Piotr Bojanowski, Armand Joulin, and Matthijs Douze. 2018. Deep clustering for unsupervised learning of visual features. In *Computer Vision - ECCV 2018 - 15th European Conference, Munich, Germany, September 8-14, 2018, Proceedings, Part XIV*, volume 11218 of *Lecture Notes in Computer Science*, pages 139–156. Springer.

Michele Corazza, Fabio Tamburini, Miguel Valério, and Silvia Ferrara. 2022a. Contextual unsupervised clustering of signs for ancient writing systems. In *Proceedings of the Second Workshop on Language Technologies for Historical and Ancient Languages*, pages 84–93, Marseille, France. European Language Resources Association.

Michele Corazza, Fabio Tamburini, Miguel Valério, and Silvia Ferrara. 2022b. Unsupervised deep learning supports reclassification of Bronze age cypriot writing system. *PLOS One*, 17(7):1–22.

Jacob L. Dahl. 2005. Animal husbandry in Susa during the proto-Elamite period. *Studi Micenei ed Egeo-Anatolici*, 47:81–134.

Jacob L. Dahl. 2007. Proto-Elamite signlist. Unpublished notes on the working signlist for proto-Elamite.

Jacob L. Dahl. 2019. *Tablettes et fragments Proto-élamites / Proto-Elamite Tablets and Fragments*, volume XXXII of *Textes Cunéiformes du Louvre*. Éditions Khéops.

Peter Damerow and Robert K. Englund. 1989. *The proto-Elamite texts from Tepe Yahya*, volume 39 of *American School of Prehistoric Research: Bulletin*. Peabody Museum, Cambridge, Massachusetts.

Teófilo Emídio de Campos, Bodla Rakesh Babu, and Manik Varma. 2009. Character recognition in natural images. In *VISAPP 2009 - Proceedings of the Fourth International Conference on Computer Vision Theory and Applications, Lisboa, Portugal, February 5-8, 2009 - Volume 2*, pages 273–280. INSTICC Press.

Tobias Dencker, Pablo Klinkisch, Stefan M. Maul, and Björn Ommer. 2020. Deep learning of cuneiform sign detection with weak supervision using transliteration alignment. *PLOS One*.

Jia Deng, Wei Dong, Richard Socher, Li-Jia Li, Kai Li, and Li Fei-Fei. 2009. ImageNet: A large-scale hierarchical image database. In *2009 IEEE conference on computer vision and pattern recognition*, pages 248–255. IEEE.

Martin Ester, Hans-Peter Kriegel, Jörg Sander, and Xiaowei Xu. 1996. A density-based algorithm for discovering clusters in large spatial databases with noise. In *Proceedings of the Second International Conference on Knowledge Discovery and Data Mining*, KDD'96, page 226–231. AAAI Press.

I. J. Gelb and R. M. Whiting. 1975. Methods of decipherment. *Journal of the Royal Asiatic Society of Great Britain and Ireland*, (2):95–104.

Borjan Geshkovski, Cyril Letrouit, Yury Polyanskiy, and Philippe Rigollet. 2023. The emergence of clusters in self-attention dynamics.

Shai Gordin, Gai Gutherz, Ariel Elazary, Avital Romich, Enrique Jiménez, Jonathan Berant, and Yoram Cohen. 2020. Reading Akkadian cuneiform using natural language processing. *PLOS One*.

Kaiming He, Xiangyu Zhang, Shaoqing Ren, and Jian Sun. 2016. Deep residual learning for image recognition. In *2016 IEEE Conference on Computer Vision and Pattern Recognition (CVPR)*, pages 770–778.

Sepp Hochreiter and Jürgen Schmidhuber. 1997. Long short-term memory. *Neural Comput.*, 9(8):1735–1780.

Mehrdad Honarkhah and Jef Caers. 2010. Stochastic simulation of patterns using distance-based pattern modeling. *Mathematical Geosciences*, 42:487–517.

Kathryn Kelley, Logan Born, M. Willis Monroe, and Anoop Sarkar. 2022. Image-aware language modeling for proto-Elamite. *Lingue e linguaggio, Rivista semestrale*, (2/2022):261–294.

Diederik P. Kingma and Jimmy Ba. 2015. Adam: A method for stochastic optimization. In *3rd International Conference on Learning Representations, ICLR 2015, San Diego, CA, USA, May 7-9, 2015, Conference Track Proceedings*.

Diederik P. Kingma and Max Welling. 2014. Auto-encoding variational Bayes. In *2nd International Conference on Learning Representations, ICLR 2014, Banff, AB, Canada, April 14-16, 2014, Conference Track Proceedings*.

Tsung-Yi Lin, Michael Maire, Serge J. Belongie, Lubomir D. Bourdev, Ross B. Girshick, James Hays, Pietro Perona, Deva Ramanan, Piotr Dollár, and C. Lawrence Zitnick. 2014. Microsoft COCO: common objects in context. *CoRR*, abs/1405.0312.

Stephen Merity, Caiming Xiong, James Bradbury, and Richard Socher. 2016. Pointer sentinel mixture models. *CoRR*, abs/1609.07843.

Mladen Popović, Maruf A. Dhali, and Lambert Schomaker. 2021. Artificial intelligence based writer identification generates new evidence for the unknown scribes of the Dead Sea scrolls exemplified by the great Isaiah scroll (1QIsa[a]). *PLOS ONE*, 16(4):1–28.

Andrew Rosenberg and Julia Hirschberg. 2007. V-measure: A conditional entropy-based external cluster evaluation measure. In *Proceedings of the 2007 Joint Conference on Empirical Methods in Natural Language Processing and Computational Natural Language Learning (EMNLP-CoNLL)*, pages 410–420, Prague, Czech Republic. Association for Computational Linguistics.

Peter J. Rousseeuw. 1987. Silhouettes: A graphical aid to the interpretation and validation of cluster analysis. *Journal of Computational and Applied Mathematics*, 20:53–65.

Nikita Srivatsan, Jason Vega, Christina Skelton, and Taylor Berg-Kirkpatrick. 2021. Neural representation learning for scribal hands of Linear B. In *Document Analysis and Recognition – ICDAR 2021 Workshops: Lausanne, Switzerland, September 5–10, 2021, Proceedings, Part II*, page 325–338, Berlin, Heidelberg. Springer-Verlag.

Catherine A Sugar and Gareth M James. 2003. Finding the number of clusters in a dataset. *Journal of the American Statistical Association*, 98(463):750–763.

Robert L. Thorndike. 1953. Who belongs in the family? *Psychometrika*, 18:267–276.

Robert Tibshirani, Guenther Walther, and Trevor Hastie. 2002. Estimating the Number of Clusters in a Data Set Via the Gap Statistic. *Journal of the Royal Statistical Society Series B: Statistical Methodology*, 63(2):411–423.

Jörg Tiedemann. 2012. Parallel data, tools and interfaces in OPUS. In *Proceedings of the Eighth International Conference on Language Resources and Evaluation (LREC'12)*, pages 2214–2218, Istanbul, Turkey. European Language Resources Association (ELRA).

Ashish Vaswani, Noam Shazeer, Niki Parmar, Jakob Uszkoreit, Llion Jones, Aidan N. Gomez, Lukasz Kaiser, and Illia Polosukhin. 2017. Attention is all you need. In *Advances in Neural Information Processing Systems 30: Annual Conference on Neural Information Processing Systems 2017, December 4-9, 2017, Long Beach, CA, USA*, pages 5998–6008.

Pascal Vincent, Hugo Larochelle, Yoshua Bengio, and Pierre-Antoine Manzagol. 2008. Extracting and composing robust features with denoising autoencoders. In *Machine Learning, Proceedings of the Twenty-Fifth International Conference (ICML 2008), Helsinki, Finland, June 5-9, 2008*, volume 307 of *ACM International Conference Proceeding Series*, pages 1096–1103. ACM.

Pascal Vincent, Hugo Larochelle, Isabelle Lajoie, Yoshua Bengio, and Pierre-Antoine Manzagol. 2010. Stacked denoising autoencoders: Learning useful representations in a deep network with a local denoising criterion. *J. Mach. Learn. Res.*, 11:3371–3408.

Xusen Yin, Nada Aldarrab, Beáta Megyesi, and Kevin Knight. 2019. Decipherment of historical manuscript images. In *2019 International Conference on Document Analysis and Recognition, ICDAR 2019, Sydney, Australia, September 20-25, 2019*, pages 78–85. IEEE.

A Additional Figures

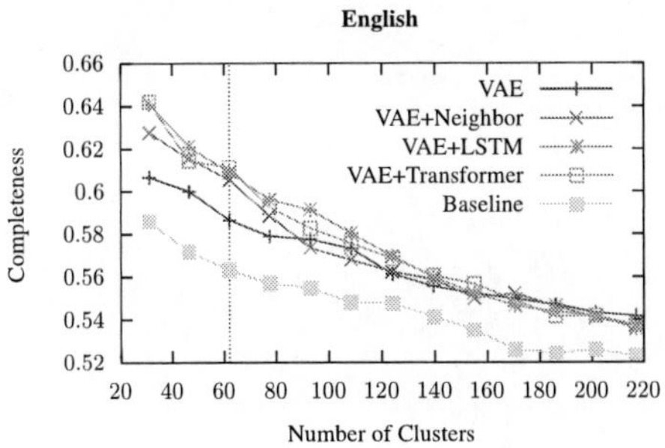

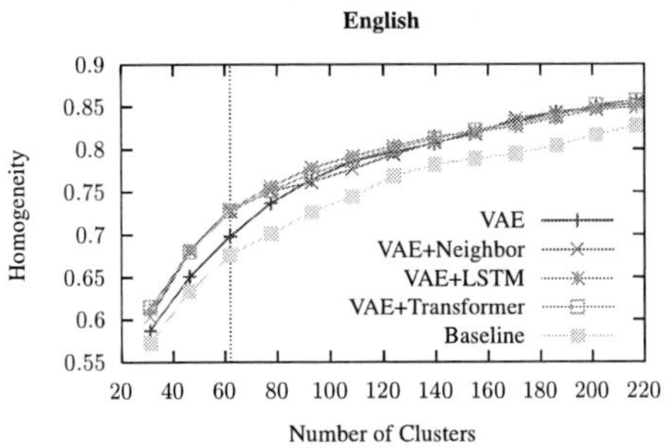

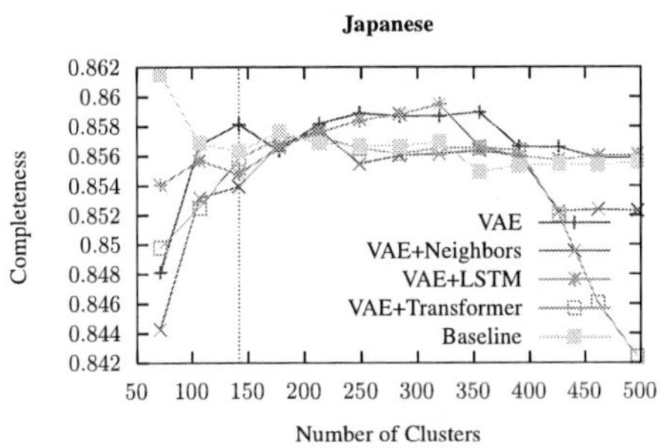

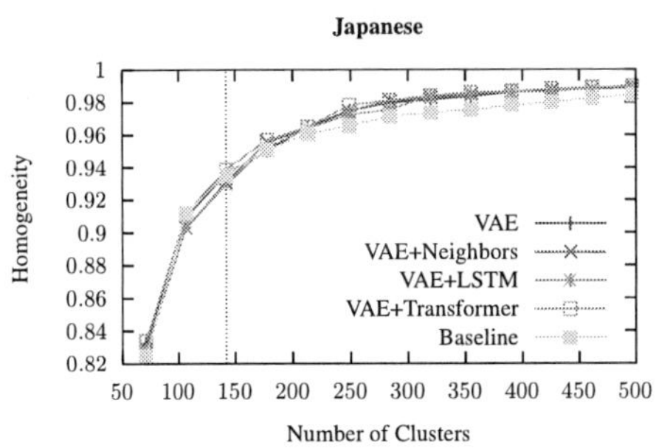

B Reproducibility Details

The code for our models will be published at `https://github.com/MrLogarithm/cawl-clustering`. All of the models in this work are implemented with PyTorch. All settings use an encoder with the following structure:

```
Sequential(
    Dropout(0.5)
    Conv2d(1 input channel, 3 output
        channels, kernel size 8)
    ReLU()
    Conv2d(3 input channels, 6 output
        channels, kernel size 8)
    ReLU()
    MaxPool2d(kernel size 3, stride
        length 3)
    Conv2d(6 input channels, 8 output
        channels, kernel size 8)
    ReLU()
    MaxPool2d(kernel size 3, stride
        length 3)
    Flatten()
    Dense(72 input dims, 16 output
        dims)
)
```

A pair of `Dense(16, 16)` layers project the encoded output to μ and σ.

All settings use a decoder with the following structure:

```
Sequential(
    ConvTranspose2d(16 input channels,
        60 output channels, kernel size
        8)
    BatchNorm2d(60 channels)
    ReLU()
    ConvTranspose2d(60 input channels,
        30 output channels, kernel size
        8, stride length 2)
    BatchNorm2d(30 channels)
    ReLU()
    ConvTranspose2d(30 input channels,
        15 output channels, kernel size
        8, stride length 2)
    BatchNorm2d(15 channels)
    ReLU()
    ConvTranspose2d(15 input channels,
        1 output channel, kernel size
        15, stride length 1)
    Sigmoid()
)
```

The VAE+LSTM model uses a single-layer unidirectional LSTM with a hidden dimension of size 16. The VAE+Transformer uses a 6-layer `TransformerEncoder` with 8 heads per layer, input and output dimensions of size 16, and 0.5 dropout. We apply a standard sinusoidal positional encoding to the Transformer inputs following Vaswani et al. (2017).

In the VAE+LSTM and VAE+Transformer models, we re-apply the reparameterization trick from Kingma and Welling 2014 to the LM outputs before decoding the image sequence. We add new `Dense(16,16)` layers to compute μ and σ at this stage, separate from those used to compute μ and σ within the VAE itself. When computing the overall KL divergence loss for these models, we sum the KL divergence from these projections with that of the VAE projections.

We train on sequences of length 50 using the Adam optimizer (Kingma and Ba, 2015) with learning rate 0.001. When computing the loss, we scale the KL divergence loss term by 0.45. The LR and loss scaling hyperparameters were tuned via a small manual grid search. We recompute pseudolabel assignments at the start of every 600th training iteration.

A Mutual Information-based Approach to Quantifying Logography in Japanese and Sumerian

Noah Hermalin
Department of Linguistics
University of California, Berkeley
Berkeley, CA 94720 USA
nmhermalin@berkeley.edu

Abstract

Writing systems have traditionally been classified by whether they prioritize encoding phonological information (**phonographic**) versus morphological or semantic information (**logographic**). Recent work has broached the question of how membership in these categories can be quantified. We aim to contribute to this line of research by treating a definition of logography which directly incorporates morphological identity. Our methods compare mutual information between graphic forms and phonological forms and between graphic forms and morphological identity. We report on preliminary results here for two case studies, written Sumerian and written Japanese. The results suggest that our methods present a promising means of classifying the degree to which a writing system is logographic or phonographic.

1 Introduction

Writing systems vary regarding how much they encode phonological versus morphological (or semantic) information: systems which prioritize conveying phonological information are conventionally labeled as **phonographic**, and systems which prioritize morphological/lexical information are labeled as **logographic** (Daniels and Bright, 1996; Joyce and Borgwaldt, 2013). While this taxonomic split is convenient as a broad-strokes shorthand for classifying different writing systems, more precise categories, as well as more precise definitions for existing categories, remain a point of ongoing research, and debate, among scholars of writing systems.

Defining what it means to be logographic has been a particular point of inconsistency in the literature on writing systems; see section 2 of Sproat and Gutkin (2021) for a review. While cases where a single character maps to an entire word would generally be considered logographic and cases where a single character always maps to a particular segment would be considered phonographic, the numerous in-between cases present points of possible contention. For example, the fact that English spells many homophones differently (e.g., *where, wear, ware*), while spelling distinct allomorphs of a given morpheme the same way (e.g., the root in ***heal*** and ***heal**th*), has motivated treating written English as somewhat logographic. (Sproat, 2000; Rogers, 2005; Sproat and Gutkin, 2021).

Relative to any particular category definitions is the question of how one might quantify the degree to which a writing system belongs to that taxonomic category. While not always framed as a matter of typology, a few methods have been used to quantify the consistency of character string-sound string mappings (orthographic transparency/depth). These include using binary consistent/inconsistent distinctions (e.g., Ziegler et al. (1996, 1997)), entropy-based measures (e.g. Treiman et al. (1995); Borgwaldt et al. (2004); Protopapas and Vlahou (2009); Siegelman et al. (2020)), and machine learning (Marjou, 2019; Rosati, 2022). With regards to consistency of mapping, results differ depending on whether one considers the perspective of the reader or the writer: it's possible to have ambiguity of reading but not spelling (e.g., English *bass*), or vice versa (e.g. English /ɹa͡ɪt/). Penn and Choma (2006) and Sproat and Gutkin (2021) more directly focused on the question of quantifying taxonomic category membership (rather than orthographic transparency). We aim to build on the work in this vein by proposing a simple metric of logography which incorporates graphic forms, phonological forms, and morphological identity.

1.1 The Study of Sproat and Gutkin (2021)

Recently, the question of quantifying category membership has been directed at measuring how logographic a system is. Responding to an earlier attempt by Penn and Choma (2006), Sproat and Gutkin (Sproat and Gutkin, 2021) propose a hand-

Proceedings of the Workshop on Computation and Written Language (CAWL 2023), pages 105–110
July 14, 2023 ©2023 Association for Computational Linguistics

ful of ways by which one might quantify degree of logography, relative to a working definition of logography.

Sproat and Gutkin discuss two different treatments of logography. By their **distinct homophones** notion of logography, a system is more logographic if identical phonological forms are not necessarily spelled the same. The rationale behind the distinct homophones approach is: given that a maximally phonographic system will spell all words based solely on their phonological form (thus not discriminating between homophones), deviation from this ideal constitutes a higher degree of logography. Their **uniform spelling** treatment of logography treats a system as more logographic if the same morpheme is always spelled the same (despite surface variation). Citing convenience and availability of reliable data, Sproat and Gutkin use their **distinct homophones** definition for their studies, though they note that the **uniform spelling** approach is also valid.

Sproat and Gutkin compare three different classes of methods for quantifying logography. Their S measure is based on the attention mechanism of an RNN that maps phoneme strings to written character strings, in context. A higher S means that a system is more logographic, since more attention needs to be given to surrounding context in order to know how to spell a word. As a simple baseline for comparison, their lexical L measure computes the average number of spellings s per pronunciation p (drawn from a dictionary D or corpus C of p types/tokens). A higher L means a system is more logographic.

$$L_{type} = \frac{1}{|D|}\sum_{p \in D} |s(p)| \quad \text{and} \quad L_{token} = \frac{1}{|C|}\sum_{p \in C} c(p)|s(p)| \tag{1}$$

Their E measure is based on uncertainty of spelling given pronunciation. For their type-based analyses, this was done as the mutual information between written forms $\mathcal{W}$ and pronunciations $\mathcal{P}$:

$$E_{type} = H(\mathcal{W}) - H(\mathcal{W}|\mathcal{P}) \tag{2}$$

The data for Sproat and Gutkin's main experiment was the Bible in 9 languages: English, Hebrew, French, Russian, Swedish, Finnish, Korean, Chinese (at the character- and word-level), and Japanese (Christodouloupoulos and Steedman, 2015); they also ran studies using data from Wikipedia for Finnish, Japanese, English, and Korean, as well as on the Bible again for additional languages. These languages' writing systems range from more (Chinese, Japanese) to less (Finnish, Korean) logographic, in terms of how they are conventionally treated by scholars of writing systems and of those languages. It should be noted that the pronunciations for their main data were automatically generated from their target texts, and their pronunciation generators did not have any homograph disambiguation (a factor which they acknowledge as a shortcoming, and address to some extent in their section 6.5).

Sproat and Gutkin's attention-based S measures most closely aligned with how logographic their target writing systems are generally considered to be: S scores were lowest for Finnish, Swedish, and Korean, and were highest for Japanese and Chinese. Their L measures were less reliable, but still somewhat consistent with expectations. While their E_{type} performed decently, it had a few unexpected outcomes, such as ranking character-level Chinese as too phonographic and Swedish as too logographic, leading Sproat and Gutkin to favor their S measure. However, it may be that these E results were a consequence of only considering pronunciations and spellings, without also incorporating morphology. A mutual information approach which also includes morphological information still has the potential to match, or outperform, their S measure.

2 Logography via Morpheme Identity

One can view graphic forms and spoken forms as two points of a triangle, with the third point being semantics or lexical identity[1]. Since Sproat and Gutkin (2021) focus on their **distinct homophones** interpretation of logography, the role of morphology (and semantics) do not play a role in their experiments. We aim to add morpheme identity to the mix, which helps to complete the missing side of the triangle. Given that traditional definitions of logography have placed emphasis on the role of morphology or semantics in how words are read and written, a complete account of how to quantify logography would benefit from including the graphic form-morphology leg of the triangle.

[1]This kind of 'triangle' model was popularized by Seidenberg and McClelland (Seidenberg and McClelland, 1989). While it's true that that work was focused on modelling how humans read, not on writing system typology, this kind of triangle schematic nonetheless serves as a useful representation of how the components of spoken/written language can connect to each other, which is relevant for classifying writing systems.

Intuitively, if a system is more logographic, then graphic forms and morphological identity will provide more information about each other; if a system is more phonographic, then graphic forms and phonological forms will provide more information about each other. We propose that the degree to which a writing system is logographic l can be quantified by comparing the mutual information between graphic forms G and morphemes M with the mutual information between graphic forms G and phonological forms P:

$$l = I(G; M) - I(G; P) \qquad (3)$$

One advantage that mutual information has in this context is its symmetry, with the consequence that it's agnostic as to whether the writing system is being analyzed from the reader's perspective or the writer's perspective. Measures such as Sproat and Gutkin's S and L metrics can only be done from one of the two reader/writer perspectives at a time (Sproat and Gutkin's experiments only took the writer's perspective); while there's nothing stopping one from getting those measures from both perspectives separately, this would give two separate measures rather than the single unified measure that mutual information offers.

3 Data - Sumerian and Japanese

As an initial testing ground, we focus on the writing systems of two unrelated languages: Modern Japanese and Ur III Sumerian. These writing systems are considered to be highly logographic, with morphemes often being spelled with a single character. Sumerian and Japanese happen to both be agglutinating in their morphology, with additional similarities including postnominal case marking, root+affix verbal morphology, and extensive use of compounding (Shibatani, 1990; Michalowski, 2004); given the role that morphology plays in our analysis, it is convenient to start by considering two languages which, by chance, have similar morphological profiles and similar writing systems. In addition, this choice of writing systems also allowed us to have one writing system (Japanese) which was considered by Sproat and Gutkin, and one writing system (Sumerian) which hasn't yet been explored in this vein. To our knowledge, this work constitutes the first attempt at quantifying how logographic or phonographic written Sumerian is. These systems were also chosen in part because of data availability and author background.

To avoid any diachronic variation within Sumerian, all of the Sumerian data were from documents composed during the Ur III period (c. 2112-2004 BC), drawn from 71,712 Ur III administrative documents within ORACC, the Open Richly Annotated Cuneiform Corpus (Tinney and Robson, 2014). This corpus was chosen for its robust size and lexical and morphological annotation. During cleaning, we removed tokens which contained damaged written forms, had uncertain readings/translations, or were proper nouns. Morphologically complex tokens, including compounds and inflected forms, were further processed into morpheme-length (rather than word-length) tokens via both automated and manual parsing by the first author. This resulted in a total of 1,875,351 morpheme-sized tokens.

Japanese data were drawn from BCCWJ, the Balanced Contemporary Corpus of Written Japanese (Maekawa et al., 2014). BCCWJ tokenizes by lemma, with each token annotated with graphic form and phonological form information. Morphologically complex tokens were further processed into morpheme-length tokens by the first author. The analyses reported here include the 5,000 most frequent lemmas, with a total of 62,929,634 morpheme tokens.

3.1 Morphological Parsing

BCCWJ and ORACC both tokenize at the word rather than the morpheme level. As such, some additional processing was needed to get morpheme-sized tokens out of morphologically complex words, particularly compounds and words with grammatical affixes. For Sumerian compounds (548 types), morphological parsing was done completely manually by the first author based on background knowledge and use of the electronic Pennsylvania Sumerian Dictionary (ePSD2)[2]; some parses were also run by someone more knowledgeable on Sumerian to double check their validity. Parsing grammatical morphology on nouns and verbs and aligning the parses with characters was handled automatically by a Python script written by the first author. Because of the complexities of Sumerian verbal morphology, automating exactly which characters mapped to which morphemes was unreliable, so verbal affixes were excluded from the analyses.

[2] http://oracc.museum.upenn.edu/epsd2/sux; http://oracc.museum.upenn.edu/epsd2/index.html.

Japanese has a rich lexicon of two-character, two-morpheme Sino-Japanese compounds called *jukugo* (Ogawa and Saito, 2006; Joyce, 2013), as well as suffixing morphology on verbs. Two Python scripts were written that automatically parsed *jukugo* into their component morphemes and that separated verb roots from affixes. The Jukugo Database at `kanjidatabase.com` (Tamaoka et al., 2017) was used to help with *jukugo* parsing.

3.2 Phonographizing Sumerian and Japanese

The writing systems of both Japanese and Sumerian are considered highly logographic. However, while Japanese texts are typically written using a mix of logographic *kanji* and phonographic *kana*, any Japanese text can be written using *kana* alone. To ensure that we have a highly phonographic system for comparison, we included in our analyses a "phonographized" version of the Japanese data that treated all tokens as if they were written in *katakana*. For example, the morpheme *abura* "oil" is typically written as 油, but can be written in *kana* as あぶら or (rarely) アブラ; in our phonographized Japanese, *abura* is only written as アブラ.

For comparison, we also devised a phonographized version of Sumerian. Since Sumerian doesn't have a set of canonical phonographic characters in the way Japanese does, we constructed a hypothetical phonographized Sumerian using the following method: for each phonological form in the corpus, we found the spelling that most frequently mapped to that form. We then rewrote all instances of those phonological forms such that they were written with that most common spelling. This creates a system which would be considered minimally logographic under Sproat and Gutkin's distinct homophones treatment of logography. Since surface phonetic information isn't available for Sumerian, phonological forms were always treated as the cited dictionary transliterations, meaning that we treat each Sumerian morpheme as having only one possible phonological form.

Sumerian was further treated in two separate ways: the first way included all available (non-discarded) data, such that graphic form types included any character string which could map to a single morpheme. To get a sense of how logographic Sumerian is at a character level, we also ran the analyses on a subset of Sumerian that only included morphemes which could be written with a single character ("MonoChar Sumerian"). For example, MonoChar Sumerian would include morphemes such as 𒉌 *i* "oil", but not morphemes such as [illegible] *šegin* "glue".

4 Results and Discussion

Results are given in Table 1. Even though the number of systems compared thus far is decidedly modest, the results are consistent with our expectations: for the more logographic systems, $I(G;M) > I(G;P)$, while the opposite is true for the phonographic systems.

The results are most salient for Japanese. The Sumerian results, while still in-line with expectations, are weaker in magnitude; whether or not this is a consequence of the smaller dataset or of an actual difference in how logographic written Sumerian was remains a point of future consideration. Additional points of comparison will be needed to get a more complete picture of whether the magnitude of the results (rather than just the valence) correlates with how logographic a system is.

With respect to the phonographized MonoChar Sumerian, the fact that $I(G;M) = I(G;P)$ makes sense given how phonographized Sumerian was crafted, and given that, for reasons stated earlier, each Sumerian morpheme only has one possible pronunciation form.

It is interesting to note that the scores for phonographized Sumerian are close to zero rather than strongly negative, i.e. written forms were about as informative about morpheme identity as they were about phonological form. This system could thus be viewed as more logographic than our phonographized Japanese, despite both systems being exemplar minimally logographic system in the distinct homophones sense. The ability to capture such a distinction marks another potential advantage of incorporating morpheme identity when quantifying logography.

5 Conclusion

The preliminary studies reported here offer a simple but promising means of measuring how logographic a writing system is. The inclusion of all three of phonological forms, graphic forms, and morphological identity paints a more complete picture of what it means for a writing system to be logographic. Ongoing work is focused on expanding these methods to a wider range of writing systems, as well as incorporating semantics.

Writing System	I(G,M)	I(G,P)	l	Writing System	I(G,M)	I(G,P)	l
Sumerian	6.950	6.819	**0.131**	Sumerian (**Ph**)	6.818	6.851	**-0.034**
Sumerian (**MC**)	6.228	6.074	**0.153**	Sumerian (**MC**, **Ph**)	6.111	6.111	**0.000**
Japanese	9.382	8.341	**1.041**	Japanese (**Ph**)	8.307	8.734	**-0.427**

Table 1: Results for the six different writing system variations. **MC** and **Ph** are abbreviations for "MonoChar" and "phonographized", respectively. See section 3.2 for details on the six variations.

Limitations

The work described here is part of an ongoing project, and our results, while promising, should be viewed as preliminary. We only report results for the writing systems of two languages, which is a major limitation for a study focusing on typology and cross-writing system variation; past studies in this vein (e.g., Marjou (2019); Sproat and Gutkin (2021); Rosati (2022)) have rightly considered a wider range of languages. While the systems we consider (including their "phonographized" versions) provide good points of comparison, the results would be strengthened by considering a wider range of writing systems (which the authors intend to do).

Finally, it should be noted that the morphological parsing done on the data used in this study may be imperfect, despite the first author's best efforts. Limitations in modern understanding of Sumerian result in some cases that should perhaps be viewed with some caution. Similarly, for Japanese, the treatment of all *jukugo* words as bimorphemic may or may not accurately reflect how such words should be analyzed in Modern Japanese. It's also possible that some non-*jukugo* two-*kanji* words were accidentally categorized and parsed as if they were *jukugo*. Certain non-*jukugo* compounds may have also escaped detection.

Given the in-progress nature of this research, code and (cleaned) datasets have not yet been made publicly available, but it is the authors' intention that these resources will be released in the future.

References

Susanne R Borgwaldt, Frauke M Hellwig, and Annette MB de Groot. 2004. Word-initial entropy in five languages: Letter to sound, and sound to letter. *Written Language & Literacy*, 7(2):165–184.

Christos Christodouloupoulos and Mark Steedman. 2015. A massively parallel corpus: the bible in 100 languages. *Language resources and evaluation*, 49:375–395.

Peter T Daniels and William Bright. 1996. *The world's writing systems*. Oxford University Press on Demand.

Terry Joyce. 2013. The significance of the morphographic principle for the classification of writing systems. *Typology of writing systems*, pages 61–84.

Terry Joyce and Susanne R Borgwaldt. 2013. *Typology of writing systems: Introduction*, volume 51, pages 1–11. John Benjamins Publishing.

Kikuo Maekawa, Makoto Yamazaki, Toshinobu Ogiso, Takehiko Maruyama, Hideki Ogura, Wakako Kashino, Hanae Koiso, Masaya Yamaguchi, Makiro Tanaka, and Yasuharu Den. 2014. Balanced corpus of contemporary written japanese. *Language resources and evaluation*, 48:345–371.

Xavier Marjou. 2019. Oteann: Estimating the transparency of orthographies with an artificial neural network. *arXiv preprint arXiv:1912.13321*.

Piotr Michalowski. 2004. Sumerian. *The Cambridge Encyclopedia of the World's Ancient Languages*, pages 19–59.

Taeko Ogawa and Hirofumi Saito. 2006. Semantic activation in visual recognition of Japanese two-kanji compound words: Interference and facilitatory effects of neighbors. *Psychologia*, 49(3):162–177.

Gerald Penn and Travis Choma. 2006. Quantitative methods for classifying writing systems. In *Proceedings of the Human Language Technology Conference of the NAACL, Companion Volume: Short Papers*, pages 117–120.

Athanassios Protopapas and Eleni L Vlahou. 2009. A comparative quantitative analysis of Greek orthographic transparency. *Behavior research methods*, 41:991–1008.

Henry Rogers. 2005. *Writing systems: A linguistic approach*, volume 18. Blackwell publishing.

Domenic Rosati. 2022. Learning to pronounce as measuring cross lingual joint orthography-phonology complexity. *arXiv preprint arXiv:2202.00794*.

Mark S Seidenberg and James L McClelland. 1989. A distributed, developmental model of word recognition and naming. *Psychological review*, 96(4):523.

Masayoshi Shibatani. 1990. *The languages of Japan*. Cambridge University Press.

Noam Siegelman, Devin M Kearns, and Jay G Rueckl. 2020. Using information-theoretic measures to characterize the structure of the writing system: the case of orthographic-phonological regularities in English. *Behavior research methods*, 52:1292–1312.

Richard Sproat. 2000. *A computational theory of writing systems*. Cambridge University Press.

Richard Sproat and Alexander Gutkin. 2021. The taxonomy of writing systems: How to measure how logographic a system is. *Computational Linguistics*, 47(3):477–528.

Katsuo Tamaoka, Shogo Makioka, Sander Sanders, and Rinus G Verdonschot. 2017. www.kanjidatabase.com: a new interactive online database for psychological and linguistic research on Japanese kanji and their compound words. *Psychological research*, 81:696–708.

Steve Tinney and Eleanor Robson. 2014. ORACC: The Open Richly Annotated Cuneiform Corpus.

Rebecca Treiman, John Mullennix, Ranka Bijeljac-Babic, and E Daylene Richmond-Welty. 1995. The special role of rimes in the description, use, and acquisition of English orthography. *Journal of Experimental Psychology: General*, 124(2):107.

Johannes C Ziegler, Arthur M Jacobs, and Gregory O Stone. 1996. Statistical analysis of the bidirectional inconsistency of spelling and sound in French. *Behavior Research Methods Instruments and Computers*, 28(4):504–515.

Johannes C Ziegler, Gregory O Stone, and Arthur M Jacobs. 1997. What is the pronunciation for -ough and the spelling for/u/? A database for computing feedforward and feedback consistency in English. *Behavior Research Methods Instruments and Computers*, 29:600–618.

Author Index

Association for Computational Linguistics
209 N. Eighth Street
Stroudsburg, Pennsylvania 18360

ISBN 978-1-7138-8223-7

CURRAN ASSOCIATES INC.
proceedings.com